AN EYE AT THE TOP OF THE WORLD

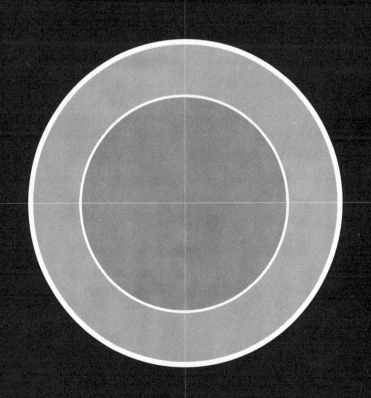

AN EYE AT THE TOP OF THE WORLD

The Terrifying Legacy of the Cold War's Most
Daring CIA Operation

PETER TAKEDA

THUNDER'S MOUTH PRESS
NEW YORK

AN EYE AT THE TOP OF THE WORLD:
The Terrifying Legacy of the Cold War's Most Daring CIA Operation

Published by
Thunder's Mouth Press
An Imprint of Avalon Publishing Group, Inc.
245 West 17th Street, 11th floor
New York, NY 10011

www.thundersmouth.com

AVALON
publishing group incorporated

First printing, October 2006

Photographs appear courtesy of the author, unless otherwise noted.

Library of Congress Cataloging-in-Publication Data is available.

ISBN: 1-56025-845-4
ISBN-13: 978-1-56025-845-2

9 8 7 6 5 4 3 2 1

Book design by Maria E. Torres

Printed in the United States of America
Distributed by Publishers Group West

*To Chuck Bird, Jonathan Copp, Sarah Thompson,
and DeAnn Masin.*

"God made man because he loves stories."

—Elie Wiesel, *The Gates of the Forest*

CONTENTS

"In the end we all come to be cured of our sentiments. Those whom life does not cure death will. The world is quite ruthless in selecting between the dream and the reality, even where we will not. Between the wish and the thing the world lies waiting."

—Cormac McCarthy, *All the Pretty Horses*

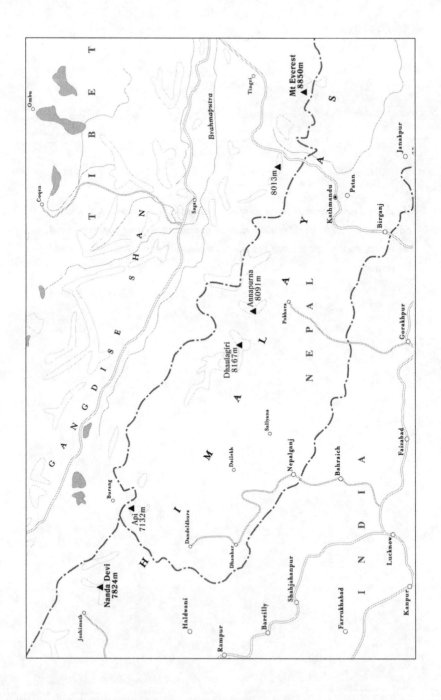

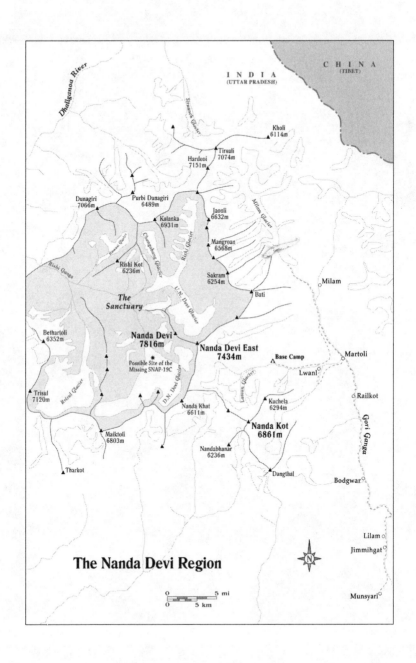

The Nanda Devi Region

PREFACE

It's not the top of the world, but it's close enough. And it's taken longer than I'd thought it would to get here. Ten hours of climbing into the rarified oxygen at 19,500 feet taps whatever mental acuity I'd retain under normal circumstances. What we estimated would be a six-hour climbing day is stretching to twice that length. Of that much I'm aware, even though my recollection of the day's events has been reduced to nothing more than a set of mental snapshots. And even these images are more comic strip caricatures than objective impressions with any depth or fidelity. However intense and memorable the morning's sights and sounds may have been, the color has been bleached out by the physical and psychological strain of a long day.

I lean into a berm of snow, formed by the edge of a deep pit where the glacial ice—deep blue where the snow doesn't stick— literally peels away from the mountainside. Half reclining and half standing, I pull slack rope through the metal grooves of a rope-braking device. The device, a folded piece of aluminum through which I've threaded the rope, is called a Reverso, and it is clipped to my climbing harness with a pear-shaped aluminum snap link called a carabiner. My clumsy hands draw the slick nylon rope through the brake—ready to clamp down like a manual version of the spring mechanism in your automobile seat belt. These machinations safeguard the human chain slowly picking its way up a near-vertical gully of ice 100 feet down the mountain. The figures below are three fellow climbers, and safeguarding their every step is a critical task.

Out of sight, they struggle, loaded down with heavy packs. We are all tied to a single rope. This thin cord, little thicker than a pencil, will stop those below from careening thousands of feet to their deaths should one of them slip and fall. I am not anchored to anything, but I've crawled over the berm, a snowy ridge lying perpendicular to their line of ascent. This should hold me—and by default, all of us—in case the worst should happen. The worst would look something like the following: the lowest and least experienced climber slips, dragging the upper two off—loading me, the fourth and highest climber, with the sudden shock of 600 falling pounds of backpack, climbing gear, and human body. Hunkering behind the snow ridge is the equivalent of lashing myself into a marlin chair while deep sea fishing. The only difference is it's not a trophy fish I have on the line, but human lives.

Despite the risk, I relax long enough to review the day's events. It all began with a surreal 1:30 AM wake-up leading to a weary struggle up deep snow and steep ice. The morning was cold, maybe 20 degrees below zero. That's cold enough to burn exposed skin and numb the toes, even nestled as they were within thick mittens and foam-insulated climbing boots. Much of the wee hours were spent plodding through crunchy snow, our footsteps illuminated by the sharp white glow of bobbing headlamps. The terrain was steeper than expected, requiring tedious zigzagging up unrelenting slopes.

Climbing some sections required swimming up molasses-like drifts that sucked us one step down for every two steps up. We took turns breaking trail through those sections in a dreary, slow-motion mountaineering rendition of a cycling peloton. As the day wore on, the sun grew to full force, at first a relief from the freezing cold, but quickly assuming an enervating quality. This development was miserably timed, coinciding with our arrival at the point where the ice and snow grew steeper. It was so steep and insecure that we'd then spent hours safeguarding our passage with time-consuming roped belays.

Lying in the snow and recalling the day's drama is a moment of beatific repose. I'm relieved to have just finished climbing through the ice groove that the others now pick through. That passage presented a snow-choked fracture leading through an otherwise unbroken— and virtually unscalable—200-foot-high ice cliff. The tottering cliff, formed by the toe of a hanging glacier, was festooned with dagger-like icicles the length and lethality of old-fashioned whaling harpoons. The cliff's surface presented such tenuous snow and ice, as to provide virtually nothing in the way of climbing anchors solid enough to stop an accidental fall. In other words, it was hard and dangerous. To a climber with my experience, this pitch, on an average weekend climbing day, is fairly commonplace. But here—in the body-sapping thin air of the Himalayas and loaded down with a pack full of food, stove fuel, and sleeping gear—the risks are multiplied. Feet can slip, and ice axes can unexpectedly pop from their lodgments in the brittle glacial ice. Compounding the risk is the haste born of climbing thousands of feet under the urgent arc of a racing sun. And it's at high altitude on what would be moderate snow and ice in one's lesser local hills, that good and sometimes great climbers meet their demise. Hence the paradoxical need for both speed, and great caution.

The ice cliff is probably the hardest we'll encounter on our ascent of this particular peak. If the weather holds, it will be two days tops, before we'll be up the mountain and on our way down. That's good news.

And the views are spectacular. The mountains march across a panorama that spreads to the north—like a topographic map that's come to brilliant Technicolor life. I live for these moments. Despite the toil, they provide clarity and purpose in a world too often drowned by requisite ambiguity and unavoidable shades of gray.

Though it's been clear all day, clouds have begun to billow and spread on peaks that form a distant horizon. I fumble for my watch, paying heed to the brake hand on the rope. The old Casio digital is buried in the inner pocket of my fleece suit. I pull it out, sliding my sunscreen-streaked glacier glasses onto my forehead so I can squint at the dial. It's around noon. The date is September 23, 2005. It's been little less than a month since three companions and I left Boulder, Colorado, for this expedition to a remote corner of the Himalayan mountain range. Our goal is to unravel a mystery whose roots are deep, well predating our own lives on earth. And at this moment, I'm convinced that we are at the threshold of success.

We are one long day, or maybe a day-and-a-half, from the summit of a hammer-headed mountain called Nanda Kot. At 22,510 feet high, Nanda Kot is merely one of hundreds of summits of a similar elevation in this great range. Her attraction to us stems neither from her height, nor her beauty—which is ample—but from the fact that somewhere on these icy flanks, lies a tangible vestige of the most bizarre and unheralded espionage escapade of the Cold War . . .

"*Though a straight line appears to be the shortest distance between two points, life has a way of confounding geometry. Often it is the dalliances and the detours that define us. There are no maps to guide our most important searches; we must rely on hope, chance, intuition, and a willingness to be surprised.*"

—Gordon Livingston, *Too Soon Old, Too Late Smart*

CHAPTER 1
THE GODDESS

Picture this. At some point during the dark and inhumanly cold Himalayan winter straddling 1965 and 1966, a strange thing happens. A storm blows in off the Indian Ocean, dropping sheets of rain on the dry plains before metastasizing into a raging blizzard as it hits the mountains. On one peak the snow collects. The individual flakes form layers, a light delicate filigree that builds millimeter by millimeter until the particles compress under their own weight. Over hours, the layers coalesce into a firm slab growing first by ounces, then by pounds, and then by tons, and more tons until, at one magic instant—perhaps the impact of a single snowflake—an unseen balance suddenly tips. Something deep in the snowpack snaps, and the entire mass, the size of several football fields, roars to life, sweeping away everything in its path.

In a mountain range like the Himalayas, this event would hardly warrant attention were it not for the bizarre cargo carried in the avalanche's roiling wake. For somewhere in this ferocious living mass of white thunder is a peculiar collection of box-shaped objects, one sprouting a six-foot, insect-like antenna. Ripped from their moorings, these objects now plummet some nine thousand feet down the sheer flanks of the mountain, the jumbled apparatus sliding down a funnel-shaped hourglass of hard snow. Gaining speed, they shoot over a black cliff band, a helter-skelter clattering mess careening a vertical distance six times the height of the Empire State building. These boxes come to rest on the glacier at the mountain's base. One, an olive drab casing the size of a fire extinguisher, lies in quiet repose in the dead silence. Then it begins to sink. Trailing a robotic dogtail of torn wires, it slowly burns through the snow, melting into solid blue glacial ice, eventually disappearing beneath the surface. And it's never seen again.

No one actually witnessed this event. But as you read these words, nearly four pounds of plutonium, locked in the glacier's dark unknowable heart, are almost certainly moving ever closer to the source of the Ganges River.

That's enough man-made poison to kill every human on earth, or to produce a radiological dirty bomb capable of paralyzing a large city and contaminating the area around it for miles.

As best I can recall, in 1987 I literally stumbled into the legend on a cold October night. On that night, I sat with five climbers swilling cheap malt liquor around a roaring campfire in Yosemite Valley. The six of us—dirty and destitute, a patchwork of stained pants, stubbled chins, and ratty fleece jackets—were living out our climbing mania on the endless walls of Yosemite granite. Some of us lived year-round in campground tents—members of the Yosemite Search and Rescue Team. Others chased the thin winter sun or cool alpine summers on cliffs, crags, and mountains around the country—a migrant tribe that lived to climb. I myself dwelled in Yosemite year-round, bussing tables at the National Park's restaurant concessions to earn money. Sometimes, I'd supplement this income with various nefarious schemes to finance my meager lifestyle or, a climbing trip.

The blaze subsided, and the raucous bullshit artistry—about epic climbs, girls whom'd spurned us, infuriating politics, and yet more climbing—ebbed and flowed. As the fat logs shrank to glowing embers, the tone of the night shifted from strident and profane to mellow and contemplative. Suddenly, my friend spoke up, filling a pensive silence that, in the absence of worthy banter, had stretched to the point of discomfort. My friend, let's call him Tucker, had a stout, low-slung build, lending him an authoritative air, the appearance of someone firmly anchored to the ground or, as was more often the case, the side of a cliff. He was one of those types whose expression becomes more earnest and animated with each passing drink. And that night he recounted the most outrageous climbing yarn we'd ever heard.

His rich, slurred delivery was peppered with the usual hyperbole—vilification of those in power, disparagement of mainstream values, glorification of our own climbing lifestyle. But somewhere before falling from buzzed eloquence to drunken rambling, the swaying Tucker managed to cast a spellbinding tale of brave climbers, CIA spooks, radioactive poison, and mountains bigger than we could imagine.

Tucker's story went something like this: A select number of elite climbers had apparently been trained by the CIA and paid huge sums of money to carry an atomic-powered spy camera to the top of an undisclosed peak. The stage of this 007-esque drama was none other than the greatest mountain range in the world, the Himalayas. But somehow this plutonium-powered device had been lost or stolen and was now either providing the fissile material in a secret Pakistani nuke or else threatening every man, woman, and child in India with deadly radiation poisoning. Not surprisingly, the CIA had apparently covered the whole thing up. That was to be expected. But for the five of us listening, the real grabber was the fact that six or seven of our own had been spies—sworn to secrecy on penalty of death. We wondered who had actually been recruited, what amount of money could possibly compel them to sell their souls for such a sinister scheme? And yet, inside, we were somehow consumed with envy at the thought of such a mission.

Morning came, the sun rose, and we scattered in search of the next climb. A few wisps of lonely smoke rose from the ashes of the previous night's blaze. And by now Tucker's campfire tale had taken on the hazy glow of legend. To me, the lost plutonium affair remained exactly that, a campfire fable of little substance, played out on an unnamed mountain and embellished with enough unbelievable details to remain nothing more than a myth. In the end, I don't think that any of us really believed that the CIA had ever paid climbers to spy on Communist China. Nor could we believe that several pounds of the deadliest substance known to man lay buried at the source of the Ganges River. One might just as easily have supposed that a Himalayan peak could glow in the dark.

Only years later would I learn the mountain's name. I would be told that the unnamed mountain had been revered by Hindus since the beginning of recorded history. It was—as I read in an old mountaineering account—the abode of their bliss-giving goddess. And I'd be inexorably drawn to this great mountain by the urge to delve beyond the shrouds of myth and legend and discover the true mystery.

My father once said something important to me that didn't mean much at the time. As a math professor with a philosophical bent, he must have read it in one of those books that tries to reconcile something timeless and esoteric like Zen with the murky real-time swamp of American living. He said it one evening as the two of us sat at the dinner table in Boise, Idaho. This was after my mom died of cancer and my only sibling, a brother, was off at Yale. My father said, "A man must embrace his fate, or at least accept it." I acknowledged the statement with a polite grunt and let him run with it. His monologue was like a background beat to the immediate business of chewing, swallowing, and finishing dinner. I was anxious to hook up with my friends—middle-class suburban kids like me who wanted nothing more than to burn up another evening passing the bong. Sitting there at the table, I wasn't nearly stoned enough to bounce such a far-out concept in my mind, nor did I really much care what came out of his mouth just then. Embracing fate was the last thing on my mind.

By the time five years had passed and I'd landed in the dirt, just in time for Tucker's fireside address, what I had embraced was climbing. I was a "troubled youth"—I got into scrapes with the law, and caused my family undue stress. As for many other immigrant children, it was hard for me to reconcile the pressures of an old culture—one that I never knew and one that originated many thousands of miles away—with the immediate reality of America in the 1980s. I was a natural rebel, adrift and unsure, and climbing gave me a creative and physical outlet. It gave me structure, goals, a peer group. This was before climbing had been defined as a "lifestyle," pursued with deliberation, or pandered to through marketing. In other words, it predated the era in which you saw down jackets by The North Face worn as hip-hop chic or the term "climbing" creep into the mainstream middle-class lexicon. But whether it was embracing fate or merely prolonging adolescence, mine wasn't the typical path of a young, middle-class Asian-American kid.

I'd quit college several years before, as well as a paid internship at the local PBS affiliate. This was after the producer told me that if I'd played my cards right I'd be running the studio some day. I looked around and saw my future. I was running studio cameras and taping shoots for the station. I was convinced that only dead fish go with the flow and through my young, and naïve eyes, I saw future peers who were professionals in their forties, some settled into lives of diminishing possibilities, whose greatest joy came from jockeying for advantage and, when necessary, backstabbing their way into the next promotion. Most others were convinced, with credibility I might add, that they were doing something of service to the community. Regardless, to me what they did looked cool. But right then, not cool enough.

I left a few weeks later while taping a live show. I literally abandoned my camera—one of three refrigerator-sized monsters, the kind wheeled around on the big pedestal dolly—leaving it trained on the on-air commentator as his image pulsed away on the flickering blue monitor. The last thing I heard was the faint crackle of the director's voice calling for a two-shot on my pair of headphones, which now hung draped over the camera lever, right where I'd left them before walking out the door.

Immediately after I took that final walk out of the PBS studio, I moved to California. I went climbing, and I never looked back. I didn't speak to my father or brother for over three years. To this day, for a number of reasons, my father and I are completely estranged. He was orphaned in World War II and, in a remarkable journey, came to the United States and went on to be a mathematics professor. His tenacity and sheer will to survive and succeed became ingrained deeply in his children. But those qualities alone could not help me thrive, especially in face of a family, fragmented by the lingering illness and ultimate death of my mother.

Though at the time I would have venomously denied it, looking back, I reinvented myself in a latter-day version of my own father. Where he chosen to boldly leave his native land as a teenager for the land of freedom, I'd chosen to drop out of the conventions of society and joined what Jon Krakauer has called, "a self-contained, rabidly idealistic society."

Climbing had given me a new family—one that acknowledged and embraced the absurd, one that didn't ask for too much in return. Life in the Yosemite Valley changed me. I became confident. I climbed well and got positive reinforcement from like-minded peers. My gait shifted from downcast shuffling to the kind of cocky, self-assured strut that only youth can carry off. I met girls, I got drunk, and I lived my dreams to the hilt.

Five years after Tucker's campfire yarn, I moved from Yosemite to

Colorado, becoming a frequent contributor to climbing journals. Somewhere along the line, while I wasn't looking, this passion of ours had become a sport, and besides churning out first-person features and departmental pap to feed the new climbing boom, I'd gotten married. My wife was a cute, quirky ER nurse from Northern California. By all accounts, I was living the dream, but when you stripped the façade away what you really had was a semi-famous twenty-eight-year-old whose lack of professional training compelled him to bus tables for the bulk of his living. Somehow, it was getting harder to strut the strut. I could pick up the phone and have a pair of the latest high-performance rock shoes FedEx'd overnight, all for free. But a living? When it comes to scoring a paycheck, climbing, with very rare exceptions, just isn't worth a whole lot to anyone but the climber.

Regardless, the flame still burned, and my climbing interests grew from rock climbing to tackling frozen waterfalls and snow-clad mountains. I don't know what my wife had expected when she married me, but it probably wasn't this ongoing obsession with climbing. It wasn't that I didn't love her, it was just that I still burned for other things. If I have one regret, it is from having wasted her time with my own vacillation towards marriage. Indeed, my true desire arrived in the form of a savage, unclimbed peak that few climbers had ever heard of. This fixation led to three expeditions, a divorce and some major credit card debt.

The peak, called the Sharksfin by virtue of its sleek dorsal fin symmetry, lies in what's called the Garhwal region of the Indian Himalayas. This mountain range is generally lower in altitude than the Nepalese and Karakorum ranges—home of the Himalayan giants of Everest and K2. For elite climbers, however, what the Garhwal peaks lack in relative stature, they more than compensate for in raw technical difficulty. The steep granite faces of the range form spear-like spires and fantastic needles of rock scraping the sky above 20,000 feet. When I first saw the Sharksfin in a picture, I knew I had to try.

I failed on every attempt. It wasn't just me, of course. To this day, despite more than twenty tries by the best alpinists in the world, the line remains unclimbed. What's its secret? I don't know. The climbing is hard, the air is thin, and the weather generates the kind of heavy snow that the Garhwal Range sheds like incessant volleys of heavy artillery. The only thing I can tell you is I know what it's like to spend six months of my life spread over four years watching all my hopes and dreams get pissed away by a flood of avalanches and endless streams of storm cloud. I can tell you what it's like to sit, stapled in place, as an avalanche roars your way with cold, implacable, inhuman speed.

Something in the mountains draws out the deepest emotions. The vast emptiness peels back the layers of pretense, leaving you with nothing but the bedrock of your psyche. You wrestle with fear, doubt, and uncertainty. What you do with those discoveries is a whole other issue, of course. For me, the ability to understand the price of a passion touches on every other issue in life. Some dreams need to be followed to the end, and I value the understanding that only comes after trying hard. So were those four years in the Garhwal worth it? More than I could have dreamed, actually. Just not in the way I'd expected.

On the last day of my final Sharksfin expedition in India, I happened upon a poster of a peak called Nanda Devi. It was tacked to the peeling wall in the sweltering hallway of the New Delhi office of the Indian Mountaineering Foundation (IMF). I knew a little about the peak already. It was surely one of the most awe-inspiring mountains in the world, a crown jewel set within an impenetrable ring of jagged peaks. My fuzzy recollections told me that wasn't until the 1930s that a human being even set foot in this true-life Shangri-La—a huge terrestrial bowl-shaped fortress of jagged peaks called the Sanctuary. And the first successful ascent of Nanda Devi itself, also in the 1930s, though virtually unknown to the general public, was a legend among my climbing peers. Indeed, to hard-core climbers it was a feat greater than the conquest of Everest. My familiarity with the feats surrounding this area of the Garhwal was more than academic; in 1999 I'd won the coveted Shipton-Tilman Grant to support an expedition to the Sharksfin. The award was named after both the first explorer (Eric Shipton) to enter the Sanctuary and first person (H. W. Tilman) to climb Nanda Devi.

Depending on whom you talk to, Nanda Devi is somewhere between the eighteenth and twenty-fourth-highest mountain in the world. While noteworthy, neither rank is particularly distinguished on its own merit, especially in a world obsessed with simplistic, misleading, and often meaningless absolutes. But, within India's two-million-square-mile landmass, Nanda Devi *is* the highest mountain. As such, she holds the bygone glory of being the highest point in the British Empire—making her, up to 1947 at least—the crown jewel of a mythic dominion upon which the sun never set. If mountains held a beauty pageant, then the Himalayas—the greatest range in the world—would be the stage and Nanda Devi, the most demure and alluring of contestants. Indeed, Nanda Devi has been called "the most beautiful mountain in the world," and earning such repute is no mean feat.

Around 45 million years ago—give or take a few million—the vast tectonic pie wedge called the Indian subcontinent collided with the Asian mainland. The voyage started nearly 150 million years earlier when the Indian plate began arcing across the globe at a lightning fast six inches per year (it was seriously fast in relative terms—faster than any other plate). One of the effects of this two-thousand-mile migration was a long-awaited collision with mainland Asia, resulting in a tortured geologic uplift of what became the Himalayas. Though tens of millions of years old, the subcontinent is still so vast and geophysically unique, it's retained the title of subcontinent. And the Himalayas still grow a couple centimeters every passing decade.

Even in India, the land of spiritual, physical, and mythical superlatives, Nanda Devi reigns supreme. No single natural feature in all the vastness of the "subcontinent" has been looked upon with such veneration and unrequited longing. Only the mythic Ganges might claim such a hold on the Indian imagination, but millions come in personal contact with the river after all, and on a daily basis. While Nanda Devi, though seen by many, is generally seen only from afar; indeed only a mere handful have felt her power in person.

The truth is, Nanda Devi is more than just a mountain. Long before the first awestruck human ever laid eyes on her majestic form, it is said that the Goddess, Nanda Devi, reigned over a pantheon of a million deities. And thus, as Mother of the Universe in the world's oldest surviving religion, Devi is worshipped by nearly a billion Hindus worldwide. To those who venerate her, Devi symbolizes all things feminine. She is the creator of life and purveyor of destruction—absolute ruler of the cosmic cycle of birth and death. As such, she balances beauty and spite, compassion and vengeance, grace and ferocity, benevolence and merciless retribution. India's Hindu tradition places Devi along side the most powerful male gods. In Hinduism, the male aspect, without Devi, is impotent.

That's a lot. But consider this. If we were to look at Devi through our Western trained eyes, we might see a divinely potent amalgam of the Virgin Mary, New Age Earth Mother, Lolita, and The Bride (Uma Thurman's character in *Kill Bill*). But even that's a crude and misleading simplification. Here's what Bruce Hathaway wrote in *Smithsonian* magazine, "She has a thousand names and faces—and countless tasks and talents. Even as a fierce warrior heroically slaying the most vicious demons, she retains her composure and radiant beauty. Westerners accustomed to a "Heavenly Father," and to seeing virginal, subdued images of the Madonna, might find Devi and her wildly vigorous feminine power quite startling. . . . Mother Goddess of India and local protector for innumerable villages, she can be quiet and nurturing. . . . On occasion she is voluptuous and alluring—a playful temptress, a passionate lover."

Devi is a force to be reckoned with, approached not with timidity, but with humility. That in mind, one can safely speculate that Devi, said to reside in her namesake peak Nanda Devi, chose her home as much for its preeminent location as for its remote austerity. It's an appropriately symbolic and literal locale, for indeed her peak is the hydrological source of the Alaknanda River. The Alaknanda is one of the three tributaries feeding the sacred Ganges. Jawaharlal Nehru, the first Prime Minister of India, himself born on the Ganges, had this to say of the river that has been exalted for millennia:

> The Ganga, especially, is the river of India, beloved of her people, round which are intertwined her memories, her hopes and fears, her songs of triumph, her victories and her defeats. She has been a symbol of India's age-long culture and civilization, ever changing, ever flowing, and yet ever the same Ganga.

As the terrestrial pinnacle of an eternal chain, it's not a stretch to say our Goddess resides at the very source—or at least one of the sources—of life for all Hindus. That's saying a lot, when we remember that the religion is over 4,000 years old and, behind Christianity and Islam, is the third-largest in the world. A religion that seeks no converts, Hinduism seems tied to India's very ground, water, and air. Ninety-eight percent of Hindus live in India, so from her high abode, Devi is their bridge between the earth and heaven—the physical and the spiritual. She dwells at the transitory link where water, purified by its passage from land to sky, turns from cloud vapor to pure snow—reentering the earthly chain of life as the snow becomes a glacier, the glacier becomes a stream, and the streams join to become the Ganges.

That being said, it is also fitting that the divine reside in such remote and unattainable splendor. And the mountain is remote.

Visible even from the distant foothills, Nanda Devi, a stunning, ice-encrusted tower of mythic stature and majesty, for thousands of years could be seen, but never touched. Unrecorded history probably holds scores who died attempting to get a closer look. Recorded history tells us that despite exploratory forays by Westerners as early as 1905, it wasn't until the 1930s that the ring of mountains guarding Nanda Devi, was ever actually breached by man.

Part of Nanda Devi's appeal comes from this self-same remoteness. For what is more alluring than beauty glimpsed, yet beauty untouched. Imagine a colossal eggshell whose jagged rim is formed by peaks 18,000 to 21,000 feet high. This serrated and nearly impenetrable ring encompasses a 100-square-mile basin of pristine alpine landscape. The moist microclimate within this core zone, known as "The Sanctuary," provides an oasis for flora and fauna found nowhere else on earth. Endangered Himalayan musk deer, snow leopard, and black bear roam lush alpine meadows and pine scented glades of Himalayan cedar. Though plainly seen for hundreds of miles year round, the only practicable way in and out of this Shangri-La is a through the Rishi Ganga Gorge, a narrow, singular slot cut by torrents of glacial melt water piercing the bedrock of the Sanctuary's western wall.

Nanda Devi's summit fell to prominent English climbers Noel Odell and Bill Tilman in 1936, and their first ascent was to become the stuff of mountaineering legend. So fixated was Tilman on the mountain's beauty, he'd spent the preceding several years just figuring out how to enter the Sanctuary. And their mammoth climbing route—nearly ten thousand feet long—was completed without the bottled oxygen that would later become a mainstay on high peaks like Everest and K2. It was also an unusually small team. Their conquest was heralded by Himalayan climbing visionary Eric Shipton as, ". . . the finest mountaineering achievement ever performed in the Himalaya."

It is worth noting that on summit day—August 29, 1936—scores of people died in nearby flooding. Observing this, one particularly respected Indian newspaper editor printed what many could not help but think—that the Goddess, having been provoked, had avenged her violation, "blindly but terribly." Even the usually taciturn Tilman was stricken with a sense of remorse. "It is the same sort of contrition," he would later write, "that one feels at the shooting of an elephant. . . . [The summit] was bought at the too high cost of sacrilege." Vengeance and contrition aside, however, Tilman's successful climb set an unbroken altitude record that would last for fourteen years.

Standing in the pressing heat of the IMF hallway, I stared at the poster, vaguely remembering what I'd heard—that Nanda Devi moved people in strange ways and made them do crazy things.

Later research would reveal the details. English explorer Hugh Ruttledge wrote,

> So tremendous is the aspect of the [Sanctuary] gorge that Hindu mythology described it as the last earthly home of the Seven Rishis [these are the seven wise men of Hindu mythology said to be represented by the seven stars of the constellation Ursa Major]—here if anywhere their meditations would be undisturbed."

If the Sanctuary held religious significance, it was as a lightning rod in an area holding (in one scholar's words), "a mythically charged geography." The Garhwal—named after the ancient "garhs" or forts dotting its unbelievably rugged landscape—was unified in the fifteenth century as a mountain kingdom, bordered by the Indian plains to the south, Nepal to the east, and the Tibetan plains to the north. Prior to unification, the Garhwal was a jagged chunk embedded in the northern boundary of the third-century Mauryan Empire (an empire spanning the Indian Subcontinent into Central Asia and encroaching on Southeast Asia). The eighth century saw the establishment of several sacred mountain shrines near the four glacial tributaries of the Ganges. These shrines grew to religious centers, becoming focal points of Hinduism. As such, the towns that grew around these centers, Badrinath, Kedarnath, Gangotri, and Yamunotri drew the faithful over the centuries with the same pull that Rome draws Catholics or Mecca draws Muslims. To this day, tens of thousands of Hindu pilgrims migrate annually from the stifling Gangetic plains to seek absolution in the crystal air and water of the Garhwal. Though later fragmented into five modern political districts, the Garhwal retains to this day both a rural backwardness and the spiritual aura of the holiest landscape in India—a true abode of the gods.

Eric Shipton—hailed as "Everest's senior statesman"—participated in all four of the legendary British Everest attempts of the 1930s. Still, he found Nanda Devi so compelling he took the 1934 hiatus from Everest attempts, jeopardizing a very real chance to be the first to stand on the world's tallest mountain (a year prior he'd turned back at 27,890 feet, 1,100 feet from the summit). This new challenge, he felt, superceded even that posed by an unconquered Everest. He wrote:

> I determined to make an attempt to force the hitherto invio-
> late sanctuary of the Nanda Devi Basin. At first this seemed
> as if we were flying too high. Here was a mountain whose
> summit was the highest in the British Empire. For centuries it
> had inspired worship and propitiatory sacrifice as the "Blessed
> Goddess" of Hindu philosophers and scribes. For more than
> fifty years it had been the inaccessible goal of explorers who,
> attracted by the impregnability of its surroundings, had failed
> in repeated attempts to reach even its foot, the reason being
> that around the 25,660-foot mountain itself stretched a huge
> ring of peaks, more than thirty of them over 21,000 feet high,
> that constituted themselves unrelenting guardians of the great
> mountain and defeated penetration.

Shipton, an explorer at heart, went on to delve into the mountains of China and Patagonia after so many years spent in the Himalayas. He was to regretfully miss the first ascent of Nanda Devi—in 1936, he was back on Everest. Tilman, not to be lured away by the pomp and prestige of the highest mountain in the world, leveraged his exploration of Nanda Devi's environs, successfully climbing the peak in 1936. He wrote simply of his and Noell O'Dell's incredulity on the summit (they had good reason to be dumbstruck, the altitude record, set without the use of supplemental oxygen was to remain unbroken until 1950), "I believe we so far forgot ourselves as to shake hands on it." Shipton, gracious even in regret, put the ascent of Nanda Devi in perspective, writing in 1937, "In my opinion the climbing of Nanda Devi is perhaps the finest mountaineering achievement which has yet been performed in the Himalayas, certainly it is the first of the really difficult Himalayan giants to be conquered. This expedition was a model of what such an expedition should be; the party was a team consisting exclusively of mountaineers; they avoided the great mistake which, to my mind, nearly all the major Himalayan expeditions since the war have made, and did not handicap themselves with a vast bulk of stores and superfluous personnel . . . above all, they avoided newspaper publicity."

Conquered or not, Nanda Devi continued to amaze and obsess. Another climber caught a mere glimpse of her in the 1940s, launching a saga whose final outcome held all the pathos and drama of a Sophoclean tragedy. The climber, Willi Unsoeld—later to become a national hero on the first American ascent of Everest (via a new route in 1963)—was at that time just an itinerant twenty-one-year-old, slumming through Europe and Asia on what we would now call a Dharma-bum tour.

Unsoeld's tale, recounted in Robert Roper's book, *Fatal Mountaineer* describes the pivotal moment,

> Sick, broke, and dressed like a beggar in rags, [Unsoeld] was eventually rescued by a medical missionary. And then one day, as Willi likes to tell audiences, "I went wandering up on a windy ridge, and from afar off I saw this superb peak, and I was absolutely smitten by its symmetry and its mystery. And the thought occurred to me, twenty-one years old and a little retarded, 'You know, I need a wife,' a logical first step in

the acquisition of a daughter. Because I suddenly wanted a daughter badly, I wanted her so that I could name her after that captivating mountain."

Roper describes Willi's daughter, Nanda Devi Unsoeld, as, "a good-looking, big-shouldered, pearly-toothed dreamboat very much in the counter-cultural style of the seventies . . . a feminist pioneer in a way, since women are still extremely rare on Himalayan climbs." Devi's lifelong ambition was to climb her namesake peak Nanda Devi. At twenty-two, her chance came in the form of a climbing expedition whose goal was to establish a difficult new route up the mountain's northwest face.

Some, including the native porters—to whom every aspect of the world was permeated by gods, goddesses, and myth—believed the Unsoeld daughter was the incarnation of the Goddess Devi herself, returning to her summit abode. To others (including not a few of her veteran teammates), Devi, despite her raw physical prowess and youthful indomitability, was dangerously naïve and lacked the experience to climb, much less survive, a serious encounter with the peak. They contended that Devi's presence on the trip was an act of hubris perpetrated by her father, whose unbending belief in spiritual growth through mortal risk was unreasonably supported by his legendary stature.

But if opinions varied, the earthly outcome could not be disputed. Devi fell ill after reaching the 24,000-foot level, 1,500 feet below the summit. The cause of her death cannot be precisely determined, though mountain medicine experts suggest an arterial clot or a heart attack was precipitated by gastrointestinal bleeding, further aggravated by altitude, exhaustion, and anemia. Her last act was to calmly utter, "I'm going to die," before lifelessly slumping forward in her sleeping bag. Devi's body was committed to the mountain with all the solemnity of a burial at sea—or, indeed, of the Goddess returning to her mountain. Later, an Indian member of the expedition wrote, "Devi lives; she has not died," adding, "She was the Goddess personified."

Though I was yet unaware of all the details, back in the IMF hallway, my unformed recollections flashed through my mind along with Tucker's late-night ramble. And they pressed in upon me at that moment like the mildewed heat of the heavy air I was breathing. I was depressed, both my physical and emotional defenses down. I'd lost 15 percent of my body weight and was now shelling out the last of my Visa-converted rupees for a third failed expedition to the Sharksfin.

Embracing fate was the last thing on my mind, but looking back, it was exactly what I was doing. I was about to return, empty-handed, to a small rented room in Boulder. There would be no one picking me up at the airport and nothing waiting for me at home save the discomfiting realization that I'd traded everything for nothing.

From past experience, I knew what lay ahead. Jet lag would induce a surreal nocturnal existence. Wake up at 3:00 AM, the mind racing with that desperate litany of self-doubt and recrimination. It had been that way from the beginning. Four years earlier, the last words I'd heard from my soon-to-be-ex wife as I was leaving for my first trip to the Sharksfin were "I can't wait around for you. I hope you have a really bad trip." And how.

The IMF staffers were well aware I was leaving after a third failure. To my face, of course, they were quite polite—solemn, in fact, to the point of condescension. But they were clearly embarrassed for me, astounded that someone could afford to squander so much money on such an obscure passion. We were either incredibly wealthy or incredibly stupid. One of the staffers now caught me looking at the image of Nanda Devi, a bold snow-draped crystal, presiding over the orange glow of a dying day. "This is Nanda Devi," he said in the deft lilt of Indian-accented English, smiling as he tapped the picture with an ink-stained finger, "She is quite closed to climbing." I asked him why. With a conspiratorial wink he said, "They say she's radioactive."

In that instant it dawned on me that Tucker's tale might be more than a campfire yarn. The mystery peak I'd heard of while sitting around the fire in the Yosemite Valley almost a decade prior must be Nanda Devi.

My curiosity piqued, I began pursuing the story. But the details of the Nanda Devi affair were so strange that they raised more questions than they answered. I pursued the story further, collecting dribs and drabs of information, even going so far as to interrogate older climbers I thought might have been involved. And when every climber I spoke with either claimed ignorance or simply stonewalled me, my suspicions were raised only higher. What exactly happened on Nanda Devi back in the days when the Beatles were singing "Love Me Do," and I blissfully slept in diapers? Did I know the climbers who'd risked their lives? When was the device going to re-emerge, and what would the fallout be?

Cursory research over the course of a year brought things into sharper focus. The puzzle pieces began to assemble themselves—a paragraph from a old mountaineering book; a moldering article from the *Hindustan Times*; a declassified typewritten memo from the sixties, its key passages blacked out with a wide-tipped felt marker; the grainy image of a plutonium power pack bolted to a NASA weather satellite. Gradually, it began to dawn on me that, however myth-enshrouded Tucker's tale originally sounded, its most incredible aspects were almost certainly true.

> *"I wanted to stress the point that our Governmental Space program was offering a lot of valuable by-products which would work to the mutual advantage and enrichment of all the world. . . . But knowledge is never wisdom."*
>
> —General Curtis E. LeMay

CHAPTER 2

A COLD WAR

Let's go to India.

I was about a year old when Captain Manohman Singh Kohli stepped through the swinging cargo doors of an Indian Army DC-3 transport plane to the cheers of a jubilant crowd at Delhi's sweltering Palam Airport. The din on that day, June 23, 1965, must have been deafening. And like all things in India, the scene must have been vast and chaotic. Absorbed by modern expansion, Palam is now merely Terminal 1 of an airport—the mammoth Indira Gandhi International—where forty years later I would debark myself some four times. On that day, Palam was the biggest game in town and played host to the most powerful men on the subcontinent. Greeting Kohli were the acting prime minister, Gulzari Lal Nanda; the new Prime Minister-elect, Lal Bahadur Shastri; and Defense Minister Yashwantrao Chavan. That India's political heavy hitters came to personally greet their newest national hero, lent a tangible weight to the importance of events that had transpired in the diminutive Kingdom of Nepal, little less than a month prior.

Seldom had a single mountain meant so much to so many. On May 29, an Indian Everest expedition—led by Kohli—placed a final team of three climbers on top of the highest mountain in the world. In doing so, Kohli and India had done what no other country had—in ten days they'd gotten four teams for a total of nine successful summiteers on Everest. It was a huge personal victory for the captain and a shot scored for the whole country. Not only did his team comprise the first Indians to stand on the Roof of the World, but to date, no single venture had put so many climbers on the summit. The news electrified India, tapping a vein of nascent national pride—for, though one of oldest civilizations in the world, independent India was a country not yet twenty years old. Recalls Kohli, "India's magnificent success on Everest placed her on the world map of mountaineering." He further noted that, "India emerged as the fourth nation in the world* to have its climbers on Everest."

---

* The People's Republic of China laid claim to a successful ascent of Everest from Tibet in 1960. Though at the time their account was doubted, later their claim was generally accepted. Here it is apparent that Kohli still takes exception. If the Chinese had climbed Everest in 1960, India would have been the fifth nation—after the British (though the summiteers in the British expedition were from New Zealand, Edmund Hillary and India Tenzing Norgay), Swiss, Chinese, and Americans.

Lying in a crib, cross-eyed in diapers at the time, I had no concept of what a climbing was. Later, some of my early childhood memories involved peaks—dreaming them and drawing them. My pictures, red and blue crayon outlines on typing paper, depicted clouds and snow-capped ranges—this despite the fact that I had seen no such thing, other than in pictures. By first grade, I'd already thumbed through countless back issues of magazines like *National Geographic*. I'd seen Willi Unsoeld on Everest and Bobby Kennedy climbing his recently assassinated brother's namesake peak—Mount Kennedy—in remote Canada. Otherworldly, the harsh landscapes of snow and ice might as well have been another planet. Even the climbers looked alien—oxygen masks, goggles, and hooded visages— especially a shot of a climber named Barry Bishop on the summit of Everest. He was an earthly astronaut on the fringe of outer space. He claimed a spot in my personal hall of heroes, right up there with Neil Armstrong and Jacques Cousteau.

India's Everest achievement helped to define the infant country's place in the global arena. It also symbolically cemented her presence in the Himalayas, which, more than just a mountain range, was the jagged physical and cultural boundary separating mainland Asia from the subcontinent. For centuries the "abode of snow" (as translated from Sanskrit) was not only the crossroads of trade and culture, but also the flashpoint for political and military rivalries. From the strategic conflict between the British Empire and Tsarist Russia for control of Central Asia—called the Great Game; to the invasion and occupation of Tibet by the People's Republic of China in 1950—the Himalayas had been a lightning rod for espionage, intrigue, and outright war. Indeed, the battles of the Sino-Indian

War of 1962—a conflict that ultimately fielded 5 million Chinese and Indian troops—took place on and around key passes piercing that same mountain barrier.

Kohli's slight stature concealed a determination and remarkable physical prowess. Then standing about five feet four inches with a 145-pound frame, Kohli was anything but imposing. But by 1965 he'd already developed a reputation for an iron will, bulwarked by his Sikh faith that drew strength from God—and his own ancestors. I was lucky enough to meet Kohli in Delhi decades later. I found his vigor and enthusiasm inspiring. Still mentally tack sharp, the old Sikh, now in his seventies, bedecked with his traditional turban and copper bracelet, worked in an office, augmented by modern accoutrements. He, like his very workplace, was an island in the physical chaos of downtown Delhi. And his recollections, deliberate snapshots of the past, had little of the sentiment or emotional overlay one would expect after the passage of forty years. Kohli, still with the posture and physical vitality of a man much younger, seemed to possess few regrets, and fewer still of the nagging doubts that plague the others who took part in the espionage from the top of the world.

Kohli, always a disciplined team player, had a strong sense of duty, both to god and country, causes greater than his own personal desires. It was perhaps this selflessness that, despite being expedition leader, led him to deny a place for himself on any of the summit teams. And the personal temptation must have been great. A few short years prior, in 1962, a twenty-something Kohli had struggled through rarified air and deep snow of Everest to within a tantalizing 330 feet of the top.

Temptations never completely leave. But even in the face of the heady kudos and heaped with the gratitude of the nation, Kohli's enviable spiritual sense and humility never seemed upset. Called "a man of destiny" by noted Indian author and ex-pat Scot, Bill Aitken, the ever-devout Sikh would later write of the successful 1965 Everest trip, "At the end of the expedition I felt overwhelmingly grateful to God. It was He who made it all possible. I was only an instrument of destiny."

A destiny of a different sort was to soon unfold. While basking in the adulation of the almost 500 million Indians, Kohli had attracted attention of an unexpected sort. On that same stifling June day, he was passed a message to meet with one Rameshwar Nath Kao. Kao, stocky and straightforward, was an admirer of Scotland Yard, the CIA, and Germany's Federal Intelligence Service or BND, was the director of a mysterious branch of India's Intelligence Bureau called the Aviation Research Centre (ARC). ARC was an appropriately nondescript designation for a secret technical intelligence agency constituted in 1963 as part of India's response to its own ill-preparedness for the Chinese invasion in 1962. As a subsection of India's Intelligence Bureau (IB), ARC was staffed by bureau officers and provided with aircraft.

The IB director, an austere and dedicated man—who had never missed a day of work—was named Bhola Nath Mullik. Mullik was short, with close-cropped hair and sixties horn-rimmed glasses, and had the ear of not only Prime Minister Shastri, but also of the CIA. It was he, no doubt, who helped acquire aircraft ranging from the rugged twin-engined Curtiss C-46 Commando to specialized Short Takeoff and Landing (STOL) aircraft like the Helio Courier—courtesy of none other than the CIA—to Russian-made Mi-4 helicopters. ARC's job was to lend air support to clandestine para-military operations. This was a critical task, given India's ongoing conflicts with both China and Pakistan—where the theaters of operation often lacked access by reliable road networks. India's frontier regions were often mountainous, and the Couriers, with their ability to use short crude runways and the Mi-4's, with an unprecedented ability to carry a lot of weight at high altitudes, were especially useful.

One can imagine it was an intrigued and mystified Kohli who met with Kao on that hot and dusty June day. At the time of the fateful meeting at Palam, Kao was only an acquaintance, and the encounter was entirely unexpected. It was obviously urgent. For the momentous event was something along the lines of an Indian version of Lindbergh's trans-Atlantic flight. The two conferred briefly behind the parked DC-3 on Palam's hot tarmac. It was a whispered meeting masked from eavesdropping by the noise of the throng. Kao, known to close associates as Ramji, said briefly, "You are required to proceed to the USA for some special training immediately." This was not a literal directive as Kohli was to be honored, feted, and decorated with awards including the Padma Bhushan medal for "distinguished service to the nation," and the Arjuna Award, the "highest national recognition of distinguished sports-persons." Arjuna was a hero and character from the sacred Hindu text, the Bhagavad-Gita. His name means "bright" or "shining." Truly, on that day, Kohli had been elevated above pale, taking his place among India's heroes. Aware of this pressing post-expedition swell of stardom, Kao knowingly added, "See me as soon as your schedule of receptions is over."

Kohli could not have known it, but Kao's request was the result of events that had taken place a year earlier in the remote Xinjiang Province of western China. On October 16, 1964, the People's Republic of China detonated their first nuclear weapon at Lop Nor Lake. In the typically shrill lexicon of Chicom Cold War rhetoric, Beijing announced, "This is a major achievement of the Chinese people in their struggle to increase their national defense capability and oppose the United States' imperialist policy of nuclear blackmail and nuclear threats." It went on and on for several pages, but shrill rancor aside, the important thing was that China had the bomb.

American reaction ranged from concerned editorials to private worries. One columnist wrote, "The long awaited Chinese atomic explosion became reality yesterday, and now the world must live with the ominous fact that a fifth nation [behind the United States, Soviet Union, Great Britain, and France] has joined the nuclear club. . . . The priority need is for action to insure that yesterday's nuclear test is the last atomic weapons experiment in human history." A secret cable from the White House to Taiwan's capital, Taipei stated, "We all noted that the President [at the time it was Lyndon Johnson] had a rather intense feeling of frustration and anxiety and believe this due [to] the suddenness of CCNE (Chinese Communist Nuclear Explosion) which he had heretofore discounted as occurring within the next three years."

The Chinese hadn't been bluffing. Their nuclear device, named an apparently cryptic "596," yielded the explosive force of 22,000 tons of TNT—comparable to the atomic bomb dropped on Nagasaki. Incidentally, the name 596 was a titular in-your-face to the Soviets, derived from the year (1959) and the month (June) when the Russians refused to hand China a prototype nuclear weapon. It's further worth noting that a National Security Council meeting was held in the Cabinet room of the White House on the Saturday immediately following the Chinese nuclear test announcement.

It was October 17, 1964. The meeting was attended by the White House staff. The test itself was cause for worry, but further concern came from the lack of intelligence on China in general, and their nuclear program in particular. One attendee was Chief of Staff of the United States Air Force, General Curtis LeMay. I'd later see the general himself staring with his eagle eyes from the pages of the same stacks of magazines that so inflamed my imagination as a kid. Everest, LeMay, Bishop. Decades later they would all converge in my life. A recently declassified typewritten document states, "The first topic, was the Chinese atomic bomb test yesterday. . . ." "One potential area of China has not been covered by photographic reconnaissance, and, therefore, could have an additional reactor (or reactors), and [CIA Director] McCone said he wouldn't be surprised if there were a plant in this area."

What better place for a secret nuclear test than the middle of nowhere in the most remote corner of "The Bamboo Curtain." Across the Tibetan border, clear into China's farthest province, the 596 with its incandescent fireball and characteristically malignant mushroom cloud couldn't have blown up a more exotic locale. Lop Nor was the legendary "heart of the heart" of Asia—where water flows inland rather than to the ocean. Depending on rainfall and evaporation, the position and size of the lake varied from year to year, giving birth to a more whimsical moniker, "The Wandering

Lake." When measured in 1928, the lake covered an area three times the size of Hong Kong. Subsequent climate change and agricultural drainage has caused its virtual disappearance.

It's safe to say that Kao's concern had less to do with any possible environmental impact on the natural wonders of Lop Nor, but more with the successful nuclear detonation, and namely its effect on India's national security. Needless to say, the Indians were not pleased with development. Indeed, they went ahead to build their own nuclear weapons in the 1970s, in what some claim was a response to China's bomb. But for now, their pleas for China to restrain their nuclear ambitions went unheeded, leading to a breakdown in relations between the two Asian powers. According to the *New York Times* of November 17, 1964, "The Chinese Communists said today that India was breaking off 'friendly contacts' such as scientific and cultural exchanges, with China after having voiced strong opposition to Peking's drive to develop nuclear arms." Indian Prime Minister Shastri (who was on hand to greet the jubilant Kohli at Palam) said, that China's nuclear weapon represented no less than, "a threat to humanity," invoking the specter of the China/Indian border war, saying that despite India's appeals, "we have been unable to get a friendly response from China."

Kao was India's leading spymaster known for his "keen intellect," a cool methodical approach, and careful study of the intelligence services of other nations. He would later found the clandestine Research and Analysis Wing (RAW), India's most powerful intelligence organ, the equivalent to America's Central Intelligence Agency. The forward-thinking Kao saw to it that RAW unlike the CIA, however, worked directly under the India's executive branch of government, reporting to the Prime Minister. Like America's National Security Agency, RAW would have no oversight from the legislative branch (the Lok Saba, or Indian Parliament). As RAW was formed in 1969, it was Kao's intelligence-gathering responsibilities as director of ARC that led him to seek out Kohli and that climber's unique skill set.

During the early 1960s, India was committed to neutrality while the Soviet Union, the United States, and the People's Republic of China hashed out their ideological differences in a game of global chess. Neutrality was at best viewed as suspect by the United States, which had just finished fighting the Korea War against communist hordes and was ramping up its efforts to stop the Red tide in an unknown slice of Indochina called Vietnam. During the late-fifties administration of President Dwight Eisenhower, his Secretary of State John Foster Dulles did much to define India's relationship with the United States. Deeply religious and "a man of complex character, full of paradoxes," Dulles found as many detractors as adherents. What was not paradoxical was his aggressive stance on communism which embraced an "if you are not with me, you are against me," mind-set. In one speech, on June 9, 1955, Dulles argued that "neutrality has increasingly become an obsolete and, except under very exceptional circumstances, it is an immoral and shortsighted conception." This statement directly undermined a key tenant of India's foreign policy—nonalignment. In some eyes, this was a tragic move, for ironically, India was (and still is) the world's most populous democracy.

India's relationship with the United States certainly wasn't helped by this American predisposition. What really hurt was the fact that the United States supplied Pakistan, America's "most allied ally in Asia," with arms. This was to drive India into the waiting arms of the Soviet Union. India and Pakistan were sworn enemies after a contentious and bloody 1947 partition that left by some estimates 13 million displaced Muslims, Hindus, and Sikhs.

Depending on whom you ask, two hundred thousand to a million died in that conflagration. Adding to the complexity, India's rather threatening neighbor to the north, China, was at odds with her own socialist brother, the same Soviet Union that plied India with jets, tanks, and guns. A shared communism did nothing to assuage the geopolitical reality of inevitable conflict on a border over 4,000 miles long (a large figure that does not count the Soviet and Chinese-controlled Mongolian border). That is exactly what the Soviets and the People's Republic faced. Such prolonged contact, when mixed with unavoidable territorial ambitions, ultimately led to border skirmishes and rivalry between the two nuclear powers. Thus it was, that the Soviets, ever seeking to offset American influence in Asia as well as wanting to neutralize the power of China, made an alliance with India a central pillar of Moscow's Asia policy.

A good soldier does his duty without regard to the Byzantine maze of political necessity. So several days later when he met Kao in the director's Delhi office, an astounded Kohli never once questioned the overarching strategic plan behind an outrageous proposition. Kao explained to an amazed Kohli that an Indian team would be trained in the United States to handle and deploy a monitoring device on a major Himalayan peak. Kohli was briefed on the growing threat of Chinese nuclear capabilities and the inability of either India or the United States to acquire the relevant intelligence.

More astounding was the proposal of the cooperative venture and
what that entailed. Years later, Kohli recalled, "The solution found
by the CIA was to mount a joint Indo-American Expedition to
plant a nuclear-powered sensing device on the high Himalayan
peaks to monitor China's missile launches. It appears the plan was
devised in Washington."

Kohli's speculation on the plan's origin seems correct. Legend has it that
a chance meeting at a Washington, D.C., cocktail party first sparked the
improbable notion—some might even call it a Faustian bargain—to
use nuclear technology to spy on the People's Republic of China from
the Himalayas. In 1964, Cold War paranoia was at its height. So great
was the perceived threat of nuclear proliferation that no plan was too
outlandish, no investment too great, and no means unjustified.

The instigators were two of the same guys I'd seen in the magazines, Barry Bishop and the General Curtis LeMay. LeMay, if you'll
remember, attended the National Security meeting following the
Chinese blast. The two were an unlikely pair. Bishop, an unassuming
climbing legend, had been a summiteer on the first successful American Everest expedition in 1963. Bishop nearly perished in a crevasse
on the descent. Later he'd lose all his toes and the tips of his pinkies
to frostbite. At a stocky five feet seven inches, Bishop was nicknamed
"Barry the Barrel" because he packed 165 pounds into the short
powerful frame. Bishop was described in James Ramsey Ullman's
Americans on Everest as "a young man of many hats and talents: a
geographer, writer, photographer and mountaineer." Many talents
indeed. On his way to the top, Bishop, as a photographer for
National Geographic, took the famous shot of Lute Jerstad

approaching the summit of Everest capped with the stars and stripes. The bold Kodachrome of a determined figure straining towards the red, white, and blue—boldly highlighted against an indigo high altitude sky—captured the imagination of the American public, as well as future climbers like myself.

A modest man, Bishop himself ended up gracing the cover of *Life* magazine. But he never let it get to his head. Wrote Gilbert M. Grosvenor, President of the National Geographic Society, "In later years he [Bishop] would play down his ascent of Mt. Everest, his participation as a member of the first American expedition to reach the summit of Everest in 1963 was a crowning achievement." Whatever credit he might not have claimed, was given anyway. Bishop and the other members of the American team were awarded the National Geographic Hubbard Medal "for distinction in exploration, discovery, and research." John F. Kennedy himself awarded the medal in the White House Rose Garden. It was a huge honor, for such luminaries as Ernest Shackleton and Charles Lindbergh were past recipients of the honor.

A man of great physical courage himself, LeMay had his own chestful of medals including the Distinguished Service Cross (second only to the Medal of Honor), the Silver Star, and the Legion of Merit. Called "Iron Ass" by his own troops, legend has it that LeMay would never ask them to do what he wouldn't. On a bombing mission in World War II, the then-colonel, himself piloted a bomber through murderous anti-aircraft fire after declaring that there would be no more "zigzagging," or evasive flying by his men. LeMay's real-life deeds and heroism made him as many detractors as supporters. He was undoubtedly the archetypal Pentagon hawk—a real-life cigar-chewing model for the rabid General Buck Turgidson of Stanley Kubrick's *Dr. Strangelove.* LeMay had been the mastermind behind the strategic firebombing of Nazi Germany and Imperial Japan in World War II. Indeed, these raids, which killed more than the combined nuclear strikes on both Hiroshima and Nagasaki, influenced his future perspective on another Asian war. In 1968, while the espionage climbers struggled on the heights of Nanda Devi, LeMay, as legend has it, let his thoughts be known on the Vietnam War. "They've got to draw in their horns and stop their aggression," he said. "Or we're going to bomb them [the North Vietnamese] back into the Stone Age."

When LeMay uttered those words, the Vietnam War was reaching a critical turning point. Though destined to rage for another seven years, the tide of American support for the war was turning, and, with it, the rejection of the political and social mores of the pre-World War II generation. I was ten years old when the Vietnam War ended. I remember seeing Soviet-made tanks on our black-and-white TV crashing through the ornate colonial gates of the South Vietnamese Presidential Palace. Like those wrought-iron gates themselves, in that moment the old order was broken. The faith of my up-and-coming generation in the United States, though not shattered, was indelibly altered. The recession, Watergate, the ongoing Cold War, and echoes of the sixties social revolution called into question the very essence of the American Dream. Those were the days of mutual assured destruction—a cynical balance of nuclear power—that overshadowed life, and human existence itself. My peers and I asked, "To what ends do we strive?" For many of us, for better or worse, the answer lay in choosing alternatives, not the conventional

path. By the time I was a teenager in the late-seventies, the rote path
was not just tarnished, it was distasteful.

Though he later denied uttering those words, LeMay's threat was
the type of language Dulles would have loved. And before you draw
any blanket condemnations, consider this—believe it or not,
LeMay *did* ponder the ethical implications of twentieth-century
total war. In his own words, "Every soldier thinks something of the
moral aspects of what he is doing. But all war is immoral and if you
let that bother you, you're not a good soldier."

The good soldier LeMay, as architect of America's primary
nuclear deterrent, Strategic Air Command (SAC), was very concerned by China's ballistic missile testing in Xinjiang Province.
Xinjiang is China's biggest and most western province. Its name literally means "New Frontier." Vast, dry, and for much of its area,
desolate, the "new frontier" was ideal for staging nuclear weapon
and missile tests, far from prying eyes. And obtaining the intelligence of China's growing capability had become an unrequited
obsession. LeMay must have winced at knowing Xinjiang was the
"area of China has not been covered by photographic reconnaissance." The reason being that though spy aircraft over-flights were
an option, they risked political fallout. The downing of Francis
Gary Powers' U-2 spy plane over the Soviet Union in 1960 had created a diplomatic furor, pushing the world to the brink of nuclear
war (if one were to heed the nuclear sabre rattling at least). Later, in
1964, the CIA sent a U-2 that actually flew a mission over Tibet.
This mission launched from Charbatia base located at a secluded
area outside of India's east coast city of Cuttack. Charbatia is India's
humble answer to America's Area 51, without the UFO hoopla and

cutting-edge technical development. Regardless, it was, "the ultrasecret airport belonging to the Aviation Research Center [ARC]." And ARC as you'll remember was Kao's mysterious aviation branch of the India's Intelligence Bureau.

The U-2 was an amazing aircraft in a world of burgeoning technology, the most advanced of which served the purposes of the military. The plane was designed to fly at extreme altitudes to thereby avoid the latest guided anti-aircraft missiles fielded by the Soviet Union and its allies. Still in active service today, the U-2 was nicknamed the "Dragonlady" because of its notoriously "unforgiving flight characteristics." "Unforgiving" is a toned-down euphemism for the U-2's sensitivity to speed and control, and its black widow-like tendency to kill those who piloted her. And many earnest aviators died while flying, or landing the plane, which looked for all intents like a big black glider with a jet engine. True to form, at the tail end of the Charbatia mission, the ungainly U-2 rolled off the end of runway after its brakes failed. Though the CIA pilot survived, the missions were apparently scrapped. A declassified CIA memorandum, dated October 5, 1964, states:

> U-2 photography would give us more precise information on the final stages of construction at Lop Nor from which we might estimate the probable time of a nuclear detonation. I (Director of Central Intelligence John McCone) said that unless information concerning the time of a detonation was of significant importance to the President [Lyndon Johnson] and Secretary Rusk [Secretary of State], I could not recommend the flight."

The document further reads,

> CIA telegram . . . October 8, stated that the primary reason
> for canceling the Lop Nor mission was the risk of an incident
> in the month preceding the presidential election.

Though CIA-trained Taiwanese pilots continued to fly U-2 missions over the PRC—some ending in death or imprisonment at the hands of the communists—American intelligence faced a technological stalemate. Risk of political fallout from U-2 flights was too great to fly over Xinjiang, And the existing satellite technology of the 1960s was inadequate to gather sufficient data. The deployed satellites, the KH-4 Corona lacked the optics necessary to glean useful images. Though a precursor to later generations of spy satellites that would render the Himalayan espionage efforts futile, the KH-4 of the mid-sixties was woefully inadequate. "Comparing the satellite optics to those of the U-2, Land [Edwin Land, a scientist who besides consulting the intelligence community, invented instant Polaroid photography] told the president that, "whereas the U-2 could photograph objects as small as 4 feet, the satellite cameras would only be able to discern objects 50 to 100 feet on a side."

And neither America nor her allies possessed a dependable spy network within the PRC. Even spying in Tibet using CIA-trained Tibetan recruits yielded limited, and inconclusive, intelligence. And with the detonation of China's first nuclear warhead in late 1964, the need grew urgent. A weapon is useless unless you can deliver it to your enemy's doorstep. But by the late-fifties, China, anticipating her nuclear teething, was already working on a ballistic missile.

Though on a technical level, China's nuclear missile program moved at a snail's pace—one to two decades behind the other nuclear powers—she did have, by 1964 a missile program, well underway. This concerned everyone, including the Soviets, who, though initially providing their socialist brethren the technical means to implement their program, terminated their assistance after the Sino-Soviet split in 1960.

Hostile nuclear-capable nation-states with the means to deliver were an emerging—and no less nightmarish—threat in the 1960s as they are today. On October 26, 1966, the Chinese one-upped their nuclear capability with the launch of their Dong Feng-2A missile (in large part, a copy of a Russian design—Dong Feng means "East Wind"). The metal tube, about as long as the eighteen-wheelers that roar down our own Interstate, was loaded with volatile liquid oxygen as a propellant—and sported a nasty cargo. Thundered from its launch pad, arcing across the clear blue skies of Xinjiang Province, the Dong Feng was tipped with a 2,838-pound atomic bomb with a 12-kiloton yield. For those of us who've either forgotten the Cold War or weren't born yet, a kiloton is the explosive yield of a thousand metric tons of the high explosive TNT. To give you an example, the Chinese Dong Feng warhead was similar to the explosive force of the Hiroshima bomb. Though small compared with cutting edge arsenals—by this time Soviet and U.S. bombs were already measured in *millions* or megatons—it still flew 500 miles to Lop Nor, where the device successfully detonated, churning up a mushroom cloud and melting the desert sand. The implications were immense. With that range, the Chinese could potentially reach America's ally, Japan.

Anticipating just such an event, the lack of solid information must have given LeMay more than one sleepless night. It must have added a stony cast to his already stern visage—as much derived from his stubborn manner as from a little known physical ailment. During World War II, LeMay became a victim of Bell's Palsy, a partial paralysis of the facial nerves—in his case on the right side. Years later, a pleased LeMay recounted, "The right side of my upper lip is immobile: it doesn't smile . . . and has helped to promote the legend that I never smile." His self-same theory on the use of nuclear weapons must have spiced up his nightmares. For when it came to communism, the general made little distinction between the use of nukes and conventional weapons. In 1949, the year of the Soviet Union's detonation of their first A-bomb, he proposed dropping, "[America's] entire stockpile of atomic bombs in a single massive attack," on that communist nation. In a scale that boggles the mind, LeMay's plan was to, "drop 133 atomic bombs on 70 cities within 30 days."

Back to the Washington, D.C., cocktail party. The details aren't recorded, even in LeMay's own autobiography. But picture the general, described as "short, fat and slovenly," bedecked in chest candy from decades of combat. His own wife, upon their first meeting—a blind double date said, "I think I'll take the fat one." LeMay is in his navy blue SAC uniform, sipping a drink, perhaps with a trademark cigar clamped in his teeth. A Washington Beltway cocktail party is something he doesn't care for, but still probably the best chance for the dedicated career officer to do anything resembling relaxation. Under it all, he must be stressed over Chinese nukes. Then picture him chatting with an equally short, stocky Bishop. Not a military guy, Bishop would be in civvies, maybe a suit. Perhaps he'd be hobbling a bit—having lost all his toes to frostbite. They are titans in their respective worlds. It's probably noisy and smoky, so they have to speak loudly to hear each other, something both LeMay—a man of "brooding silence and intense concentration"—and Bishop—reserved and "exceedingly modest"—are unaccustomed to. No doubt they've already known of each other. LeMay, a trustee of the National Geographic Society, has been featured in the yellow magazine's pages as the man behind the technological wonders of Strategic Air Command (SAC). SAC's sister is the American Space Program.

Though the first-hand details of the actual cocktail party meeting are forever lost—both men are deceased now—it's easy to imagine LeMay's interest, when Bishop recounts the unobstructed line of sight into western China he'd enjoyed from the summit of Everest. It was an ethereal experience. He could only have described it as such—like soaring through the jet stream with one's feet planted on earth. As Norman Dyhrenfurth writes, "Barry and Lute spent forty-five [minutes on the summit]. Their picture making done, they looked around them: out across mountaintops into miles of space; at their own mountaintop, falling away on all sides beneath them." Maybe that's the start of the conversation, for LeMay, "unsophisticated, taciturn, dedicated, tactless to the point of rudeness," knows a little something about soaring through the jetstream. He's the fiercest warrior of the jet age. LeMay dislikes socializing, "except with a few intimates, those with whom I can share a reverence for the past, and an awareness of the challenges to come." So maybe in Bishop he's found someone at the party who can connect with his sense of mission. And someone he can talk to without navigating the political minefield that's eventually going to blow him out of his berth as Air Force Chief of Staff.

When they get to the actual talk of spying on China, they probably move closer to escape prying ears. One account of the meeting has them discovering a "synergy" that "suddenly became obvious." Bishop knew the Himalayas and appreciated the scientific and photographic aspects of high-altitude climbing. LeMay, whose air force was responsible for tracking tests by nuclear states and threshold nations, felt a pressing concern about China's nuclear program. For him, the ability to peer into Xinjiang and glean information about Beijing's atomic tests held merit. "An era of covert mountaineering was about to begin." And so, from a rather casual exchange emerged the unlikely inspiration: recruit America's best high-altitude climbers and set about placing a nuclear powered observation device atop the world's greatest mountain range.

I'd give my left arm for the details of that chat and the more formal meetings that must have followed. Those details are lost. Barry Bishop died in a one-car accident near Pocatello, Idaho, in 1994 at 62, having just retired. LeMay, after leaving the air force in 1965, went on to a political career. The regrettable high point, of the general's political life, was as vice-presidential running mate for the later-repentant segregationist, George Wallace. LeMay died in 1990.

It's all history—and one that won't die away with its protagonists. When Indian and American strategic interests regarding the Red Chinese bomb aligned in the mid-sixties, that development corresponded with a brief warming in relations between the two nations. The diplomatic defrosting was due in part to the American aid provided during the Sino-Indian border war. And having just ended that inconclusive conflict, India stood to gain on the national security front from the timely partnership. As the CIA and Indian Intelligence had been jointly running intelligence operations for several years, "the project was turned over to the agency." What this meant was that through the CIA contact in India, ARC director Kao, word was, "passed [in] the message on to Mullik," who after listening to the concept, "was agreeable in theory." Mullik as you'll recall was the powerful Director of India's Intelligence Bureau.

The buck probably did not stop there, but it certainly sinks out of sight. I use the word "probably," because the key high-level players are now deceased and I've discovered no official statements on the matter. I cannot prove a higher-level connection with the project. To do so would be playing a game of journalistic pin the tail on the donkey—with no donkey in sight. Certainly, the operation had, "approval from the highest levels" as Jim McCarthy puts it. An outspoken former Manhattan trial lawyer and leading American climber, he was a CIA recruit in the Nanda Devi escapade. But all we know is that from the American side the affair was given the, "tacit green light," by somebody in power.

Though brushed under a carpet of secrecy, the story never fully died. In May 1978—around the time I started rock climbing—journalist Howard Kohn (who later authored the nuclear exposé *Who Killed Karen Silkwood?*) published an account of the espionage escapade. I didn't see the story at the time, appearing as it did, in a budding *Outside* magazine that covered a wide range of outdoor activities. By then, I'd fallen into the world of the hard-core technical climber, a path that would for a time sever the ties with my more tradition-bound ancestry. My periodical tastes ran strictly along the hard-core niche climbing mags. I, and the few thousand other read-ers of these tiny publications, would have it no other way. Little did I know that my path would lead full circle to the great mountain ranges, that enthralling alien world, depicted in those glossy pages of *National Geographic*.

Later, I'd dig up Kohn's story. Though plagued with inaccuracies—the article drew mostly from second-hand reports—it confirmed, to me at least, that the rumors had credibility. Enough at least, to keep me hot on the Nanda Devi trail.

I later learned that the choice of remote sensing locations was a peak called Kangchenjunga. Bishop made the decision. His choice was based on the requirements set down by technological and polit-ical necessity: the peak must have sufficient line-of-sight altitude to listen in on Tibet, and it must be entirely within Indian jurisdiction. The schedule was also urgent. By June 1965, Bishop had already collected the American climbing team for a training mission on the 20,320-foot high Mount McKinley. Also known as Denali, the Alaskan peak provided a convenient arena to familiarize the climbers with the nuclear-powered sensing device—and meet their Indian counterparts.

He wasn't long in choosing the Himalayan objective. As Conboy writes in *Spies in the Himalayas*, "By the process of elimination, Bishop arrived at Kangchenjunga as his mountain of choice. It was sufficiently tall, it shared a border with Sikkim [which was effec-tively under the control of India], and it was not on the Tibetan frontier. The CIA technicians concurred with the pick."

For me, it's mysterious why Bishop chose Kangchenjunga. As one of the best high-altitude climbers in the world, Bishop should have known what the CIA technicians did not. That is, that Kangchenjunga—whose name means Five Treasures of the Snow because of its five distinct summits, the highest of which was 28,169 feet high—was one of the most massive and complex mountains in the world. One could argue that it was a more difficult climb than Everest. As such, it had seen only one ascent and was not to see another until 1977, long after the espionage missions faded into dark depths of the classified Cold War. From a climber's perspective, getting up the peak by any means would be the crowning point in one's climbing career and would be well-nigh impossible, lugging a 125-pound sensor. Perhaps Bishop secretly wanted to climb the peak. What climber wouldn't? And what better way than on a government-sponsored junket. It's true that after the choice was made to place the sensor on Nanda Devi, Bishop all but disappeared from the hands-on role in the espionage expeditions. Was the 8,000-meter Nanda Devi not big enough to attract the Everest veteran? In truth, it was probably the minimum height requirement of 27,500 feet (set by the CIA) that drove Bishop to his choice. Plus, his amputated toes may have negated any chance to climb Kangchenjunga. Still, the minimum altitude pressed by the CIA encompassed only five peaks in the world! And only Kangchenjunga resided entirely within the Indian control.

As the project gained momentum, it became clear that there had to be an alternative. During a debriefing following the Alaskan junket, Kohli himself stated in a written account, "even if there was no idea of putting any equipment [in this case the sensor] on the summit, the chances of just climbing the mountain would be one in four. With the additional task of carrying four extra loads and

installing them on the summit, the chances would become extremely
remote. The entire plan, in my view, is almost impossible."

Kohli recalls the reaction, "Kao was stunned at my outright rejection of Kanchenzonga [a different spelling for the same mountain]
as the chosen spot. . . . Kao advised me to tear up my report."

We only have Kohli's viewpoint on what happened next. During
the same meeting with Kao where he stated just how ludicrous the
Kangchenjunga destination was, Kohli threw out three possible
alternatives. They were Trisul (23,360 feet), Nanda Kot (22,510
feet), and Kamet (25,446 feet). Apparently there was some previously
unspoken fudge room in the CIA's minimum height requirements—
a pattern that was to unfold over the years. In the end, all three were
rejected on the grounds of either altitude, or in Kamet's case, its
proximity to the Tibetan border. At a few kilometers from Chinese
controlled territory, "Kamet was voted down because it was . . .
theoretically susceptible to a Chinese raid."

I can't tell you how the decision was made, but during a three-day
interval following his meeting with Kao, Kohli was handed word
that, "after further consultations . . . the CIA now wanted to them
to climb Nanda Devi." How this all transpired is again lost to us.
During an interview, Kohli said, "I don't know why the CIA chose
this peak next and I don't know why they kept reducing the height
requirements for their objective." Whatever evidence might exist
lies with the CIA, and they are not talking. We do know that eventually the CIA, continuing to loosen their altitude restrictions,
approved elevations for sensor placements as low as 20,000 feet.

The odds of a successful sensor placement on Nanda Devi were better than those presented by Kangchenjunga. But only barely. As of 1965, despite attempts by seven international expeditions, only six climbers from three expeditions had stood on Nanda Devi's summit and at a cost of three lives.

With a line of sight into Xinjiang province, the transceiver, once placed atop Nanda Devi, would be able to intercept radio telemetry signals transmitted between the Chinese missile and ground control. Powered by a plutonium battery pack, the device would then beam the information to a CIA listening station in the flat lowlands of India, where the data could be analyzed to gain insight into the range, speed, and payload of the Chinese missile.

Perhaps the project was doomed from the outset. National security and political pressure forced a tight and rigid timeline. The American contingent was hastily assembled and underwent a brief course of high-altitude training on Mount McKinley (Denali) in the summer of 1965. I can personally attest to how ferocious and intractably cold and fierce that mountain can be. The CIA training expedition's original intent was to climb the mammoth South Face of Denali. Forty years later, I considered climbing that same gigantic, avalanche-swept face. Even with the latest high tech gear, and modern training, I never even made it to the base.

So it's no surprise to me, that the sixties spy team abandoned their attempt. After Denali, the espionage efforts shifted almost immediately to Nanda Devi. With logistical support from the Indian military and several clandestine paramilitary groups, the American climbers, accompanied by CIA handlers and Atomic Energy Commission technicians, joined their Indian climbing counterparts in early September 1965. For big Himalayan peaks, most expeditions arrive in mid-August to allow time to approach, reconnoiter, and safely climb their objective before the onset of the bitter Himalayan winter. And Nanda Devi, most majestic of all, would prove oblivious to the dictates of superpower politics and the imperatives of timely intelligence gathering.

Though Denali was a failure as a climbing exercise, it served other practical purposes. Besides familiarizing the climbers from two continents with each other, the expedition unveiled the exotic device they hoped would be their eye at the top of the world.

> "A breed of aimless wanderers can be found in California, working as mason's helpers, carpenters, parking cars. They somehow keep a certain dignity, they are surprisingly unashamed. It's one thing to know their faces will become lined, their plain talk stupid, that they will be crushed in the end by those who stayed in school, bought land, practiced law. Still, they have an infuriating power, that of condemned men. They can talk to anybody, they can speak the truth."
>
> — James Salter, *Solo Faces*

CHAPTER 3

THE MISSION

It's no secret that in 1954, a nuclear lab called the Mound, located in the quiet agrarian community of Miamisburg, Ohio, began testing the practical applications of radioactive polonium. The Mound got its name from the nearby prehistoric Indian burial site, a 2,000-year-old pile of dirt about 65 feet high. The Mound lab, besides building parts for nuclear weapons, saw the first successful effort to convert nuclear heat to usable electric energy. And by 1958, the Mound delivered the world's first radioisotope thermo-electric generator (RTG).

A few years later, the first satellite equipped with an RTG power source was successfully launched. Using polonium-210 as its fuel source, legend has it that the satellite broadcast President

Eisenhower's farewell speech. Ike's speech became famous, for it contained the first public reference to the threat posed by, "the military-industrial complex."

When I say power source, I mean that the RTG created the electricity to run onboard electronics and later, small propulsion motors. RTGs don't use self-sustained atom splitting, or fission to create heat. They depend on "natural" nuclear decay. In other words, RTG's don't blow up, melt down, or chain react. Still, polonium burned hot and fast, so much so, that it was soon supplanted by plutonium-238. The plutonium required less shielding from nasty penetrating ionizing gamma radiation—the invisible killer that generates the greatest fuss and panic when people think of radiation. Plutonium-238's half-life (the amount of time it takes for half of the atoms to decay) is far longer than polonium-210 by a factor of almost 230. That extended lifespan was a big bonus, especially considering the unprecedented power demands of the emerging Space Age. And it was plutonium that the CIA used in the spy device.

Reflecting the Cold War's unbridled enthusiasm for atomic power, the RTG principal was incorporated as the electrical power source for what soon became designated as System for Nuclear Auxiliary Power (SNAP). The SNAPs turned radioactive heat into electricity, through what's called the Seebeck Effect. As legend has it, in 1821 a doctor turned physicist named Thomas Seebeck, was making a pot of tea. In the process, "he twisted two wires made of different metals and heated a junction where the two wires met." Maybe Seebeck, known as a hands-on guy, was fixing the handle to his teapot. Whatever the circumstances, the Estonian-German researcher produced an electrical current. This current, later dubbed thermoelectricity, resulted as heat flowed from the hot to the cold junction. He didn't know it, as he finished his tea, but he'd go down in history for discovering the Seebeck Effect.

Basically, all this means is that you can create electricity with heat. And what later became known as thermoelectric generators—*thermo*, meaning heat and *electrical* meaning . . . well, you get it—are now fairly common. If your house has hot water, then chances are you have a thermoelectric generator lurking in your basement. But don't fret. Your basement isn't hiding a lump of plutonium. Your household thermoelectric generators runs off heat from the boiler and powers the pilot-light valve.

Unlike what lurks in your basement, the Nanda Devi SNAP, designated Model "19C," hid not one, but seven plutonium rods in its graphite core. At SNAP's heart lay the metal lozenges glowing with the orange heat of radioactive decay. Fuelled by no less than 1,900 grams of alloyed plutonium—Pu-238 (with a half-life of 87 years) and Pu-239 (with a half-life of 24,400 years)—the unit was expected to power the four-part Nanda Devi sensor assembly for two years, unattended.

The SNAP generator was a round metal bin with five radiating fins for heat dissipation. When mounted on its tubular metal monopod and supporting by cables, the SNAP looked like, "a metallic mushroom."

When fully installed for the first time ever—on Denali in 1965—the collection resembled a remote weather station. A later photo revealed, a crowd of climbers and technicians milling amidst a grove of weird boxes sprouting from thin metal stalks. And, towering over it all, a six-foot long antenna intended to ultimately collect and transmit telemetry data, namely radio signals from Chinese missile testing.

As I was discovering, Ian Fleming neither conjured up a more exotic spy gadget—nor plot.

Having the right elements is neat, but I began to realize that it's one thing to stumble on a great story, it's another thing to try and tell it.

By the time I came to realize that I was the guy to spring this tale on an unsuspecting world, I was well on my way to losing my rudder. For years, I'd climbed and made money working in restaurants or writing the odd story for the magazines. Companies like Marmot, a sponsor, helped immensely in keeping my head above water. I'd written two books, the first so horrible that if I could wipe every trace of it off the map, I would. The second was an overview of climbing told in a not quite how-to style that was more dues paying than heartfelt prose. Come the turn of the millennium, I'd been lucky enough to find a job working in the Internet world. I'd parlayed what I'd learned from tapping out stories for climbing magazines into a budding career of sorts—as a content developer for a company that produced Web sites. It was all very alluring and engaging for the most part—smart, motivated people in a techy, creative, professional environment. Yet working for a company never evoked the passion and meaningful engagement of the writing I'd done in the past.

The pull of climbing, though waning for a time, never entirely relinquished its grip. The gravitas of experiences, of knowledge, and of doing something for its own sake, was its own addiction—and as far as anything in life goes, not a bad one to have. I remember returning to the office after a successful Alaskan expedition, whose highlight was an ascent of Denali, the highest peak in North America. Walking into the office, I was sunburned and skinny after weeks in the realm of thin air and ice. Two days earlier, I'd been flying in a small plane over the Alaskan wilderness. Now, my collared shirt felt baggy and my suede shoes ill-fitting—almost as if I'd put on a costume that suited neither my identity, nor my physical being. The climbing seemed far more real and relevant than the hundreds of emails that had built up on my electronic desktop during my two-week absence. The time spent climbing, even if was stuck in a tent with a smelly partner, was better than the endless meetings. I felt like a cog in a machine, one of many machines grinding to an inevitable and impersonal end.

A few months later, in 2003, I left the company where I'd worked for two years, striking out to unravel the myths and riddles of Nanda Devi. Had I known how difficult this process would be, I might have balked, for more than once in the following three years I'd come to the breaking point. And in those moments it was of little comfort that—as I was to discover in my research—the obsession with Nanda Devi had racked up a high human cost for many others.

The heart of the story wasn't in a dry sum of the facts. Much of those remain obscured by the passage of time and the American government's absolute lack of acknowledgement or accountability. What gave the vast tale meaning was the human interplay with the elements in the story. It was plutonium, the Cold War, sacred mountains, and climbers that made the story so fascinating that I couldn't walk away. And what better narrative thread to tell the story than climbing? What better vehicle to bind the diverse various pieces together? From those thoughts grew the notion to retrace the steps of those same Indian and CIA climbers who risked their lives for a cause both patriotic and personal. I wanted to climb Nanda Devi. proposing to "acquire a visceral first-person perspective by treading the same raw edge that the Indo-American spy expedition walked, following the very route used to place the surveillance device in the first place." Thus the timeline unfolded. To attempt Nanda Devi in the summer of 2005, accompanied by a climbing partner and a photographer.

I'm no saint, and it wasn't just the lofty pursuit of the "true" story I was after. I saw a chance to hit a career home run *and* appease the climbing jones. Besides conveniently providing a fascinating story, Nanda Devi was a perfect step in a climbing career that still, to this day, has aspirations as lofty as the highest summits in the world. It was also a chance to make a sweeping statement; to justify the years spent casting my soul upon the daily hotbed of the vertical; to make up for that which I should have done better.

It's a treacherous line to marry passion and the true course of one's life. And it's too often a mistake to mix business and pleasure, especially when the success of one is so closely linked to the success of another. There were some major impediments to my plan, not the least of which—as pointed out by the clerk in the sweaty halls of the Indian Mountaineering Foundation—was that Nanda Devi was closed to climbing. What would have been the crowning touch to my plan, was to almost become the death of my ambitions, one that had already in its indirect and insidious manner, cost me my job and my girlfriend at the time. Putting all one eggs in one basket and going for the gusto is a lovely and romantic notion—provided one wins. And a year into the project, I was looking like anything but a winner.

Through a close friend in India, I spent more than six months and thousands of dollars of my own money, in the serious attempt to acquire a special permit to climb Nanda Devi. Another close friend loaned me some money to help—a debt that I eventually paid back and one that ultimately bore no fruit. Then, on May 11, 2004, I was forwarded the following:

Dear Sir.

In the order of the above mentioned letters, this is to bring to your notice that the given mountaineering expedition could not be given sanction on the reason [the word "pretext" had been marked out in black pen and replaced by "reason"] of the area lying in Nanda Devi National Park.

An identical copy, written in Devanagari (Sanskrit) script, accompanied the rejection letter. The beautiful horizontal sentences flowed across the fax page, each letter dropped down in flowing vertical letters, reminiscent of Arabic calligraphy.

Beautiful script or not, the message was an unhappy one. No permission to climb, because the mountain—and the entire Sanctuary—was off limits, with no exception. I was devastated. It was like stepping up to the plate with loaded bases in the ninth inning—and striking out. Personally, though there was a lot at stake —the money, my self-esteem, and my ambition—nothing hurt worse than failing.

This bad news came on the heels of several rejections from literary agents, Their responses could be characterized by one typical message, "I'm extremely sorry to report that I'm probably not the right agent to represent the project."

I was fearful that I'd lost some magic, some charm that had always seen me by and seen my dreams come true. And I was learning that selling something this ambitious was a brutal, merciless task. A lot of its viability hinged on getting a permit to Nanda Devi. A lot of the potential to get permission hinged on first selling the project. And the drive required to capture the story required a corresponding detachment from the outcome—something I found hard to acquire. I was learning that great ideas are a dime a dozen and it takes an element of desperation and grit, just to get an agent, much less a publisher interested. Know-how helps too, something that I certainly lacked and paid for it more than once. It wasn't a fast easy street, but in its own way, Devi was teaching me a hard—and valuable—lesson. That unlocking her secrets demanded nothing less than absolute commitment.

But a glimmer of hope still twinkled on the distant horizon. I discovered that besides the attempt to spy from Nanda Devi, the CIA had also targeted a mountain called Nanda Kot. Nanda Kot, an attractive summit, lay a few miles from and several thousand feet lower than, Nanda Devi. The tabletop, snow-draped summit also lay *outside* the forbidden Sanctuary. The CIA technicians, over the course of the eight espionage expeditions, progressively lowered the minimum height requirements for the SNAP and its transceivers. So after the disappearance of the Nanda Devi device, the Agency approved the placement of the spy station on the more accessible, Nanda Kot.

This historical accident was for me, a piece of good fortune. At the very minimum, I figured I could retrace the CIA footsteps on Nanda Kot *and* at least get a glimpse into the Sanctuary by climbing a high pass called Longstaff's Col (*col* is a French term for a gap or saddle in a mountain ridge). The col was adjacent to the mighty Nanda Devi, and the perspective would at least give me the on-ground feel for what those climber-spies of the sixties experienced. The pass also granted a clear view of their base camp and the tortured glacier where, to this day, the lost device resides. Better yet, Longstaff's Col—named after the turn of the (nineteenth and twentieth) century Scottish explorer Tom Longstaff who pioneered some of the biggest and hardest mountains in the Himalayas—led to the only established climbing route up Nanda Devi's equally stunning sister summit, Nanda Devi East. I'd love a chance to climb the mountain, which was as aesthetic and alluring as the main summit—and nearly 25,000 feet high. That route might yield clues to the CIA mystery. And, as yet unclimbed by any Americans, it was a world-class challenge in its own right.

Thus, discouraged but undefeated, I kept after the project. Late one night, a few months before leaving for Nanda Kot, I joked with a friend, "I'll finish this story, even if it kills me."

"There was no way I could turn it down. I was willing to change my whole life at that point to do this project—I was a surgical resident, I was married and just had a child and yet, I was very willing to give all that up not knowing how long the project would last or what my involvement would be," so says Dr. Robert Schaller II when recalling being approached by the CIA in May 1965 to take part in the first of the series of clandestine expeditions to Nanda Devi.* In April 2005, about five months prior to my departure to that mythical corner of the India, I was finally lucky enough to interview Schaller.

Schaller's statement echoes my obsession with climbing in general, and Nanda Devi in particular. His frightfully reckless and instant reaction reminded me of the ignited passions of Tilman, Shipton, and Willi Unsoeld. Today, Schaller, a tall, still-handsome surgeon with a full shock of white hair is now in his early seventies. Though "crippled by arthritis," as he puts it, Schaller still practices pediatric surgery in Seattle, Washington. Just like the rest of us, he survived his affair with Nanda Devi—if just barely.

Back in 1965, Schaller was a thirty-year-old surgical resident in Seattle. He was an attractive target for CIA recruitment. Besides his medical background, Schaller was patriotic and gung-ho, so much so that when informed of the particulars of the trip, he saw it as, "an opportunity to serve my country in a unique fashion." The cloak and dagger aspects must have been compelling for "the recruitment was just like out of a James Bond movie," recalls Schaller. "I was in the hospital in my white coat and white pants and even white shoes. This person literally wearing a trench coat and dark sunglasses in the building—sidles up to me and introduces himself and opens up his jacket and takes out this airline ticket. He tells me a little bit about the project. And he says, 'Do you want to go to the Himalayas?' "

* Of eight total CIA expeditions including the maiden, shake-out trip to Denali, American climbers and/or American Atomic Energy Commission specialists were present on five. Schaller was to take part in four of those. Legendary climber Tom Frost was also on the same trips as Schaller. Four out of the other five American climbers played varying roles on one or more of those trips. Of that five—four were veterans of the 1963 American Everest expedition.

His curiosity piqued, Schaller listened on. The encounter—at his hospital workplace—explained why his friends had been calling him and asking if he was in trouble. They'd been fielding calls from the FBI, who were doing a background check on the young doctor. The thousand-dollar-a-month retainer was another incentive for a cash-strapped Schaller. "That was a lot of money for a surgical resident," he recalls, "I was only making a few hundred dollars a month as a resident so this was a tremendous boon to me," adding, "although I didn't do the project for the money it was a nice thing to have . . ." What cost $1,000 in 1965 is now worth six times that much, putting the salary benefit (though most of the climbers would only be gone for stints that lasted three or four months at most) at $72,000 per year in current dollars.

Persuasive as it must have been, the clincher for Schaller was the climbing. For as I would discover for myself nearly twenty years later, a Detroit-born Schaller remembers that, upon first seeing the mountains, "It was almost like falling in love for the first time." The effect was more than passing infatuation for, "Seeing the mountains made me whole—it filled something in me that was missing."

And it wasn't just mere climbing. The fact that Nanda Devi was the prize sealed the deal. Schaller says, "I have to admit my first motivation was a very selfish one. It was the opportunity to go to the Himalayas to one of the sacred peaks of the world—Nanda Devi. That was my first motivation even before I knew about the project."

Patriotism was a driving force for more than one of the American climbers. Schaller, who would later wear the uniform of a lieutenant colonel as a teaching army doctor, says, "I believed in my country. And I believed that what we were doing was right."

McCarthy concurs. "I felt that America needed to know what China was up to," he says. "Back then, the threat of nuclear weapons and ballistic missiles was as real as anything and I wanted to serve my country."

All American participants swore an oath of secrecy and endured psychological screening and lie-detector tests—the purpose of which, I assume was to weed out any potential security risks. Schaller recalls being given a pseudonym based on the identity of, "a real dead person." His moniker was Norris P. Vizcaino. "I don't know who he was, and they wouldn't tell me," Schaller recalls, "But [the CIA] said it was a real person."

Legendary Yosemite climber Tom Frost takes his oath of secrecy regarding the Nanda Devi caper so seriously, that to this day he is the only surviving spy climber who won't discuss the matter. A staunch Mormon, Frost, a successful engineer and inventor, remained tight-lipped when I attempted to interview him on the phone. "I'd be glad to talk, but I don't know if I can answer any of your questions," said the otherwise polite and affable Frost. When pressed, he said, "I have nothing to say or any recollection of what you are asking about—but good luck."

I was lucky enough to interview Dr. Schaller a few more times after our initial meeting. I had been connected with him by his son, whose name was also Robert. The younger Robert, this one Robert Schaller III, is a budding filmmaker. To this day, he labors under his own Nanda Devi addiction, hoping to tell her many tales on film. Less of a passionate climber than his father, Robert the filmmaker was a baby when his father first left for Asia on the CIA payroll. Looking back, the doctor says, "Leaving for Nanda Devi was the beginning of the end for my marriage," adding, "I'm afraid that it was not the best thing for my children either." When seeing the father and son together, I noticed a plaintive quality to their conversations, especially when talking about Nanda Devi. It was as if the mountain—which ironically sundered their original bond—had become something to share. And like the father/daughter Unsoeld pair, Nanda Devi became a concrete symbol upon which to build a common bond.

To his country and mountains at least, Dr. Schaller was unswervingly committed and motivated. He was also in many ways, typical of the eight total American climbers who volunteered for Himalayan duty over the years.* Schaller was an accomplished mountaineer, whose belief in the cause was complimented by a useful professional background. Of his American compatriots, four were members of the 1963 Everest team. They represented a mix of doctors and professional guides along with two engineers, and a lawyer. Schaller and Tom Frost participated in the bulk of those espionage trips. Besides the Denali excursion, they climbed on two Nanda Devi expeditions and one trip to Nanda Kot.

It was a dangerous enterprise. Paula Lehr, future wife of spy climber Harthon "Sandy" Bill (they later separated) heard a few details. "I got an idea of how serious things were when I heard about the huge life insurance policies taken out on these guys." She adds, "I can see how all those trips would have an adverse effect on their marriages."

---

* Eleven total American climbers participated if you count the Alaska training mission prior to the first Nanda Devi expedition. Barry Bishop, Mount Rainier National Park ranger Gil Blinn, and medical doctor Dan Wolfe trained on Denali, but never made it to the Himalayas.

And the loss did not end there. While helping to locate and recover the lost Nanda Devi sensor, Schaller made history with the greatest alpine climbing feat ever accomplished by an American to that date, by climbing alone to Nanda Devi's summit. He kept a journal and took photographs, recording in word and image the outrageous details of that expedition. The film and journals were confiscated by the CIA, and like his amazing climbing feat were hidden from the world. This enforced secrecy denied Schaller not only the accolades of his peers, but also the understanding of a wife who was understandably distressed over a husband who mysteriously disappeared for months on end. With three other climbers, Schaller also won an intelligence medal from the Agency. It was draped around his neck, only to be locked away in a vault at CIA headquarters in Langley. He also lost his marriage, alienated his children, and now finds himself "disappointed by a government I don't trust anymore."

"The radioactive half-life of plutonium, 24,000 years, becomes an ominous figure that signifies the endurance of this bargain with the devil, and almost seems to forebode the inevitable restitution in the future. It seems hardly coincidental that the Latin name "Pluto" refers to the god of the dead and ruler of the underworld, from the Greek ploutos, wealth. This sinister origin of plutonium is what imbues it with those supernatural powers that inspire its popular characterization as "the most poisonous substance known to man," despite scientists' objections that other substances are lethal in even smaller concentrations."

—Alexandra von Meier, Jennifer Lynn Miller, and Ann C. Keller, *The Disposition of Excess Weapons Plutonium: A Comparison of Three Narrative Contexts*

CHAPTER 4

A DEADLY SUBSTANCE

If there were such a thing as *The Complete Idiots Guide to Plutonium,* it might start with something like this:

Say you held two identical half spheres of plutonium 239— one in each hand. They are the size and shape of split coconut shells. You'll have to grasp them tightly because they would feel unnaturally heavy—twice as heavy as the comparable sized dumbbell plates in your local gym. The sweat, and there would be plenty, would make your palms slick. There'd be an unpleasant, almost pulsing warmth in your hands described by one researcher as feeling, "like a live rabbit." For the time being, the warmth is the only ill effect. On a playful whim, you decide to clap the two dull, silver-green, half-spheres together, like a pair of miniature cymbals. "What harm could it be?" you think. The very instant the halves clap together you are washed with an eerie blue glow. There's a blast of unbearable heat, and a disagreeable sour tang filling your mouth. You promptly vomit. Even if you managed to drop the shell halves and run (though even an Olympic sprinter could not run fast enough to escape the radiation) you'd still die. But only after suffering from excruciating burns, severe diarrhea, vomiting, and total disintegration of body functions.

Plutonium is funny stuff. It is a metal, but it doesn't act like any metal you or I have ever seen. As illustrated in our imaginary *Idiot's Guide*, just changing the *shape* of a plutonium mass leads to an uncontrolled release of energy—the same energy that holds *all* matter together. The fact that it changes its chemical properties based on purity, density, mass, temperature, and so forth, is not all that special (most elements do this to one degree or another). What is strange is how quick, unprovoked, and *dramatic* these changes are.

Another illustration, this one historical, occurred in May 1946 in a secret laboratory in Los Alamos, New Mexico. Martin Zeilig wrote that on that date Dr. Louis Slotin, a slightly built, bespectacled Canadian physicist was conducting what was whimsically called, "tickling the dragon's tail." He was essentially bringing two halves of a beryllium-coated plutonium sphere into close proximity to convert the plutonium to a critical state. A critical state is one in which a nuclear chain reaction occurs, releasing energy in the form of light, heat, and radiation. Slotin was no newcomer to the process. While helping develop the atomic bomb, the thirty-five-year-old had already done the incredibly dangerous procedure dozens of times. He'd also had been warned by Nobel Prize-winning nuclear physicist Enrico Fermi that, "if you keep doing that experiment," he would not live through another year.

> With his left thumb wedged into a cavity in the top element, Slotin had moved the top half of the sphere closer to the stationary lower portion, a micro-inch at a time. In his right hand was a screwdriver, which was being used to keep the two spheres from touching. Then, in that fatal moment, the screwdriver slipped. The halves of the sphere touched and the plutonium went supercritical.

Slotin, who bravely stood his ground, shielding the seven others present in the room, "knocked the spheres apart, but deadly gamma and neutron radiation had flashed into the room in a blue blaze caused by the instantaneous ionization of the lab's air particles. Louis Slotin had been exposed to almost 1,000 rads of radiation, far more than a lethal dose."

It was suggested that "it was as though Slotin had been fully exposed to an exploding atomic bomb at a distance of 4,800 feet."

He died nine days later, "after an agonizing sequence of radiation-induced traumas including severe diarrhea and diminished output of urine, swollen hands, erythema (redness) on his body, massive blisters on hands and forearms, paralysis of intestinal activity, gangrene, and a total disintegration of bodily functions."

It's rumored that Slotin was buried in a lead-lined casket. Whatever the truth to that is, the incident, and its gruesome aftermath (it's been suggested that three of the seven observers present died as a result of the radiation exposure) underscores the plutonium's mythic, hysteria-inducing qualities.

What Slotin essentially held in his hands on that grim spring afternoon, a half a century ago, was the core to an atomic bomb. It is impossible to understand plutonium without understanding its origins in a human context, as a bomb-making material. Popular beliefs hold that plutonium is a man-made material. That's true in a way, but plutonium existed before earth itself, in the depths of space as a by-product of supernovae—or exploding stars.

What's more, in the early 1970s, French scientists made a startling discovery in the sweltering equatorial African nation of Gabon. In a uranium mine called Oklo, it was discovered that a self-sustaining nuclear chain reaction of natural uranium deposits, regulated by groundwater, took place over the course of several hundred thousand years. Over that interval, an estimated four tons of plutonium were created as a by-product of the natural reaction.

Fear not. The four tons has long since decayed away, since all this happened two billion years ago. Chances are it won't happen again, not within a humanly comprehensible time frame. It wasn't until 1941 that plutonium was "discovered." A short five years later, plutonium was arguably the most important strategic material in the world. And it was the material of choice for the second of two atomic bombs that ended the bloodiest war in history.

Indeed, it was plutonium's extraordinary response to shape and density that made it the material of choice for nuclear weapons. It is some amazing stuff. Eileen Welsome, in *The Plutonium Files* writes, "Small amounts undergo spontaneous combustion in air, therefore, it must be handled in an atmosphere devoid of oxygen. Depending on its chemical compound, it can be blue, green, purple, yellow-brown, red, or pink." Nobel Prize-winning chemist Glenn Seaborg led the team of scientists who first isolated the element. He wrote:

> Plutonium is so unusual as to approach the unbelievable. Under some conditions, it can be nearly as hard and brittle as glass; under others, as soft and plastic as lead. It will burn and crumble quickly to powder when heated in air, or slowly disintegrate when kept at room temperature. It undergoes no less than five phase transitions between room temperature and its melting point.* Strangely enough, in two of its phases, plutonium actually contracts as it is being heated. It also has no less than four oxidation states. It is unique among all of the chemical elements. And it is fiendishly toxic, even in small amounts.

Plutonium really should have been called "plutium," but as Seaborg, said, "we liked how plutonium rolled off the tongue." Seaborg, a tall Berkeley graduate of Swedish ancestry, first isolated

---

* To give an idea of what this means, imagine a glass of tap water on your kitchen counter. If it acted like plutonium, the water would freeze, melt, boil, condense, refreeze, and sublimate as it went from room temperature (70°F) to 212°F (water's boiling point).

the element little more than a decade after its equally mysterious namesake planet—Pluto—was discovered. Being element 94, it made sense to call it such, as it closely followed the discovery of element 93—neptunium, named after the planet Neptune. Known for his "enticing, whimsical" sense of humor, Seaborg also facetiously suggested the symbol Pu (as in a child making a face at a foul odor and saying "Pee-yoo!") for this newest of elements. Overlooking the more logical, and obvious, Pl, Seaborg's suggestion passed the naming committee without a hitch.

As a pioneer on the frontier of atomic energy and radioisotope research, Seaborg, who died in 1999, co-discovered a host of elements, and continued to be involved in the name game. The naming of element 106—seaborgium caused no little controversy as it was the first—and to date—only element named after a living person. For a while, the International Union of Pure and Applied Chemistry declared that no element could be named after someone still walking the earth. The decision was rescinded in 1997 and for the remaining two years of his life, Seaborg was the only person in the world who could write his address in chemical elements: seaborgium, lawrencium, berklium, californium, americium (Glenn Seaborg, Lawrence Berkeley National Laboratory, Berkeley, California, United States of America). As long as there is a periodic table of elements—and that will be as long as human society lasts, Seaborg's name will live.

Without World War II, we might never have cared about plutonium. Perhaps like neptunium, it would have been relegated to the esoteric realm of elemental obscurity were it not for the discovery that plutonium was more fissionable than the hard-to-produce uranium-235.* This meant that it was more apt to chain react uncontrollably—a big bonus if one is building a bomb. The discovery of this property took place in March 1941, mere weeks after plutonium's discovery and months before the Japanese attack on Pearl Harbor.

As America entered World War II, plutonium, and its bizarre proclivities, became a matter of national security. Scientists, years before, had realized that such material could be used in the production of a new and radical weapons. Indeed, the patent for the atomic bomb was filed by a brilliant Hungarian-Jewish scientist named Leo Szilard** well before the war and well before plutonium's "discovery." This event was absolutely visionary as it predated the discovery of nuclear fission. Fission, no less than the splitting of the atomic nucleus is the foundation of all nuclear energy generation, whether for weapons or peaceful power. Szilard after fleeing the Nazis to London in 1933 reportedly read an article written by the "father of nuclear physics," Ernest Rutherford. A giant in the scientific world, Rutherford refuted the then-theoretical concept of atomic energy as

---

* Though as late as September 2002 researchers at Los Alamos created the first nuclear critical mass using neptunium along with enriched uranium, thus discovering that the critical mass of neptunium was less than previously predicted. This prompted U.S. officials to move the nation's supply of enriched neptunium to a site in Nevada in March 2004.

** Szilard was known as "an eccentric, lightning-quick thinker who seemed fond of startling people with strange, seemingly incongruous, yet extremely perceptive statements and questions." Besides being credited with predicting World War I as a boy, Szilard claimed to have forseen the details of World War II. Perhaps such unhappy ruminations led to his real-life phobias, for he "made a habit of residing only in hotel rooms, with a packed suitcase always on hand." As the one who first foresaw the atomic bomb, it's ironic that Szilard later stood in firm opposition to the use of nuclear weapons on civilians. In 1945, he drafted the Szilard petition, later signed by 155 scientists working on the atomic bomb, asking President Truman to consider a demonstration of the unprecedented weapon, before using it against Japanese civilians.

"moonshine." An uncowed Szilard was reportedly "so annoyed at this dismissal that he conceived of the idea of the nuclear chain reaction [fission] while waiting for traffic lights to change," on Southampton Row, a busy street in London's Bloomsbury district. A year later, he filed his now-famous patent, and four years later, German chemists successfully demonstrated the patent's underlying principle of nuclear fission.

So disturbing was the prospect of this new "isotope blast" (as the notion was called in 1939 newspaper headlines), that no less than Albert Einstein himself wrote a letter. The great man himself, in no small part prompted by Szilard, warned President Roosevelt of the stakes in the nuclear game. Outlandish as it was, the message was not unheeded. Ultimately, the U.S. government would spend $2 billion ($27 billion at today's money, a figure that approaches the Gross National Product of North Korea in 2004) in a race that was "without a doubt the most concentrated intellectual effort in history." That effort, code named "The Manhattan Project" ended World War II with the first and to date, only use of a plutonium nuclear weapon in warfare.

It's strange to think that rapidly compressing a six-pound, baseball-sized sphere of plutonium could level a city and instantly kill more than a third of its population. But that's exactly what happened on August 9, 1945, when a lone B-29 called *Bock's Car* (named after Captain Bock who usually flew the plane)—a four-engined aircraft so awe-inspiring it was called the *Superfortress*—dropped the world's first operational plutonium weapon on the unsuspecting populace of Nagasaki. It wasn't the first nuclear strike. Three days prior, on August 6, another B-29 dropped an atomic bomb on Hiroshima, a

Japanese city of little strategic importance but noteworthy as being untouched by prior bombing. This lack of damage made Hiroshima ideal to evaluate the effectiveness of the bomb, that and the fact that it was the only targeted city without POW camps. What made *Bock's Car's* mission unique, was that the Hiroshima bomb was the first—and only—nuclear weapon in history that used uranium 235 as its "explosive" material. In its detonation, the uranium bomb, euphemistically called "Little Boy" used up nearly the entire global stockpile of hard-to refine material—underlining the practical aspects of the easier-to-produce plutonium.

To compress the core of plutonium and create the necessary chain reaction of splitting atoms, engineers used a technique called implosion. To do so, they layered regular explosives like TNT around the plutonium mass. The conventional explosives, detonated with extremely exact timing, compressing the plutonium with such speed and pressure that the fissile material went "supercritical" or in other words underwent a sustained nuclear chain reaction, thus releasing the atomic bomb's hallmark heat, blast, and deadly radiation. The creation of this "critical mass" is euphemistically called "assembly." And to do so, engineers used explosives patterned in a truncated icosahedron—a pattern of 12 regular pentagonal faces, 20 regular hexagonal faces, 60 vertices and 90 edges. It was the kind of shape favored by the likes of Buckminster Fuller, and it looked like, if anything in the world, a partly deflated soccer ball.

All this might seem a bit overwhelming but of course, in truth it's a ridiculously oversimplified description. Remember, the Manhattan Project blended theoretical physics—like Einstein's groundbreaking formula of $E=MC^2$—with hands-on precision engineering hurdles.

It was driven by the urgent deadlines prompted by the biggest, bloodiest war in history. In seven short years, the Manhattan Project took an unproven theory and created something so very real and menacing that future decades lived under the threat of wholesale annihilation.

Though the Manhattan Project encompassed unprecedented and baffling complexity, the effects were simply devastating. Nagasaki, a major Japanese seaport and production center for ordinance, ships, and other military equipment was also at the time, a city of (by most estimates) 240,000. When the plutonium bomb dropped at 11:02 AM, at least 70,000 people died instantly. A Japanese report tersely characterized post-bombing Nagasaki as "like a graveyard with not a tombstone standing."

One survivor described the horror as so unbearable, that, "for a long time afterwards, I wanted to die,"

William L. Laurence, a writer for the *New York Times*, was the only reporter allowed into the Manhattan Project. He gives us a different perspective, this one from 32,000 feet while observing the Nagasaki bombing from another B-29. In addition to being a writer, Lawrence was also on the War Department payroll and was expected to put the proper spin onto the story. Nevertheless his account conveys the raw, unbelievable power unleashed by a few pounds of plutonium.

> A tremendous blast wave struck our ship and made it tremble from nose to tail. This was followed by four more blasts in rapid succession . . . a giant pillar of purple fire, 10,000 feet high, shooting skyward . . . had reached the level of our altitude . . .

Awe-struck, we watched it shoot upward like a meteor coming from the earth instead of from outer space, becoming ever more alive as it climbed skyward through the white clouds. It was no longer smoke, or dust, or even a cloud of fire. It was a living thing, a new species of being, born right before our incredulous eyes. . . .

Then, just when it appeared as though the thing has settled down into a state of permanence, there came shooting out of the top a giant mushroom that increased the height of the pillar to a total of 45,000 feet. The mushroom top was even more alive than the pillar, seething and boiling in a white fury of creamy foam, sizzling upwards and then descending earthward, a thousand old faithful geysers rolled into one.

It kept struggling in an elemental fury, like a creature in the act of breaking the bonds that held it down. In a few seconds it had freed itself from its gigantic stem and floated upward with tremendous speed, its momentum carrying into the stratosphere to a height of about 60,000 feet.

When one considers that all this came from a chunk of plutonium, little bigger than a softball, it's no surprise to consider the alarm and elemental fear stirred by the mere mention of the material. For plutonium is as complex and incomprehensible as it is powerful.

Plutonium in space is a hot topic today. The other night I was at a party hosted at the house of a professor of astrophysics and planetary sciences. The subject of the missing Nanda Devi RTG came up, and it was amazing to hear the polarized viewpoints ranging from the knee-jerk environmentalist to passionate defender of the use of radioactive materials in the space program. On the one hand, I was hotly accused of having my scientific facts wrong in a teaser piece published in a magazine article. On the other, I was also lambasted for soft-pedaling the threat of plutonium. What struck me as more significant than the variety of views was the absence of definitive facts behind the health effects of plutonium and the risks inherent in its use.

Here are a few facts. The SNAP-19's plutonium is not like what you'd find in a nuke, nor is it the thick green glowing waste depicted in *The Simpsons*. Rather, it consists of those seven fuel capsules, small rods inserted in a graphite block. They were arranged in a radial pattern—one axial rod dead center with the remaining six arranged evenly spaced and equidistant, like a compass with six cardinal points. The metal plutonium rods were doubly encapsulated in "leaktight" casings with the first layer being a half-millimeter of tantalum, a highly corrosion-resistant, hard, blue-gray metal. Tantalum is used in surgical instruments and electronics. In this case, it was chosen to inhibit the corrosion of the plutonium fuel, which when exposed to air oxidizes rapidly and under certain conditions, ignites spontaneously.

The outer casings of the plutonium rods were composed of a nickel alloy with high strength, resistance to temperature change, and inertness to oxidization—hence its use in coins like our own five-cent piece. The 2.5 millimeter—the width of your computer headphone jack—material was composed of Haynes-25 alloy, a mix of cobalt, nickel, chromium, and tungsten, combining according to its manufacturer, "excellent high temperature strength with good resistance to oxidizing environments." In turn, the graphite block was used to regulate the heat of plutonium's radioactive decay. According to the Indian government report in 1978, the fuel block was "encased in a cylindrical aluminum casing which is 14 inches in diameter and 13 inches high. The total weight of the entire assembly was 38 pounds."

Experts in radioisotopes point out that predicting of the possible effects of the plutonium power pack on humans is sketchy at best due to the number of unknowns. The material itself poses some questions, as it is an alloy primarily composed of Pu-238 with 18 percent Pu-239. Pu-238, gives off far more heat than Pu-239, which in turn, is the fissile material that "explodes" in nuclear weapons. Pu-238 has a half-life of 87 years. Alloying the two yielded the most effective combination of lifespan and energy generation. The SNAP was expected to last decades whether in the depths of space or on a bleak mountaintop.

Any assessment of the SNAP's potential to pollute the watershed and therefore harm humans needs to be qualified with the knowledge of the events leading up to its disappearance. Over a year before I left for India, I had the chance to meet and climb with outspoken former Manhattan trial lawyer Jim McCarthy. As I've mentioned earlier, McCarthy was a member of the CIA trip that lost the SNAP on Nanda Devi.

"My dad was pissed when I went off to Alaska and Nanda Devi. He'd been the undersecretary of Naval Intelligence and said, 'You won't like these guys (the CIA).' Every so often during the interview, McCarthy dropped an f-bomb, most often in the context of a colorful polemic like, 'The intelligence community, they are largely fucking assholes.'

"I had an epiphany. I had this vision right then and there of exactly what was going to happen. I said, 'Jesus Christ!' and start yelling. 'Do you have any fucking idea what's about to happen?' I could see it with absolute clarity. We're going to lose a SNAP generator, powered by plutonium, in the headwaters of the fucking Ganges!"

So recalls McCarthy. He's retired now, but as a dominant force in American rock climbing of the 1960s, McCarthy was one of the first picked by Bishop to be on the espionage team.

McCarthy's epiphany came as a storm, bearing down on Nanda Devi, was forcing the hand of M. S. Kohli, who as leader of the espionage effort in the field, was calling for a general retreat. The CIA-sponsored expedition was stalled on Nanda Devi after several weeks of climbing, on the flat shoulder of Camp Four, at an altitude of 23,750 feet. It was a large expedition, as big as anything ever fielded, even on Everest.

The Indian contingent consisted of Kohli, and Indian climbers Harish Rawat, Sonam Wangyal, Gurcharan Banghu, and Sonam Gyatso. All the Indians had an Everest summit or at least Everest experience under their belts. And all worked for the Intelligence Bureau. The American crew was comprised of Lute Jerstad, Tom Frost, Sandy Bill, Dr. Robert Schaller II, and McCarthy, with CIA case officer Bill McKniff. To round out the large, helicopter-supported expedition were nineteen Sherpas and a cook.

Things had been smooth, progress steady. Then heavy storms moved in. The highest climbing team on the mountain consisted of six Sherpas supervised by an Indian climber Gurcharan Banghu. They were a scant 2,000 feet below the summit. In their possession was the SNAP-19C, the two transceivers, and the sensor antennae. Banghu, a radio expert and veteran of the previous spring's Indian Everest expedition, radioed the worsening situation to Kohli. The date was October 16, 1965. The fall launch placed the expedition late in the climbing season. According to Kenneth Conboy, "The snow was continuing . . . and it had reached the point where the lives of the men were in definite jeopardy. [Conboy reports that American team member Lute Jerstad, now deceased, suggested that] everyone on the mountain should begin coming down to Base Camp. Having run out of options, Kohli concurred." Kohli and attending CIA case officer Bill McKniff, radioed their higher ups, based in New Delhi, for approval of the decision, which was granted.

If retreat down the mountain was sensible, Kohli's next decision was questionable, and its aftermath haunts the world forty years later. He decided to cache the generator and its deadly contents. "It had been hard enough hauling that load [the sensor and nuclear generator] up to Camp Four," writes Conboy, "So it seemed foolish to repeat their efforts next season." Kohli then directed the climbers to deposit the device in a shallow niche. The intention was to retrieve the sensor the following spring. Kohli must have thought that from the highpoint, it would be a much easier job to hump the heavy device to the top the following year. That's a reasonable strategy, and one that's fairly commonplace among climbers. But in his epiphany, McCarthy saw the flaw in the plan. Besides the ever-present hazard of the sensor getting dislodged by avalanche, especially over the ensuing six winter months, McCarthy says, "I do not have a high opinion of Indian climbers. Neither they, nor the accompanying Sherpas, were technically savvy enough to adequately secure the device—I know, I climbed with them."

That in mind, McCarthy is adamant that it was a mistake. He recalls, "Kohli was just outside the tent. He's talking on the transmitter. His headphones are on and even through the Indian accent, I can understand what's happening. He's ordering them to abandon the generator."

That's when the shouting started.

McCarthy says, "That's when I realize what's happening, that they're going to dump the fucking generator and go down the mountain. I'm like, 'What the fuck are you doing? You can't do that. Have them bring it down! Are you crazy?' I'm yelling at the top of my lungs."

According to McCarthy, McKniff nearly had to pull him off of Kohli. McCarthy recalls, "He says to me, 'You are creating an international incident!' Which of course, I was. He went on, 'It's their country, they get to run it how they want.' "

If one is to believe McCarthy's story, and I see no reason to doubt it, then it was like diplomatic brinksmanship at 16,000 feet. Kohli, in a written account of the critical moments, makes no mention of any such incident. Says, Dr. Schaller, "I wasn't present when that confrontation happened." But he adds, "I know that Jim was appalled by the idea and said as much—as he's apt to do. Things were intense in Base Camp, and leaving the generator was a bad mistake." In an account of that fateful decision, author, Kenneth Conboy writes, "Kohli gave his approval, then radioed New Delhi for retroactive consent [to leave the device]. Again, those in the capitol deferred to the reasoning of the mountaineers."

What's unquestioned is that Kohli's authority prevailed. Conboy writes,

> Banghu oversaw measures to safeguard the device on the slope. There were five loads in all: four cardboard boxes containing elements of the sensor, and one for the generator. Finding a suitable cavity adjacent to the Camp Four tents, he and six Sherpas wrapped the boxes with nylon rope and secured them to the rock using pitons and carabiners. Special care was taken with the generator, which was anchored by extra rope. Nearly a third of the load was sheltered inside the cavity.

However securely the SNAP and its sensor equipment were cached, we know that upon return the next spring, Banghu, accompanied by six Sherpas, "looked to his left toward the shelf where he had secured the sensor eight months earlier. Banghu's breath caught in his throat, as his brain began to register the sight before him. The rock shelf where he had left the boxes was completely gone, as if a massive knife had surgically severed that one corner of the slope."

All that remained according to Banghu, was a crushed cardboard box used to hold one of the transceivers. Below, on a shaky slope of loose rock, there were some severed clumps of wire and odd bits of plastic.

It was obvious that, short of an Indian plot to use the elaborate circumstance to pilfer the plutonium from under the noses of the CIA—a theory supported by the fact that there were no Americans immediately present, at its caching in 1965, or at the discovery of its disappearance in 1966, but you can discount that theory since the plutonium in the SNAP, was not the type desirable for weapons (only 18 percent was the fissile Pu-239).

However, over the ensuing decades and two subsequent search missions, McCarthy's prophetic vision acquired substance. Official Indian government analysis in May 1978 lists the following possibilities:

- The device could have fallen on the southwest face of the mountain.
- Though damaged outwardly as a result of the fall from where it was left, it could still be intact.
- It could have been buried in the glaciers in the mountain.
- It could have been buried in the debris on the slopes of the mountain.
- It could have fallen into the mountain streams and finally reached the gorge of Rishi Ganga.
- As a result of multiple impacts during the fall the device might have been very badly damaged/disassembled and thus scattered all over, in which case radioactive material would have got released in the environment.

From his first-hand experiences with the mountain and the device, McCarthy believes the first three. "Yeah, it got avalanched and got stuck in the glacier and God knows what effects that will have."

In general, Kohli's assessment that he delivered to the Indian Prime Minister in 1978, concurs with McCarthy's intuition. According to Conboy, Kohli "concluded with two likely scenarios about the fate of the missing device. His gut feeling was that it hit the snowfields softly and landed intact on the glacier. By now its heat would have caused it to sink to the very bottom of the glacier, making it impervious to detection from the current generation of alpha and neutron meters. The less likely possibility was that it had hit a rock on the fall, broken apart, and been strewn across the glacier."

Had the device broken up during the fall, there would, no doubt, have been telltale traces on the search expedition's Geiger counters. Though there were some anomalous spikes in the search party's Geiger readings, these were dismissed as resulting from malfunctioning equipment.

The aforementioned Dr. Schaller, now a retired pediatric surgeon, also believes the device is locked in the heart of Nanda Devi's glacier. He says, "The generator puts out enough heat so that it would melt any of the ice around it eventually. I believe that it ended up on the bedrock underneath the glacier on the south face of Nanda Devi and it might eventually be crushed by rock."

Were the device to be crushed under tremendous glacial pressure and its deadly contents spilled, how soon would the indications appear from the silt and water testing? Factor this possibility with the alarming trends in the global climate. Global warming is causing the recession of glaciers from the Cordillera Blanca of Peru to the European Alps, to Alaska. This would lead, says one expert, to an earlier emergence of debris and artifacts from the foot of a glacier. If one were to boil water containing even a minute speck of material, what would the results be?

The closest studies come from the battlefields of the Middle East. Depleted uranium, essentially spent nuclear reactor fuel, is used in antiarmor munitions due to its high density and resultant kinetic energy—great for penetrating modern tank armor. Depleted uranium is 40 percent less radioactive than natural uranium. Still, it is both radioactive and chemically toxic, and many scientists like Dr. Siegfried Horst Guenther, who studied the radioactive health effects in Iraq after 1991, are convinced that the inhalation or ingestion of even microscopic DU particles can cause mutation, leukemia, disease, and/or neurological problems. Some point to DU as one of the toxins linked to Gulf War Syndrome. But, depleted uranium is about as toxic as garden dirt when compared to plutonium—a substance so deadly that less than *one-millionth* of a gram is fatally carcinogenic.

What would be the effects of an unwitting villager stumbling onto the device and opening this hellish Pandora's box?

On September 29, 2003, Dr. Gordhan N. Patel spoke before the House Committee on Government Reform, Subcommittee on National Security, Emerging Threats and International Relations. His testimony gave a chilling account of a 1987 nuclear disaster precipitated by the release of 1,400 curies of Cesium-137. Said Patel,

> A scrap merchant stole a radiation therapy source from a hospital (which was closed) in Goiania, Brazil, in 1987. It contained a small amount (size of a cigarette lighter) of highly concentrated radioactive cesium chloride. He cut the source and the powder was released and contaminated the area. The radioactive dust was tracked throughout Goiania. Nearly two hundred people were exposed to high doses of radiation. Four died, including a four-year-old girl who had eaten a sandwich after playing with blue radioactive powder. She was

buried in a lead coffin sealed in concrete. Pavements, buildings, etc. needed to be scrubbed and scraped. Contaminated soil had to be dug up and carted away. Some homes that couldn't be cleaned were carted away. Decontamination took six months. The radioactive material created 5,000 cubic meters of waste. More than 100,000 people (~10 percent population) demanded screening. Everyone wanted to be monitored. The long-term socio-economic effects were devastating. Goiania suffered a 20 percent drop in gross domestic product. Tourism dropped to zero. Demand for food and other products plummeted.

If such a small amount of radioactive material could cause that level of calamity, what would happen if the SNAP-19 plutonium fell in the wrong hands? It is sobering to note that the SNAP-19C retains fully 23,500 curies (curies are a measurement based on the radioactivity of one gram of radium) or, 3,360 curies per battery capsule—in other words, twenty times the fallout described by Patel.

Consider this horrifying possibility. What if someone were to pre-empt such a scenario, only to unleash upon the world something more terrifying? What, indeed, if someone were to deliberately search for the nuclear material, in hopes of making a nuclear weapon or even just a king-sized dirty bomb?

Dr. Iggy Litaor of the Tel-Hai Academic College in Tel Aviv, Israel, says, "The real threat of the material lost on Nanda Devi is the dirty bomb. Such a device could yield the entire Lower Manhattan uninhabitable, creating a worse economic disaster than the Great Depression."

A dirty bomb is simply conventional explosive, like TNT, salted with radioactive material intended to disperse the life-threatening nuclear material, thereby contaminating a large area.

Litaor notes that such a crude but effective device is far, far easier than to build than a sophisticated nuclear fission weapon. It usually takes the resources of a developed nation—with cooperation of other like-minded countries to build an atomic bomb. Bearing the Goiania example in mind, the effect of a dirty bomb is more psychological than material. The TNT blast might kill mere dozens, but the psychological effect of radiation contamination would absolutely paralyze any area remotely contaminated. How many of us would return to work in a building that had even a negligible chance of contamination? Such a bomb would terrify a whole city. It's the ultimate terror weapon.

The testimony of Henry Kelly (president of the Federation of American Scientists), before the Senate Foreign Relations Committee in March 2002 gives some indication of its capacity to harm. Speaking of a radiological device with a tenth of the SNAP-19's potential, Kelly noted:

> Areas as large as tens of square miles could be contaminated at levels that exceed recommended civilian exposure limits. Since there are often no effective ways to decontaminate buildings that have been exposed at these levels, demolition may be the only practical solution. If such an event were to take place in a city like New York, it would result in losses of potentially trillions of dollars.

Adding that millions of people would leave the affected area in a state of panic, Kelly further noted that it would be a logistical nightmare to relocate so many people in such a short time.

Is such a thing possible? Though a hard question to answer, several incidents over the past fifteen years demonstrate how very plausible this would be. In 1995, Chechen rebels directed a TV reporter to a park in central Moscow where she found a package containing about fifteen pounds of explosives and Cesium-137. In March 2006, the United States Government Accountability Office, anticipating just such an eventuality, successfully smuggled enough radioactive material to "to make two dirty bombs," prompting a Senate subcommittee review.

As early as 1987, Iraq tested a crude radiological device, according to intelligence reports. Twenty operatives for Osama bin Laden have tried and failed to buy enriched South African uranium on the black market. In the fall of 2001, American-led forces discovered documents in Afghanistan containing detailed information on the making and deployment of a dirty bomb. Al Qaeda recently paid Jose Padilla (Abdullah al Muhajir) $10,000 to carry out a dirty bomb attack before he was arrested.

In the post 9-11 world, the means, motive, and opportunity are all there. David Albright, president of the Institute for Science and International Security says, "There is a 10 to 40 percent chance that terrorists will conduct a successful attack with a crude 'dirty bomb' in the next five to 10 years." That was in 2002. The clock is ticking.

Accidental discovery and potential terrorism aside, nagging fears remain four decades after the disappearance on the Nanda Devi

SNAP unit. Shyan Bhatia of the *Deccan Herald* reported on April 25, 2004:

> Captain M. S. Kohli is wracked by doubts about a radioactive sensor that was left behind on Nanda Devi and its effect on the environment. He is concerned that he may have unwittingly contributed to the pollution of the Ganges by placing a radioactive sensor on the slopes of Nanda Devi. The missing sensor poses a long-term health hazard to millions of Indians who drink from the river and bathe in its sacred waters. In part atonement for his actions, he helped to set up the Himalayan Environmental Trust in 1989."

"In the beginning God inhaled and created all life. This is the Hindu creation myth. They have the same word for breath and spirit, as did the ancient Greeks. Over the years, I've realized that my brother is basically writing his own creation myth, although it's couched in evolutionary terms, since he's a vertebrate morphologist and studies the evolution of breathing. . . . All his tests and experiments with lizards, fish, birds, and dogs rest on the underlying theory that the lungs and the pulmonary system always change and evolve toward increasing stamina and endurance. . . . Always, the changes are driven by the need for more breath, and, to be metaphysical, more spirit or soul."

—Scott Carrier, *Running After Antelope*

CHAPTER 5
TO INDIA

Expeditions are always more than just mere vacations, and it takes more than luck to go on them. First off, they are a lot of work to prepare, and, secondly, they require you to put your life on hold for months—something that might sound great. But if it were all that easy, everyone would be doing it.

Through the spring and across the stifling summer months, I worked, sometimes feeling like the travel agent, tour organizer, banker, and entertainment director for the expedition members who contributed to the effort in varying degrees. Once bitten, twice shy, and on past trips key organizational work had been sorrowfully neglected. Offers of help are nice, and I got plenty, but without follow-through or attention to specific details, I worried that help was more a hindrance.

Granted, it might have been my obsession with Nanda Devi and my fear that things wouldn't be done right that prevented me from spreading the work out. I had a professional responsibility that made this more than just a climbing trip. My agent had arranged a deal with a publisher that spring, and so this was a step in my writing career. The other team members shared various levels of involvement in the expedition. Of the four others, Jonny Copp and I shared the greatest passion for the destination. And if I was a committed climber, then Jonny was even more so.

At thirty one years old, Jonny had those tall, Keanu Reeves-like good looks. Unlike Keanu, who probably goes to the gym to pump up for that next action thriller, you'll seldom if ever catch Jonny in a gym. Jonny trains by doing. And what he's done in climbing is no less than world class—a blend of vision and genetic athleticism, with a full-speed-ahead approach that dwells on the possibilities, not the problems. He'd started climbing after high school and was smitten. A mutual friend who was a freshman with Jonny once told me, "Jonny would show up for our class—I think it was science or a chemistry makeup. There would be about 200 people in this large lecture hall, and he'd walk in fifteen minutes late, covered with chalk (used to keep a rock climber's hands dry), sit down in the very back, and promptly fall asleep."

Chuck Bird, packed levity and good humor into a medium frame capped with thinning brown hair and soulful blue eyes. An avid skier and sometime climber, Chuck was a self-proclaimed "baron of leisure." He is so much so, that he'll often neglect basic things with shrugging slacker-generation carelessness. I once pulled a hefty bags-worth of garbage from his beat up Toyota Forerunner. The junk consisted of McDonald's wrappers, beer bottles, underwear, and a glove he'd been missing for two years. I didn't dare touch the old french fries and what must have been twenty dollars of quarters and dimes glued to the exposed metal floor by a dark brown viscous substance.

A little less than a year ago, Chuck met Sarah Thompson, an attractive twenty-something with big blue eyes. They met at Neptune Mountaineering, a Boulder outdoor store specializing in climbing, backcountry skiing, and wilderness travel. It's at Neptune's that Chuck works as a pedorthist—basically an expert in the design, fit, and function of footwear and orthotics. He builds custom footbeds and inner liners for mountaineering boots, ski boots, and other outdoor footwear. His job is half science, half art and Chuck—the man with the magic touch—takes a real hands-on sensitive approach to people's foot problems. Because he truly cares, it's not uncommon to see Chuck swarmed—like a Hollywood hairdresser or counselor—with needy clients, jealously claiming their appointed minutes. The needy as often as not are girls, and it was in the shop that Chuck and Sarah met. Though she was obviously interested in more than just a boot fitting, one can hardly call Sarah needy. As a laser research engineer who "designs, builds troubleshoots, integrates lasers and laser radar systems," Sarah is mature and steady, though thirteen years Chuck's junior. And she's coming on the trip.

Sleep was rare in the weeks prior to India. The pressure was intense. We had some late-breaking conflicts with the Indian government and some shifts in personnel. A few months prior to leaving for India, we'd had our film permit denied. That effectively killed the goose that laid the golden egg, since money to support the expedition from a media company was predicated upon shooting film of our adventure. No film, no money. Luckily, Visa stepped in—at 19 percent interest.

Gabe Rogel, a friend and photographer who lives in Idaho, near the Tetons, called telling us he could only share the first few weeks of the trip with us. He'd been an integral part of the expedition from its nuts-and-bolts inception the previous winter. It turned out that he'd taken a berth on another expedition. The fact that the other venture was a fully sponsored jaunt to Tibet might have made a difference for him. I do know there was some pressure to accommodate the sponsor, but whatever the reason, his presence—affable, funny, energetic—would be missed badly.

The really bad news came on August 6, 2005. That day, I received a fax from the Indian Mountaineering Foundation. The message made me shake. In three brief sentences, I was informed that permission to climb was denied. No explanation was given: and we had tickets in hand for an August 27th departure. It was astounding. Either the bureaucracy in India had dropped the ball—something I'd not remotely experienced on three prior expeditions—or the powers that be didn't want me to tell this story. On seeing the fax, Jonny commented, reflecting the pretrip ups and downs, "I don't know what good news is anymore."

But we weren't to be put off so easily: After much lobbying via email, we were finally awarded permission to climb. We'd found an unexpected ally in an Italian expedition that wanted to climb Nanda Devi East. The team's leader, a very competent Italian climber named Marco Dalla Longa, was my age, 41. He himself possessed an enviable alpine resumé spanning the Peruvian Andes, Yosemite,

Patagonia, and Himalayas. Later, we discovered that, like so many others including myself, Dalla Longa felt an instant passion for the peak, despite having only seen it in a picture prior to the expedition. "From a photo, he just loved this mountain," recalled their Indian agency field manager. "It was like he just knew he had to try it."

Our ages and love for Devi were not the only things we shared. He too had been denied a permit. The good news was that Marco's expedition was well connected with their national organization—the Club Alpino Italiano, which in turn drew a lot of water with the prestigious Union Internationale des Associations d'Alpinisme, an international federation of climbers and mountaineers.

The day before departure, I woke up about 10 AM with a hideous hangover. I had gone to a gathering of friends the night before, attended by the close-knit Boulder climbing subculture. It was a good mix of the tribe. Some younger climbers were there, an example of how the scene transcends the usual age barriers. Some were older—my age—and some older still. I hoisted a few with friends with whom I'd shared storm-bound bivvies and tense moments on climbs all over the country. For some, it was a break from kids and busy schedules that had crept into their lives. For others, it was merely a chance to party down with bacchanalian fervor. For everyone, it was fun.

The event was at Jonny's—partly a going-away celebration, partly a celebration that we were finally going at all. Between the appeals from both sides of the Atlantic—and from within India—permission was granted little more than two weeks from boarding the plane. The party felt like releasing the steam from a pressure cooker.

Monumental hangover aside, it didn't help that just leaving on an expedition gives you a feeling of dread, and you get that certainty that if there weren't such momentum, you could just as easily stay home and forget the whole thing. I checked my voice mail and got a few encouraging messages from friends around the country. It's an unspoken understanding that when you get on the plane for the mountains, it could be the last time your foot ever leaves the pavement of the good old USA. It's good to drop out on a happy note—hence the parties and a slew of well-wishing phone calls—because that might just be how you are remembered.

Two days later, on August 27, I got ready to leave. I crawled out of bed after only a few hours of sleep—I'd been up until 1:30 AM, after packing until 11:30 PM It pays to pack thoroughly. Once you get on that plane, there's no chance of acquiring critical things like boots, tents, climbing hardware, and so on. Even the small stuff—Pringles potato chips, extra socks, batteries, or contact lens solution—becomes critical after a few weeks in an isolated base camp, and we'd be more isolated than the vast majority of expedition camps throughout the Himalayas. That includes the metropolis of Everest Base Camp, or the tent-studded, if pleasant, meadow of Tapovan, where I'd spent six months of my life over the years. After a half-dozen major expeditions, you'd think I'd have it down. As it was, I'd later discover I'd forgotten one of my sleeping bags, down booties, sandals and footwear to fill the gap between my Nike running shoes and the next-generation mountaineering boots.

DeAnn was there to help me. She and I began dating last March. She's a leggy climber who lives in Boulder, and over the years I'd admired her whenever I happened to see her across the room at the climbing gym. She's got the ripped physique of an extreme rock climber, contrasting with delicate facial bone structure, a pixie nose, and big brown eyes. Like a lot of girls in Boulder, she turns heads—and she certainly turned mine more than once. You might say she's cute, but that would be a disservice, because though a pretty freshness that peeks out from time to time, it usually vanishes quickly and abruptly.

DeAnn and I finally met at the local bouldering gym. Bouldering is a facet of the overall climbing game where one climbs on small rocks, executing gymnastic moves of extreme difficulty. It might take hours, days, or years to master a particular sequence, or you might never climb them at all.

These days, bouldering has become the most popular branch of climbing, and it has revolutionized all facets of the sport with its explosion of extreme difficulty, athleticism, and engaging social dynamic—think about the skateboarding explosion when posses of kids threw off the uptight strictures and the limited set of moves that characterized the sport up to that point and started doing tricks for their own sake. They, like the boulderers of today, were the vanguard of new-school difficulty and attitude. They did it without any pretense or expectations. Somewhere in all that, the bulk of new climbers discovered something that my generation by and large overlooked or forgot—climbing is fun. The youth boom also tapped into a wider genetic talent pool—no longer was climbing such a disenchanted fringe lifestyle as in my era, but it became something that children and teenagers can easily share with friends and family. More than anything, what tapped into the vast pool of middle-class suburban kids was the climbing gym. These indoor facilities created year-round training zones—no longer were you forced to quit your job or drop out of school to climb (though some still do). In a sense, climbing gyms brought the mountains to the flatlands of suburbia. These indoor walls, made of steel frames with rock-like sand and plastic resin surfaces, grew so popular, that today you'll find one in every major urban area of the United States.

Rock-gyms also brought about a profound change in the social fabric of the climbing scene. That's how I met DeAnn. For in my day, climbing was a male bastion—and a lonely one at that.

It's been suggested that climbing gyms are the new singles bar for the vertical athlete. Indeed, go to a gym and you'll see stacks of hotties straining away on the walls wearing skimpy sportswear. For you ladies, fear not, you'll see plenty of shirtless ripped guys grunting and sweating in a venue that doesn't promote the impairment, bad choices and the sometimes bogus interactions like the local theme bar.

For one thing, DeAnn—a fiercely independent creature herself —understands my passion. Though she's not drawn to the high mountains as I am, she can understand how that passion is a unique gift to those who have it and it's that respect that makes me mad about her. As a pediatric ER nurse, DeAnn deals with the intensity of life and death. She understands tragedy in more than just the abstract sense. She shows her support today, as we load up her van with six duffels weighing nearly seventy pounds each. She drives us to the airport, which is a great help. Though we both have declared our love for each other, there's a part I sense in the both of us that still straddles the fence. She's never really been in love—or so she tells me. And I, stung once by a divorce and now stubbornly independent, have spent a great deal of my life pursuing my dreams in a solitary manner—alone in many ways because certain things should be faced alone.

Whether I'm different now or if I've met the "right" person, I'm not sure. What I am sure of is that DeAnn doesn't play any games of relational brinksmanship nor seeks to change me in ways I cannot be changed. She also calls me on my flaws, but for some reason it isn't offensive and never threatens the bedrock of our mutual respect.

Another big bonus—there's no hideous display of sentiment at the airport either. As the time ticks, I file that into the plus category of relationship details. It's hard enough to leave, and harder still to endure someone else's emotional claptrap. It's not that there's no sadness or worry, it's just that we know the other. We know what's at stake. And by releasing that person into what is to be, we show our respect.

DeAnn helps Jonny and me unload our bags, and after one last kiss and the hint of a tear, she's off. Jonny, who periodically astounds me with a subtle pearl of wisdom, says, "Every good-bye is the birth of a memory." Our memories start on the curb surrounded by a sea of black, yellow, and brown duffels the size and shape of punching bags. Jonny's a travel veteran and immediately tries the $20 bribe to the curbside skycap ploy. It costs $70 for each extra bag you put on the plane, and the trick is to try and weasel your extra baggage— two in our case—into the system before checking in at ticketing. It's worked in the past but the skycap—who's obviously done his job for many years—gazes upon the piles of luggage and furrows a brow. He's still holding the twenty, as if weighing the value of the bill against the possibility of actually checking our mountain of crap without the excess baggage fee for the 7,000-mile flight. "I can't do it," he says, a little crestfallen. "It's too much to slip through." He has the decency to hand Jonny back the twenty and we hunt down a cart to ferry our load to check-in.

Checking in at the airline counter is the first step in getting to India, but an expensive one. With two extra bags, it looks like we'll have to pay $50 each to get them to L.A. and then recheck our luggage for international travel and pay another $70 each. That comes to a total of $240 to get our luggage to India. You'd think there was a better way, but shipping is a huge hassle, and the savings are negligible.

We begin our race to the other side of the world at 2:30 in the afternoon and by the miracle of modern time zones, we arrive in Los Angeles two hours later at only 3:25. Jonny's parents are there to meet us. I can see where Jonny gets his ebullient manner—and physical stature. They are a full of vigor and earnest in that classic American manner. His dad, a barrel-chested guy with a shock of thick white hair, shares out a beer as we walk to the connecting terminal. We meet with Chuck, Sarah, and Gabe at the Air India terminal. As Jonny and his folks order burritos at the Mexican fast-casual joint in the airport, I help Chuck and Sarah usher their gear through security screening.

Gabe Rogel is also at the luggage terminal. It's good to see Gabe as he is a ball of energy, with a smile that lights up the entire airport. We are about the same height—short at five feet seven inches. Having road-tripped in the past for weeks on end, we are familiar enough to tease each other about being long-lost brothers—one Jewish the other Japanese. Our brotherhood takes on new meaning at the airport when we coincidentally show up with the same haircut (close cropped about two millimeters long—mine thinning in a preamble to middle-aged baldness), blue jeans and the exact same brown patterned causal Marmot shirt. The effect is too exact to be left unnoticed by even bystanders. We make the most of it as we skip along to boarding—holding hands and wiggling our butts mock life-partners leaving for a tropical vacation.

Airfare usually constitutes a little less than a third of total expenses. We were lucky this time around as we had our international airfare underwritten. Mr. Venkatesan Dhattareyan, assistant director at India Tourism's New York City office, generously allowed us complimentary airfare. As a result, we were flying Air India on a sparsely occupied 747. On the plane I had plenty of time and space. The flight—which is supposed to take around twenty-four hours total—goes from L.A. to New Delhi with a brief layover in Frankfurt. We are lucky, as we board: I notice the flight is only half full as near as I can tell. After we dutifully take our seats, we glance around until the plane taxis out. Then we scatter, each of us taking an entire row to ourselves. Chuck and I treat ourselves to Ambien—after the flight lands, we won't be getting much sleep in a time zone twelve-and-a-half hours different from ours.

Despite the fact that I'd been to India on three previous expeditions, on some level I still braced myself for the transition into a culture that, despite the homogenizing effect of globalism, remains to me on many levels utterly baffling.

The world's most ancient civilization, birthplace of not one but two of the world's major religions, and one of the world's youngest nation states, India has been justly called a land of contrasts. It is also a place of paradoxes. Baffling to the Western mind, with its predilection for order and urgent need to grasp and hold onto ingrained traditions. As Stanley Wolpert, who studied and lived and lectured on India for four decades, writes, "Everything is there, usually in a magnified form. No extreme of lavish wealth or wretched poverty, no joy or misery, no beauty or horror is too wonderful, or too dreadful, for India . . . nothing is 'obviously true' of India as a whole."

I'm reminded of another facet of Indian travel in a copy of *Newsweek International* in the magazine flap of my seat. Thumbing through the pages I see an article by Indian columnist Shashi Tharoor called "Brown-Out in Calcutta." He writes,

> My French friend Rene had just finished a three-year stint as a cultural attaché in Kolkata, formerly Calcutta. During his medical exit-check, the doctor asked how many packs of cigarettes he smoked a day. "I've never smoked in my life," he replied. The doctor couldn't believe it. After three years of breathing Kolkata's polluted air, Rene's lungs resembled those of a chain smoker.
>
> Globalization may be transforming India, but there's one dismal constant: pollution. India's cities are among the world's dirtiest. The air in Kolkata or Delhi is all but unbreathable in winter as car-exhaust fumes, unchecked industrial emissions and smoke rising from countless charcoal braziers get trapped by descending mist and fog. When the Australian cricket team played in Delhi, its coach complained the smog-laden air gave the home team an unfair advantage—by impairing his players' performance.

From my experience it's an accurate picture—at least of the urban areas. New Delhi, where we will debark, is one of the four most polluted cities in the world. The plus side to the pollution is that it is a by-product of India's emergence as a major economic power. She is the second largest producer of computer software, has her own satellites, and is one of seven nations possessing a nuclear arsenal.

I put the magazine away, pondering the drama and anticipation of landing in the dense population of Delhi, with smog and packed streets, its amazing beauty and vibrancy, with all its accompanying disorientation and fascination. And the smell. Oddly enough, there is a tinge of it in the cabin of our Air India 747 as we streak across the sky, chasing the setting sun at 30,000 feet. It's distinct, unlike anything I've ever experienced in the States. To describe it in its components falls pathetically short of the real thing—but I'll try anyway. Diesel, curry, dung, smoke, incense—and the scent of three thousand years of human habitation—permeating the hot, humid air of the climate where things are born, grow, and die rapidly, simultaneously and often very publicly.

It's small wonder that, given the industrial pollutants, human waste, agricultural runoff, and myriad other conventional (and deadly) forms of pollution that India faces, the plutonium story has faded and is largely forgotten. Though the occasional brief news item pops up in Indian newspapers, it's been over twenty years since the lost plutonium was given close scrutiny.

I pull out my copy of Howard Kohn's *The Nanda Devi Caper*. The headline blares: "THE SPY CLIMBERS: How a CIA Expedition Lost a Nuclear Generator in the Himalayas." The cover shot, of a guy holding a trophy-sized trout with a shit-eating grin, didn't do much to enhance what became a controversial story. When it hit the newsstands, Kohn's exposé captured enough essential facts to wring an admission of culpability from the government of India's Prime Minister, Morarji Desai. A few days after word of the impending article, "suddenly and unexpectedly reverberated around the world," Desai addressed the Indian Parliament on April 17, 1978,

> Mr. Speaker Sir,
>
> Honorable members are quite understandably exercised over the reports that have appeared in the Press here on news items which appeared [in] the United States about the attempt to locate a nuclear-fuelled power-pack on the heights of Nanda Devi. The failure in this attempt has raised just apprehensions about the possibility of contamination of the waters of our sacred river Ganga. I can assure the House that all of us share this concern of the Honorable Members as well as by the people at large at the possible hazard to our environment and people.

If the article shook India, it garnered less notice in the United States. I guess if the plutonium isn't in one's backyard then it's less of a concern. However, on the same day, the *New York Times* reported, "The [United States] State Department would neither confirm nor deny today the statement by India's Prime Minister that the planting of a nuclear-powered monitoring device in the Himalayas had been a joint project of India and the United States."

The *Times* then quoted State Department spokesman Tom Reston: "Just note that Mr. Desai has addressed this question in some detail out in India, and I would refer you to this statement."

The issue generated more buck-passing by the CIA. Senator Alan Cranston received a letter requesting information on truth of Kohn's article.

Dear Sen. Cranston:

I would like corroboration of a recent news report authored by *Rolling Stone* editor Howard Kohn and appearing in the journal *Outside.* That report is based on personal interviews the author conducted with former CIA agents and other sources from the intelligence community. It states that a nuclear powered spying device containing plutonium 238 was placed in 1965 by the CIA on the Himalayan peak Nanda Devi in India; that the devise was accidentally buried in an avalanche; that efforts to retrieve the device failed, and so it was abandoned in spring 1966. This decision to abandon the device was allegedly concealed from both President Johnson and Prime Minister Gandhi. According to scientific testimony in the account, the outer shell of the generator in the device could corrode in twenty to thirty years, thereby releasing lethal radioactive material into the spring runoff that feeds the Ganges River system. Are these statements and allegations true in any way? If so, there is little apparent meaning to the concept of "national security" for this or any other country on earth so long as such "intelligence" agencies are given cartes blanches.

The CIA responded to Cranston's subsequent query with the following:

> Thank you for your letter . . . I am advised that it is the policy of the CIA not to publicly comment on speculations about its intelligence activities which may appear in the media from time to time. You should be aware, however, that the CIA does report on its activities to oversight committees in both Houses of Congress. They are the Senate Select Committee on Intelligence . . . and the House Permanent Select committee on Intelligence . . . These two committees and others in Congress maintain a careful scrutiny of the activities of the Central Intelligence Agency.

The unidentified letter writer (the name was blacked out in the document—picture an old type-set memo with lines marked out) drew upon two suppositions presented by Kohn's article that remain in question. The one about the SNAP's casing is based on Kohn's words "would eventually corrode and release its poisonous core. Handling or inhaling plutonium can be fatal, and it would be impossible to retrieve the radioactive material once it escaped into the snow." The statement is true on several accounts, but the picture painted—a giant eggshell spilling a toxic green yolk that quickly seeps into the ground—is anything but accurate.

India hits us in the early morning hours of August 29. Even around midnight, local time the atmosphere presses in like a warm curtain of velvet as we pass through customs. Stepping outside, we slide through a sea of hot molasses. We are a train of five travelers; rickety carts piled high with clumsy baggage, led by our travel agent pick-up guy, a short cheery fellow named Krishna.

It's sometimes debatable whether to hire an agency to run one's logistics while on an adventure. To operate, shielded under the service and guidance of a travel company at once insulates us from the rigors of true India, while expediting the process of getting to the mountains. It's the old trade-off of time versus money.

The next day, we discover another benefit. Our agency, Ibex Expeditions, is run by a friend, who for the last four Indian trips has facilitated our travel, logistics, and government liaison.

Though our first meeting was over eight years ago, Mandip Singh Soin is the same tall, charismatic, and articulate Sikh, with a beard that now shows streaks of gray. He's cut out in the classic mold—handsome, King's English with the charming Indian lilt, and turban. He's also a good diplomat, as he demonstrates in a meeting with the Indian Mountaineering Foundation. We sit around the table, five team members, Mandip, our liaison officer, and the IMF Director, a harried-looking man named Colonel N. K. Bhimwal. Even with the air conditioner, a window-mounted affair chugging out a dampish vapor one could hardly call cool, the room is stifling. With an hour of sleep and jet lag, we are red eyed and half-asleep. But Mandip deftly guides us along, smoothing the rough edges of conversation while representing our needs.

The key issue brought up is the negotiation over what's called a field permit. It is customary that, once one climbs or seriously attempts an officially sanctioned objective—in our case Nanda Kot—we have the option to attempt something else in the area.

That's of course, contingent on approval by the liaison officer—usually a military officer, policeman, or other officially approved individual who has mountaineering experience. I've gone down the field permit road several times, and if possible, we'd use the option to attempt Nanda Devi East.

The IMF director seems reluctant to discuss the field permit. It's almost as if, having been grant permission in the eleventh hour, we'll see no privileges added. We get some help from an unexpected quarter when our Liaison Officer steps in to point out the regulations explicitly state the privilege. He does so in clear terms and in language that bespeaks years of command and bureaucratic wrestling.

Lieutenant Colonel S. V. Singh is a tall rangy officer who commands a battalion of India's famously ferocious Ghurkas. As a line officer—his tiger-striped camo uniform and chest of campaign ribbons speaks of long combat service—he punctuates his statements with quick hand chops, finger often tapping the table as he drives home an argument. He is a man I instantly respect and who, for some reason, likes us within minutes of our meeting earlier in the morning.

The next few days are spent in transit, a flurry of buzzing autorickshaw rides in streets so smoggy that visibility is limited to a few blocks; shopping trips for items like food, isobutane canister fuel for our mountain stoves, and umbrellas; a search for a bank for cash withdrawal; then a day of bus travel across the northern extreme of the vast red earthed Gangetic plain—toward the foothills of the Himalayas.

To experience India is to accept a microcosm of the human experience—condensed, vast, and dizzying. Each minute of travel reveals a thousand slices of life as we pass from the urban zone of Delhi's environs through a series of towns divided by intensively cultivated fields of bright green. Wheat shimmers, even through the blasted slate monotone of an atmosphere laden thick with particulate matter, both organic and industrial. The white static of background din overwhelms with tens of thousands of untuned motors, blaring rhythmic bhangra music, horns, and the voices of millions. I spy a Palam airfield from the road, where Kohli was simultaneously greeted as a national hero and recruited to spy on the People's Republic. An adjacent tarmac is lined with Mil 8 transport helicopters, descendants on the same Soviet family tree as the Mil 4s used to shuttle climbers, SNAP units, and plutonium from the lowlands to the mountains. The helicopters squat, gray in the smog, with drooping rotor blades blooming like the bare wires of denuded umbrellas.

We cross the wide Ganges, our bus groaning over a bridge as I watch children play in the sluggish, gray-green soup. Plutonium is the least of their worries as the Ganga—as it is now officially known—flows through the lives of millions carrying a daily influx of 1 billion liters of raw sewage, chromium, benzene, DDT, and an annual cargo of tens of thousands of half-cremated human corpses. Khem Singh, the Ibex agency field manager and friend, with whom I've spent many weeks on three other India expeditions, rides with us. He sits next to Dipender, our cheery Nepalese cook. Along with S. V., the driver and his assistant, we are a total of ten people with three quarters of a ton of gear, food, tents, and kerosene.

At a traffic light our brakes squeal in protesting halt, engine idling as our exhaust belches up a bit more misery for the inhabitants of a roadside hovel, made of tin, wood scraps, and bright blue tarps. A woman holding a pathetic child approaches, drawn by the flash of pale skin. She ignores me and goes for Sarah, who on her first Indian adventure can't help but be visibly moved by the beggar's anguished eyes.

Prosperity, beauty and life itself booms on the streets of every town we pass. Hindus, Sikhs with turbans, Muslims in robes and skullcaps move in swirling undifferentiated masses, many with cell phones—younger kids in faux-designer baggy jeans and American-style baseball caps. Brilliant colors, whether traditional saris, movie posters, garlands of flowers, or mounds of curry powder contrast with the dirty streets and mildewed stucco walls. Gradually, as we navigate the narrow highway, packed with ox carts, motorcycles, bicycles, autos, busses and lumbering orange lorries, the towns thin out, and it's possible to glimpse the paddies and fields of pastoral India and a few of her villages that number in the hundreds of thousands.

By late afternoon, we've navigated through the foothills to the town of Ranikhet, a charming former hill station of the British Raj. At 6,000 feet above sea level, the air is refreshing, and we catch a brief glimpse of distant snow-capped mountains. They burn crimson in the setting sun as birds caw and crickets chirp in cadenced harmony. Mandip meets us at his summer bungalow and treats us to barbequed chicken, marinated in spices and local yogurt.

The next morning, Nanda Devi appears, a snow-hooded, wispy white apparition floating above the horizon like a distant dream—mysterious as the moon. My heart stops. She indeed is ethereal. Fit for a goddess.

> *"In my benign walks around sanctuary meadows, viewing peaks and considering some of the achievements on them, studying the religious feelings of the local people and noting the natural glories in the rare beauty of the forests and the riotous sexuality of the flowers, I followed my innermost instinct to worship. . . . Intellectual enquiry into the nature of the Goddess, I discovered, shrunk her stature and any investigation of her temples invited serious disappointment."*
>
> —Bill Aitken, *The Nanda Devi Affair*

CHAPTER 6

FROM THE TRAILHEAD

By 4:30 PM the next day—August 31—we are sipping sweet, milky, cardamom-scented cups of Indian tea, called chai. We are in Tejam, deep in the foothills after a dusty, twisting drive through stunning riverine valleys thousands of feet deep. Our views have included waterfalls hundreds of feet high, crystal blue rivers gushing past precipitous mountainsides laced with complex terraces holding fields of wheat, corn, lentils, and potatoes. Tejam is one of dozens of similar villages of narrow laned shops, concrete houses, cows, and muddy streets we've passed through in the last eight hours. Tejam does hold the distinction of being the way station for the three CIA expeditions that spied on China from Nanda Kot. Back then, the road ended here; now lumbering trucks kick up dust for an additional forty miles of rugged hair-raising roads that teeter at the very edge of cliffs and sheer mountain faces.

As I sit rinsing down the parching dust with another sip of chai, I recall that somewhere around these very hills, is the location of the CIA listening station tasked with retransmitting data from the mountain, on to Delhi, and ultimately to Washington, D.C. Schaller showed me a slide of the secret outpost—reportedly able to deliver the telemetry to Washington within three minutes of reception by the sensor—it looks vaguely like a wide spot in the river valley near where we now wipe the grime from our foreheads. "Vaguely" could mean any number of things, and the location, called the Field Research Unit, is just as uncertain as the exact location. Needless to say, the relay station, nothing more than a two-room house with antennae sprouting from the roof, is long since deserted.

We arrive in Munsyari at 9:30 PM after twelve hours of basting in our own sweat. We are beat after the long bus ride and are still digesting the wonders witnessed during a combined twenty-four hours of staring out the windows.

The path from Munsyari—one that will ultimately take us to our Base Camp at nearly 14,000 feet—starts by going downhill. We debark the bus at 3:30 PM after a winding ride, descending 1,600 feet from Munsyari's main bazaar; a muddy square enclosed by a loose circle of yellow stucco shops and corrugated tin-walled dhabas. Dhabas are India's hole-in-the-wall eateries, often wedged between tandoor shops; with their charcoal oven baked tandoori chicken and specialty breads; and sweet shops with their glass-cased array of colorful baked or fried confections. Dhabas serve a simple fare and are the best value—monetarily and often culinary. If you want to get the local flavor, go to the nearest dhaba. Here in the Himalayan foothills in north India, they serve up rice, dhal (yellow or red lentils in a thin spicy sauce), and chapattis with the odd deep fried dish. The dishes are fresh, cheap, and convey the nuances of local produce and flavors.

The trailhead lies at a nondescript pullout marked by a high concrete arch, through which passes a path of rough rectangular granite blocks diving steeply down the hillside. We are eager to leave after a three-hour delay in town, during which S. V. and Khem Singh do a magnificent job of unraveling some mysterious paperwork issues between the local governmental authority, the IMF, and the regional office of the Indo-Tibetan Border Police. There is much running about, phone calling, text messaging, and faxing. Such a high tech hoop dance is incongruous with the muddy streets, wandering cows, and goats that nuzzle heaps of garbage.

Sometime during midmorning, S. V. pulls me aside with a worried look. He holds his phone, one with the mini keypad to send text messages and surf the web. It's far more sophisticated than my cell phone at home. S. V. casts me a worried look. "Mr. Pete," he says, "There might be some problems." It's funny to be treated with such formality, coming as I do from such a rampantly anarchic subculture in an outwardly nonhierarchical country. All I can muster is a solemn, "Do your best S. V.," adding "Thanks."

Bureaucratic inertia is part of the Indian experience especially when dealing with a project demanding some degree of coordination between administrative entities. There often seems to be an unwillingness in India to put any effort into making something happen, especially if it requires stepping out of a set procedure. That mindset is perhaps, a hand-me-down from the era of British colonial rule. One might assume that the British version was more efficient because, at the beginning of the twentieth century, the 1,500 British administrators of the Indian Civil Service ruled a country of over 300 million Indians. That is an unfair perspective considering Imperial rule is less cumbersome than running what is now the world's largest democracy. India, having grown threefold in the past one hundred years, is as successful as any in letting people have a say in how things are run. But it's always slower and more complex. What's undeniable is that India presents the confounding contrast of a guy speaking on a cell phone in a mountain village, haranguing an administrator probably sitting hundreds of miles away at a desk with a pen and damp piece of paper. It seems that, like all offices throughout the world, but especially so for India, hidebound strictures and processes of colonial times don't integrate with streamlined expectations of the information age.

As I've mentioned, India is a land of very stark contrasts. An example. On the high tech end, say, technology outsourcing, we can't help but think of the subcontinent. If you've ever used a handheld or computer some of those 1s and 0s were no doubt crunched with Indian-written code. Dial an 800 help desk number for software or credit card questions—you've probably gotten Mumbai or Bangalore. The other side of that coin—I've also seen payments of thousands of dollars be recorded in triplicate with a piece of carbon paper so old and worn out, it was it was no more than a limp transparent onion-skin of lavender parchment. And, the administrators all work on Indian Standard Time, a real time zone (and one of the only in the world deviating from Greenwich Mean Time in half-hour increments—most time zones are adjusted in whole hours for simplicity) and also a euphemism for "it will get done when it gets done." That often means a time frame that falls nowhere near our western expectations.

It's all a mystery to us, and because we have hired Ibex Expeditions to manage these details, we occupy ourselves with trivialities. I join Chuck, Khem Singh and Sarah for a plate of pakora at the dhaba. Pakora, one of my favorite Indian snacks, are delicious deep fried potatoes with cauliflower and onion breaded with chickpea flour and flavored with pepper, salt, cumin, and coriander. The deep fried delight is served with the ubiquitous chutney—in this instance a fiery red pepper paste. We sit in flimsy plastic chairs watching Bengali tourists depart in diesel-belching trucks for a tour of the area. The Bengalis, known here in the hills for their prolific travel are easily recognized as they, almost without exception, over-dress for the climate. Maybe the climate of the scorching Bengal, which sits astride the Ganges before emptying into the Indian Ocean, makes the inhabitants sensitive to cold. They always appear bundled up—the women in thick jackets and the men wearing woolen balaclavas, even on days like today where half of our Americans group is wearing shorts. It's heartening to see that even in a relatively impoverished country like India, people budget travel into their lives.

The pakora is a good and greasy meal—just the thing to fatten up with before leaving on our trek. My mouth is still watering from the rich spices as I wipe my fingers on my pants and walk into an adjacent phone booth for a last phone call home. I've found it easier to call the U.S. than to send a postcard or letter. It's another one of those paradoxes about India that's difficult to grasp. The last postcard I sent home—though quite cheap (8.5 rupees or about 20 cents)—arrived a few weeks *after* I returned from a two-month expedition. I've found that using the phone booths are simple. You walk into the stall manned by an attendant, pick up the phone and dial 001 plus the number you want to connect with. A fax-like machine spits out a printed receipt when you are finished. All you have to do is pay the attendant and you are off. The connections are remarkably clear—much clearer than half the cell phone conversations I've had in the States. Today I leave a message for DeAnn. It's a twelve and a half hour time difference. That makes my call about 11 PM. She's either at work at the hospital on the night shift or sleeping as I get her answering service. Despite not actually talking, it's great to hear her voice. It has that crackling nasal intonation that I could recognize anywhere. When I hang up, I make another call— this time to the credit card company to chase down my pin number for a cash withdrawal. It's a surreal contrast from the noisy shit- splattered streets to the cool, clinical and crystal clear voicemail prompts, emanating from across the Pacific. Maybe this call—to an 800 number the United States—is getting forwarded back across the ocean to a city in lowland India. No such luck. The voice prompts have a Texas twang and tell me, "There's no service avail- able at this tahm . . ."

The cost of the calls—five minutes total—blows me away, adding up to a mere 14 and a half rupees, or 32 cents—a bargain considering what it would cost to call anywhere overseas from the U.S. Every town or village has at least one phone booth. They are, as I've said, usually a small booth that's almost always part of a sweet shop or tea stall. They are clearly marked from the outside with a canary yellow sign bearing the initials STD and/or ISD. If one didn't know better you would think that every village had a clinic for an alarming proliferation of sexually transmitted diseases, but that's certainly not the case. The initials stand for Subscriber Trunk Dialing, and International Subscriber Dialing, both obsolete holdover terms from British nomenclature.

Phone duties done, Chuck and I then wander through the town in search of Coca-Cola. It's not an easy pursuit. Munsyari is built on a hillside, so our search takes us up and down the muddy streets. Whenever we find a promising shop, Chuck asks the patron, "Do you know where we can get Coke?" After asking, he makes the hand tilt and uplift chin gesture, which, combined with the word "Coke" generates nods of universal understanding. The attendants send us off to the shop next door. They do the same in turn, and so it goes as we pass down to the last shop on the street. At the final stop, a bare stall perched on stilts holds nothing more than a few bottles of orange liquid, stacks of candles, dusty packets of cookies, and clear plastic jars full of individually wrapped candies. The guy behind the peeling linolium counter promptly directs us back to the original store. It would have saved us a lot of time and walking if someone just said, "There is no Coca-Cola in town." But as I've noticed in Indian foothills, there is a curious reluctance to say no, as if it was rude to do so.

Jonny scoffs at the notion of spending energy trying to get something as grotesquely American and consumer-driven as a Coke. That's one reason he goes on trips like this—to get away from products and attitudes that to him, undermine all that is unique and valuable in an emerging country like India. When we catch up with him, he's getting a haircut.

If you were to walk into a salon in America after a few 10–12 hour days of sweaty, dusty travel with no shower, you'd probably be politely asked to leave and not return until you've cleaned up. But here in a land whose resources and infrastructure cannot sustain such frivolity, the barber doesn't even bat an eyelid. It's a reminder of how good we, a fractional minority of the globe, have it in America. It's also yet another reminder of how we, in many ways enjoy the abundance of such things—like the gallons of clean hot water we carelessly pour on ourselves—at the expense of the vast majority of humanity.

Jonny never pays for haircuts in the States. He either does it himself or has Stacey, his girlfriend, do it for him. Of all the people who could capitalize on good looks, Jonny could doll himself up like a male model and cut a swath through the ladies, but that's not his style. He has a sense of himself that few I've met have and, it's a sense that is, for the most part devoid of superficial vanity. The other night, he described how as a wide-eyed twenty-one year-old, traveling alone in India, he sat down under the shade of a tree to get a haircut from a barber whose open air shop consisted of a chair, a pair of scissors and a broken mirror hung from the tree trunk. Jonny had been waiting for a bus. He'd been waiting for days because there was no set schedule of bus service, and he was getting worried because his supply of rupees was running thin. A monkey had stolen his passport in a place called Hampi. Hampi, with great fields of burnished granite boulders carelessly tossed amidst religious statues and bullet-shaped Hindu temples is known in climbing circles as a great place to rock climb. Jonny had been doing just that, when one of the many monkeys in the area pilfered through his pack, skampering off in a cloud of scattered rupee notes. Cutting through red tape to get a new passport was almost a scarier proposition than having no passport at all, and Jonny had been dipping into his monkey-depleted wallet to complete the required travel between consulates and district police stations. He'd spent more than his fair share on jarring sleepless all-night train rides to acquire the necessary paperwork. The barber was halfway finished when the bus unexpectedly rumbled into the village with a belch of dust and diesel. It was now or never, so with the top of his head shaved and the sides still shaggy from weeks of travel, Jonny threw some rupees to the barber and boarded. Picture Jonny running to the bus with a crudely tonsured head in the heart of a very nontouristy South India. He squeezes on board a bus so crowded with rural locals that the suspension creaks with every bump. The man seated next to him was agape at the sight of a tall, strapping, white guy sporting a reverse Mohawk. He blurted out in broken English the first thing that came to mind.

"Sir," he said, "You look like a superhero!"

Jonny's hairdo no doubt raised some eyebrows at the U.S. Consulate and gained no additional respectability with the passage of time. And he never fixed it. The "superhero" coiffure wound up immortalized on his new passport.

Back in Munsyari, waiting for the red-tape to unravel, Sarah sits on the bus knitting and exploring the *Lonely Planet* guide to India. She took Dramamine yesterday to counteract the motion-sickness generated by the endless bumps and switchbacks of the hot and dusty mountain roads. It's left her a bit dozy and slightly with-drawn. "Sorry, I'm not being that social," she says, through heavy-lidded eyes. I assure her that it's not an expectation. It must be over-whelming for her, being only 26 and having never been to Asia much less a place as alien as the India foothills. Her notes from August 30, confirm this, "dramamine induced haze compounded by culture shock," followed by "make two purchases unassisted—feels like a real sense of accomplishment," on September 1. The speed of arrival, the whirlwind of meetings, errands, and rapid departure to the hills is enough to make all but the most experienced heads spin. I had a friend who after arriving at an overseas airport become so intimidated by the new environment, he immediately turned around and rebooked a flight back home. I remember when he got home, haggard after only 36 hours. Through red-rimmed eyes he spoke two words, "Fuck that . . ."

Travel like this is like a drug trip except the user is mainlining not an illusion, but an alternate reality. Gabe, like the rest of us, is a vet-eran world traveler, so he's absolutely uninhibited, shooting endless photos of dirty streets, cows, people, and scenery that ranges from ethereal terraced hillsides of vibrant green to the five distant sum-mits of the Panch Chuli peaks. The Panch Chuli's, or "five pointed ovens," as the translation reads, hover in the distance as they scrape the sky at almost 23,000 feet. According to legend, the Pandavas—great warrior princes of Hindu myth—cooked their last meal on the Panch Chuli massif before ascending to Heaven.

We are all itching to do some ascending ourselves. S. V. is the man to help us. He's revealing himself as an efficient liaison officer who not only understands bureaucratic inertia, but also how to overcome it. As a veteran of every one of India's major armed conflicts of the past decade, our LO also begins to expose an alter-ego—hard-drinking, chain smoking, no-nonsense man who is not afraid of dressing people down. Later, he'll regale us with tales, but for now he sticks to his official duties, waiting perhaps for the endless days in Base Camp. In the meantime, he and Khem Singh dash between various offices, alternately faxing, text messaging, and telephoning Delhi, Dera Dun, and Uttarkashi. With a neatly trimmed mustache and piercing dark eyes, S. V. can conjure up a hard temperment, that unsentimental side derived from years of modern warfare, where often the enemy, the goals, and the means to fight are filtered through off-color shades of ethical gray. S. V. is also a class act effectively hiding his underlying disdain of petty officialdom. But every so often the mask slips, and the frustration boils to the surface. "I just had some choice words with Mr. X," he fumes at one point. He adding with some bluster, "These bastards care nothing for what is happening beyond their damn offices!"

For an hour, we all brace for an extended stay in Munsyari—perhaps lasting days. But as mysteriously as the problem arises, it gets resolved. An hour later, we pass under the concrete trailhead arch and begin a trudging descent past tea stalls and pointy Hindu temples. The river's rumble grows in strength. When we arrive at the bottom of the deep V-shaped valley, the roar drowns out all but the closest conversation. The river, called the Gori Ganga is swollen by late monsoon rain and snow, coursing down from the high elevations. In Hindi Ganga means "river" or "flow," while Gori is "fair" or "white." Gori, sometimes spelled Gauri, is a reference to Parvati, the fair-skinned daughter of the lord of the Himalayas. Parvati incidentally, is one of Devi's incarnations, thus the milky river crashing down from the distant peaks on the roof of the world is, Devi's river. So, as we trudge up the trail on our first eager day of foot travel towards our goal, we are ever reminded of the awesome beauty—and power—of the Goddess whose domain we now enter.

It's a six-mile hike up the valley on a path that occasionally traverses far above the raging Gori Ganga. The air is thick and humid, and the lush broad-leafed vegetation and occasional banana tree lends a near-tropical feel. The path is of a uniform width, perhaps six feet, composed of ancient granite blocks worn smooth by the passage of countless feet and hooves. A good many of the blocks are vertically placed. In some sections they resemble row after row of blunt incisors that contour the valley wall, sometimes set in grooves hewn from living rock.

Our path is ancient, tracing its origins back to at least the sixteenth century when the region was settled by tribes migrating from the parched deserts of Rajasthan, 500 miles to the southwest. This path was a trade route where wool, gold, turquoise, and ponies from Tibet were traded for wheat, barley, rice, and sugar from India. Over time, this region developed its own unique culture, one that fostered seasonal agriculture and animal husbandry, migrating between settlements of varying elevation as the seasons changed and the years passed. Those centuries of peaceful trade were interrupted at sunrise on October 20, 1962, when the China's People's Liberation Army invaded India with overwhelming force on two separate flanks—in the west in Ladakh, and in the east across the border of the North-East Frontier Agency, later renamed Arunachal Pradesh. Though these areas of actual conflict were geographically distant and relatively isolated, the inability to reach a political solution and the resultant war closed the entire 2,000-mile border. After that, trade became impossible. And with the passing of trade, so went a way of life.

Some historians argue that the invasion was merely an ever-expansionist China laying claim to territory in a twentieth-century expression of an ongoing geopolitical game that had already spanned centuries. Others argue that Indian Prime Minister Nehru's "forward policy" of establishing small military outposts on the frontier, baited the PRC into an offensive. Both sides point the finger at each other as instigators of the conflict. Regardless, this policy placed the Indian military in an untenable position as it faced an overwhelming, well trained, well equipped, and acclimatized Chinese army. Depending on whom you talk to, some claim China still occupies tens of thousands of kilometers of Indian territory. Others state that both sides have withdrawn to prewar boundaries.

No matter what perspective Indian and American cooperation grew after the U.S. airlifted supplies to strengthen India's defense. In some eyes, this revealed a tacit alliance between the two democracies. As mentioned earlier, alliance or not, relations between India and the U.S. prior to the Chinese invasion were frosty at best. The U.S., unsatisfied with India's nonalignment policy, sought a strong ally in the region. They did so by becoming a major arms supplier to Pakistan, India's enemy. With the Chinese invasion, America became an erstwhile arms supplier to the Indians, eager to stem the tide of communism, whatever the cost. Thus China's incursion opened the door for cooperation and in only a short time, both nations would join forces to spy on China.

Chuck, Jonny, Gabe, Sarah, and I would not be walking this path were it not for the fateful cooperation between India and the CIA. We can thank the border war too, for the chance to see such lush grandeur in splendid isolation. Prior to 1962, this very path must have been a bustling highway of foot and animal traffic. Indeed, Tilman hiked down this very road almost sixty-nine years ago to the day, experiencing the hustle bustle of an active trade route. He later wrote,

> Tibet produces very little grain and is largely dependant on imports from India. . . . The figure of 400 tons of wool for the year 1907 is an impressive one when the route and the means of transport is considered. The Bhotia traders and their households come up to Milam and Martoli in the spring and establish depots there, and in the course of the summer they make two or three journeys into Tibet. . . . Goats and sheep are the principal carriers, but yaks, jibbus, and mules are sometimes used. . . . There is romance in trade and not least in this carried on in the grim defiles and over the stern passes of the Himalayas.

Though once a veritable thoroughfare of people and animals, today our team of five, plus S. V., Khem Singh, Dipender, and 42 porters comprise the vast majority of travelers.

It's good to stretch our legs and feel the trail under our feet. We carry little more than daypacks with water, some food, and raingear. Jonny and Gabe tote cameras and often race ahead to capture images as we stroll through the breathtaking scenery. We gain about a thousand feet of elevation over a little more than six miles of hiking.

"It must be a hundred percent humidity," Chuck says as he pulls the clingy wet synthetic T-shirt from his chest in a vain attempt to vent. Our sweat, even in the 80-degree heat fails to evaporate and coats us with an oily sheen.

If the climate's not refreshing, at last the views are. Our trail skirts steep hillsides, thousands of feet high. In some places, these walls compose vertical expanses of granite dotted with clumps of spiky vegetation. Other faces, equally steep, hold trees, grasses, and shrubs. Only the tropical environment could encourage vegetation on the impossibly sheer walls.

It's all very Tolkeinesqe and mysterious—a real treat after days of smog, diesel, and dust. *Lord of the Rings* could have been filmed here except that the inhabitants are brown, not white. I separate from the group and have, for the first time in days, a chance to be in my own head without managing or worrying about details. Sometimes, I like being left alone. It's a new side to me, for in the past I've always craved or needed company or presence of others to feel at ease. I've learned that there is a difference, at least for myself, between being lonely and just being alone. Though I might come across as aloof (or even arrogant), I now, more than ever require solitude and my own inner dialogue. And my own company is company enough as I stroll along, marveling at the palpable history and mythic vibe in this deep and narrow gorge.

It's more than just my imagination, for the events spanning the centuries are indelibly cast on this very trail. Here is where countless generations plied their wares as traders between continents and cultures. Here is where hardy souls cast off on long hazardous journeys in search of holy Mount Kailash—the legendary central pillar of the Hindu and Buddhist world—and its companion Lake Manasarovar. Those lie across the border, maybe a hundred miles due north. This is also the same path trodden by Kohli's espionage expedition and countless other Himalayan aspirants.

Here also are shrines. Some are stately structures made of concrete and stucco, draped with green, red, and yellow prayer flags, adorned with brass bells, and littered with rupee coins and cigarettes—offerings to Shiva or Devi. Others are mere heaps of stone that build to blunt points drawing the eye skyward and invoking the phallic profile of the persistent Hindu fertility symbol. One such humble shrine bears a smoldering incense stick placed with deliberation on a crude alter. As an offering to the deities, it casts its sweet smoke like a vaporous prayer to the heavens. It must have been lit by one of the porters only minutes before, for I can see them a few hundred yards ahead, a knot of a half-dozen dull dots bent under our red and yellow climbing duffels. They plod along, the sounds of their footfalls buried beneath the torrential thunder of the Gori Ganga. As the group bobs around a curve of our fairy-tale path they disappear one by one. I am blissfully alone again.

The magic is broken when I round a bend an hour later and there's S. V. standing, chatting on his cell phone. He raises two fingers as he sees me coming into view. That means he's getting two bars on his Nokia. As I pass, he gives me an acknowledging tip of his hat before carrying on with his conversation. Though I don't speak Hindi, the gestures and verbal intimations indicate a call to his wife. The fact that he's getting a signal deep in this river gorge shows the pervasive spread of technology. Soon, the unseen march of global communications will span even this, the greatest chain of mountains in the world. I walk on as S. V.'s voice rises and falls, the animated conversational pitch echoing—through the heart of an ancient land.

We arrive at the settlement of Jimmighat—nothing more than a small level expanse at the base of a huge wall upon which steep green grass and foliage clings. The elevation is high, nearly 6,000 feet. Still, we linger in that subtropical zone where wet-loving bamboos, ferns, and palms only begin to give way to deciduous trees and evergreens. This valley seems to funnel the wet air that moves north in its timeless monsoon flow, thereby creating a microclimate extending the subtropical flora to higher elevations than the norm. The effect brings an exotic flavor to our trek, one that is completely unexpected.

That night, as September 2 becomes September 3, I wake up at 2:00 AM to the drip of water. I switch on my headlamp, which as my years of experience dictate, I keep handy in either the side pocket of the tent, or in my sleeping bag, where I know I can find it. The harsh beam of the light, made more intense by my sudden consciousness, reveals a steady trickle of water, falling directly on the chest of my sleeping bag. The roof of our tent, which Jonny and I pitched on the irregular granite cobbles of the guest shelter patio, is a complex mass of stitches and zippers. Intended to vent moisture, the actual result is a jumble of leaky stitches and zippers that the rain relentlessly penetrates.

I jury rig a towel and wrap my sleeping bag in my rain jacket. It helps, but the damage is done. My bag is an amazing ultralight down cocoon whose outer shell fabric is made to be featherweight, not water-resistant, It's an age-old lesson that down, once wet, stays wet and unlike synthetic insulation, ceases to retain heat. Climbers caught in storms in wetter areas have died from choosing down insulation instead of synthetic. I certainly won't die from this unexpected soaking, but the damp chills me to the bone. By the time we get up and have breakfast after a sleepless night, I feel a restless chill, the first signal of illness.

Jonny's not had a peaceful night either. Besides getting wet too, he has a wild dream that is so vivid and disturbing, he wakes up and feels compelled to write the details down. He furiously scribbles in the light of his headlamp as I pull my bag over my head and try to fast-forward into morning. In his dream, Jonny flies in an aircraft. He's reading a newspaper. Upon glancing up and looking out the window, he realizes that the plane is about to crash. In his words,

> I see with complete certainty that the jet-liner I'm on will be smashing into the side of a rocky, icy mountain, I can see the tall pillars jutting from the mountainside and it's horrifying. Then the lights go out. Impact seems to take forever. With the first jolt, I imagine the front of the plane collapsing. Thoughts race, family, friends, dying, pain, one chance, eternity, but then I think no—too fast. The next jolt dislodges me from my seat and I feel a piece of metal hit my foot and set me spinning. Air is rushing around. It's constant and powerful. I can see myself just spinning now in a black space. I'm losing the sense of panic and catastrophe and I wait, like one might wait for the sunrise. I can only listen as all is now black. Only the rushing of air continues. Finally I am almost

bored, but not quite, as I hear another sound break the silent roar; it is a cricket. And the silent roar, a river.

A dream like that in a place like this, is odd enough. Does it foretell disaster? Is it a warning from the deities presiding over this mythic environment? Do we take comfort from the death-like serenity that followed his unconscious journey to the edge of mortality? Odder yet is the fact that for Jonny, this dream is a sequel of sorts. Two years ago on the first night of his first climbing expedition to India, Jonny found himself, once again sleeping by an equally holy river. This time the river was the mighty Bhagirathi—another of the Ganges tributaries. Jonny recalls,

We were having an argument—my sister and I, and then my dad, and then their faces changed and it was my girlfriend I was arguing with. Then, as if someone had died, the scene grew black and full of grief.

Slowly, the scene changed again. People I didn't know were fighting and it was red and loud, and there were guns and war broke out. Someone cried in terror and then someone else in triumph. The scenes began changing rapidly and even the gender of the people was becoming abstract: people laughing and groaning with ecstasy, people eating and chanting, people dying and being born.

The pageant of human life began to stream like a reel of 16 mm film accelerating through the projector, the sounds and colors bleeding together until they began to cancel each other out. We were moving from color to black and white, the sounds merging. Overwhelming neutrality without extremes (without emotion), began to overtake—faster and faster the scenes pulsed through—until there was only gray light and white noise.

Then . . . I just listened. Eventually I realized my eyes were open. I was in my tent and the white noise, the sound of everything, was the sound of the rushing river.

Two expeditions, two trips, two eerily similar dreams. I'm not sure what to make of it, but Jonny writes,

> It proves to me that places can talk, that there is a certain intelligence that is so old, that it's frightening at first. But we are all part of that vast and flowing river—whether we run from it or not. What matters in our individual lives is how we perceive that overflowing surge: beautiful, chaotic, serene, bloodthirsty, righteous, wordless? When places talk, do you listen?

Daylight comes to wash the mystic echoes of the past night from our minds. After a breakfast of eggs, toast, and chai, Khem Singh announces that the path ahead is washed out by a monsoon-fed stream. There are two sections apparently demolished by the raging waters and crossing the second sounds sketchy. It's so precipitous that we'll need a rope to cross the flood-exposed cliffs. From what Khem tells us, there's a rope already in place, but despite the additional safeguard, half the porters are taking a steep bypass. In the process, they'll gain a bruising 3,000 feet before dropping back down to rejoin the trail for the final two-and-a-half miles to tonight's camp.

All told, today's hike, without the longer detour is a good ten miles. That in mind, the five of us decide to risk the washout and avoid the longer, steeper detour. The trail issues explain the absence of the ponies that usually carry loads on this route. It's always baffling how Khem knows everything that's happening. You never see people running up and giving reports or documents being passed around, so sometimes it seems as though he acquires information by osmosis. I've been lucky enough to have Khem on every Indian expedition, and this is the fourth in eight years. Over that time I've benefited from his ability to get things done.

He's a little shorter than me, which makes him about average in stature for these parts. He retains a modest demeanor—to us climbers and trekkers anyway. I've seen him lay into slacking porters, and just the other day Jonny watched as Khem lambasted a shopkeeper for overcharging a few rupees for an umbrella. His English is fairly good, and when he listens, he looks at the ground or at some indistinct point in space and furrows his brow like a man in deep concentration. In other words, he's scrupulous, dedicated, and a good guy to have on your side. As an arranger, there's no better in the Garhwal and Kumaon (the region of the Himalayas adjacent and immediately due east of the Garhwal) than Khem. Today, he wears a green and black Marmot rain jacket.

"Sir," he says, addressing me with a firm and forthright tone. "Do you know this jacket?"

I sift my brain, which this morning, is a junkyard of relevant details, commingled with useless junk.

Sensing my hesitation, Khem adds, "A very nice man from America gave this to me."

I am about to congratulate him on getting such a nice gift from some random guy, when it dawns on me that he's wearing a jacket I gave him in 2001, four years prior. The shell is faded now, and the logo is barely legible, but I can see that he wears it with pride. It's nice to see someone get the most out of their equipment. I myself have gone through four jackets since that trip, all of which were retired, more on fashion limitations than for wear. I make a mental note to leave him another jacket when this trip is done.

By 7:15 AM, we are hiking along a precipitous trail following the left, or west, side of the valley. Again, the hills are vibrant green with the tops of the canyon obscured by a thick mist billowing thousands of feet above. The trail is periodically cut by gushing cascades, which provide a great excuse to stop and fill our water bottles. Chuck and Sarah carry high-tech water filters with silver-impregnated ceramic elements that strain out protozoa, bacteria, and viruses with 0.2 micron diameter pores (a micron is a millionth of a meter). With no residual aftertaste like what iodine or bleach treatments leave, we are free to enjoy the best-tasting water we've had in our lives.

After drinking the tepid commercially bottled Indian water— guaranteed to contain no viral or bacterial bugs, but reportedly high in pesticides—it's a real treat. (Some popular bottled drinking water brands in India, including Kinley—bottled by Coca-Cola, Aquafina—bottled by Pepsi, Bisleri and Aquaplus, contain upwards of 79 to 104 times the level of pesticide residue allowed by the drinking water standards of the European Economic Community. Pesticide residues include HCH, Malathion, and DDT.)

It takes two hours of hiking to reach the point where the trail diverges. We can see some of the porters humping our bags up the fearsome path, bypassing the main route. We cross the first destroyed section of trail under the watchful gaze of a half dozen mud-coated workers. I'm walking in back, and it's fun to watch the locals oogle Sarah. She's wearing shorts and a shirt clingy in the humidity. She's an uncommon sight, cute, without the overt girly-ness (and she's the only white girl for a hundred miles around). Sarah has that sandy blonde, blue-eyed beauty, and a smile set off by a pair of prominent front teeth, vaguely reminiscent of Sponge Bob's girlfriend, Sandy Cheeks. Comic strip comparisons aside, her real-life achievements speak for themselves, as she's an engineer and the only true trained and technical professional among us. All that is lost on trail workers, who are a more restrained version of an American construction crew. I make eye contact with one guy after he tears his gaze from Sarah, whose form now recedes up the trail in a flash of tanned thigh. He' s embarrassed and after a brief moment, averts his eyes vigorously returning to stack flat chunks of granite—a few of what must be millions, stretching for a hundred miles into Tibet—in the retaining wall of the new causeway crossing the stream.

Sarah is oblivious to the covetous attention. She's coming out of a career cycle where she "burned really hot, so much so, I burned out." Immediately prior to the trip she'd worked long hours developing advanced laser technology under a government contract. Ironically, as we hike, her company is about to be acquired by Lockheed Martin, the aerospace and advanced technology company formed by the 1995 merger of Lockheed Corporation and Martin

Marietta. It was Martin Marietta that fabricated the SNAP-19, way back in the early 1960s.

The bombardment of seventy-hour workweeks, straight out of college, never let up until the evening before Sarah hopped on a plane to India. She was spent, "scraping bottom." Now, on a much-needed sabbatical and contemplating a career about-face, she, "suddenly found myself walking through the most amazing scenery. It was funny how the views were not exceptional to the others. It was just simply a part of their lives."

The walkway and the hand tools the crew wields must be the same seen here over the centuries. They have hammers, Pulaski-looking hoes (without the axe), and hand drills that are nothing more than long metal rods with chisel tips. I see fractured boreholes in the stone, evidence of the dynamite used to hollow out the cliff-side and quarry for construction material. The workers assemble the flat raw granite plates into interlocking layers, like brick walls without the mortar. In some places, it's hard to tell what is holding the structure up, as the piles often grow in widening tiers up from single blocks that appear to sit on blank rock. With no OSHA regulators standing around, it's difficult to confidently tread the narrow chock-a-block path, poised as it is, Indiana Jones-style, over a long drop straight into a crashing Gori Ganga.

Our fears are not unfounded. This section of path has claimed lives. In 1967, returning from successfully planting the SNAP-19 on Nanda Kot, Kohli nearly perished in the river near this very spot. He recalls,

We had to cross a stream but found that its water was flowing very turbulently. A few kilometers down, I discovered a spot which looked very calm and decided to cross the stream there. I did not suspect any danger and therefore moved along, feeling the bottom of the stream with my ice axe.

As I reached halfway, I noticed that the ice axe did not touch the ground. Before I could retrace my steps I was swept away by the current into deep water. . . . The water was ice cold and I lost control. For a while I entered a whirlpool and got churned. I was moving down with the swift current, like a lifeless object.

The water, freezing glacier melt, dragged Kohli down, instantly soaking his padded clothing. He was mercilessly ricocheted off boulders—like being pummeled by Mike Tyson.

About 66 feet below was a vertical fall. I resigned myself to the fate and said my ardaas [a Sikh prayer entailing complete surrender to the will of God] in a fraction of a second. Gyan Singh saw me. Without thinking about his own safety, he quickly jumped in . . . [and] held me by my waterproof jacket and spinning me with full force against the bank. Simultaneously, a Tibetan constable who was watching the drama, jumped into the water and pulled me out to safety.

Gyan Singh, a radio officer in the Indo-Tibetan Border Police was later awarded the Police Medal for risking his life to save Kohli. The constable was a member of the Special Frontier Force (SFF). The SSF was a Tibetan commando unit in part trained and funded by the CIA with an infusion of American dollars. Writes John Kenneth Knaus, in *Orphans of the Cold War,* of the SFF, "The U.S. provided light arms and instructors for this clone of the Green Berets. American interests were served by the firsthand intelligence gathered. . . . Moreover, the cooperation broke down old barriers between the U.S. government and the previously aloof Indians."

According to Conboy, the SFF, "In theory . . . would parachute onto the Tibetan plateau and strike the Chinese rear in the event of renewed Sino-Indian hostilities along the Himalayas." In reality the planned-for war never erupted, and on this mission the "determined and ferocious unit" was reduced to acting as porters for the grueling load-carrying required by the rough terrain. Conboy writes, "These commandos had an earthy, primitive aura. Most had inadequate footwear, including a few with sandals, but this lack was more than offset by their focused, serious demeanor. With little exaggeration, they looked like they were spoiling for a war."

They wouldn't have their war on the CIA spy trips, but they still faced mortal risk. Kohli's rescue, nothing short of miraculous, was followed the next day by yet another miracle. He later wrote,

The following day, my colleagues arranged for two ponies and we headed towards Munsyari, along a narrow footpath which overlooked the fast flowing Gori Ganga, some 10,000 feet below. The mountain ponies have a strange habit of strutting along the edge of the footpath. My baggage was being carried by one such pony and I was on the second pony ten feet behind. Looking at the Gori Ganga several thousands feet below . . . I decided to dismount and walk.

Five minutes later, I saw the pony carrying my baggage disappearing into thin air and heading for the swift stream 10,000 feet below. I thanked my stars for the second narrow escape within 24 hours.

Though the drop-off into the river is nowhere near 10,000 feet deep, above or below the washout, it is formidable. Jonny, gazing down the potential fall line—over a cliff, past a cobble-studded clay wall, and into a boiling mass of froth, comments, "That's deep enough to kill you ten times over." Kohli's book, *Miracles of Ardaas*, whose title is akin to a contemporary Christian publication like, *The Incredible Power of Prayer*, attributes his survival of these, and many other instances, to, "the unshakeable faith in the divine power of Ardaas." I am not one to argue on such issues, but there is no doubt that these two accidents underline the hazards that face us on this path.

Another hour of traipsing through conifers, chestnut trees, and the occasional stand of bamboo brings us to the second washout. I turn a blind corner as the trail traverses a cliff, hundreds of feet above the river. There's a lineup of porters sheltered in an alcove, waiting their turn to cross a two-hundred-foot gap in the granite wall. Down the middle of the gap rushes a waterfall. I can see the remnants of trail—blocks scattered in the rocky bowl—the waterfall shoots straight off into the angry frothing water of the Gori Ganga. The Gori flows with dun-colored "glacial milk," which textbook calls, "a solution of ionically dissolved elements and a suspension of the finely ground rock dust ground from the living parent rock of the mountain by glacial friction."

What that says is that the rushing water is freezing cold, and much denser than say, the water that runs out of your faucet. It's fast and heavy enough to carve solid rock into wild shapes and twisted forms. I move ahead in the queue to check out what we are up against.

The waterfall has swept whatever causeway existed, leaving a bare expanse of blank rock pounded by the falls. All those who wish to pass must shimmy down a rope—perhaps 25 feet long—to a shelf system traversing below the falls. This shelf terminates after 80 feet in a jumbled pile of loose rock, immediately blocked by a wet section of near-vertical rock, 60 feet high. A fall from almost anywhere would end up at best in snapped bones, at worst in death, after a terminal plunge into the river.

By the time my turn arrives, I am eager to get it over with. Gabe and Jonny are mere dots on the other side. Whether by accident or plan, they stand on solid ground, cameras ready to capture what we can only hope will be the hardest and most dangerous part of the journey to Base Camp. Though I am a climber, it's still with some trepidation that I gingerly grasp the rope. I first use it only for balance. Then forced by the steep holdless stone, I trust my entire weight to it. Were it a normal climbing rope, anchored to climbing hardware maybe a nail-like piton or bolt, I'd have no trouble trusting the whole setup. The trouble is, the anchor is a pole of metal—one of those long drills I mentioned earlier—buried an indeterminate length in the rock. I can't see how solid it is. For all I know, someone pounded on the thing for a few minutes before leaving it buried an inch deep. That's not my only concern. The rope I grab is a thick waterlogged hank of grayish brown fiber. It could be hemp. It could be manila. What's for certain is that it's not the tried and true nylon I, as a modern climber, am used to.

Behind me I hear a crash. "Oh shit," I think. "Someone just took the plunge." Out of the corner of my eye, I see a dark object fly down the cliff, slamming into the bowl. It turns out that it's just our luggage. Quite understandably, the porters do not wish to shimmy down the rope with sixty pounds on their backs. They have opted to drop the baggage down a shallow slot in the cliff, and upon crossing, retrieve the baggage and carry it across the bowl. They still have to climb the final stretch with the bags lashed to their backs. I wince as I see one of our pieces of expensive wheeled luggage take the tumble. "I wonder if my laptop is in there. . . ." My thoughts are interrupted by a voice, "Please sir." It's one of the porters. He's wearing flip-flops with a tractor-tire tread, dark shapeless pants and a soaked, full-button long-sleeve shirt. He jerks his head adding, "Please, this side—only." I gather from the gesture that he wants me to get out of the way. His sunken smoker's chest heaves with adrenaline as suspended above me, he clasps the rope in a white-knuckle grip, obviously terrified of the drop. I scoot down, brace myself on the sloping shelf leading under the waterfall and hold my arms out as if volunteering to catch him if he takes the dive. I obviously don't inspire much confidence as the man retreats back up the rope to the safety of the six-foot drill bit.

The queue is getting longer, and everyone in line is growing visibly impatient, so I get out of the way and let a different porter pass. This man, fearless and nimble yells at the first frightened guy who finally commits to climbing hand over hand down the rope. It's like watching *Fear Factor*, except the contestants aren't as attractive, the penalty is maiming or death, and the prize for surviving is the porter day rate of four dollars and fifty cents.

The final climb up to where the trail continues would be roughly the equivalent of an American technical climbing grade of 5.7. This is a respectable level of difficulty for intermediate climbers. Throw in some running water, a sixty-pound load, bare feet, and a possibly fatal fall and you have today's true-life drama.

I hate to keep calling them porters. They are villagers and towns-people who spend only this time of year, the off-season, harvesting tourist dollars. For them, humping luggage isn't a career, rather, a seasonal odd job that helps pay the bills. By and large, they are, by American standards, shorter than average. To a man they are fit, much fitter than the gym rats or weekend warriors in the States. They are not concerned about cosmetic fitness. For them it is a matter of survival. This is surprising for most of them chain-smoke the peculiar leaf cigarettes indigenous to India, Pakistan, and Nepal. Called bidis, these cheap, handmade cigarettes are about the diameter of a firecracker, the length of a pinkie, and made from shreds or flakes of tobacco wrapped in a green tobacco leaf. The final unfiltered product is slim and tapered on one end that's tied with a colored thread. They cost about 15 rupees or 30 cents for a pack of 20. Incidentally, the Portuguese introduced tobacco to India in 1605. Today, India produces more tobacco than the United States and is not surprisingly, the world leader in oral cancer.

As I stand on the other side of the washout, I wonder what the life expectancy of some of the porters is. They stand in knots, steaming, even in the midmorning warmth from their dousing in the waterfall. They puff their bidis, smiling and relaxing, much like any other group of working men in the world on cigarette break. A few have deep tubercular coughs and sunken smoker's chests. Still, they can carry tremendous loads with less exertion than I can—even were I at peak fitness.

One guy is taller that the others. His name is Bachan, and he puffs at his bidi with an easygoing grin. With the laid-back demeanor, brown hair, green eyes, and fair skin, Bachan could pass for a surfer on a Southern California beach. Of course, you'd have to clean him up a bit and lose the threadbare homespun wool jacket and Chinese-made chappals. Chappals are Indian flip-flops with an added flap wrapping the big toe. Many of the thrift-minded porters wear these cheap sandals. And below the ankle they are a podiatrist's nightmare of twisted feet, crooked toes and long-since fallen arches. Chuck, mutters, "Amazing," as the men shoulder their burdens. Some tote double-loads breaking the one-hundred-pound mark.

We are luckier than some expeditions who've faced down porter strikes and outright abandonment. That is one of the advantages of working with an agency. An agency like Mandip's insures that such things don't happen. I shudder to think of the result were the porters to pose a sit in on the trail below the washout.

Tilman's successful Nanda Devi expedition experienced just such a setback in the middle of the Rishi Ganga gorge. Their predicament— the walk-out by thirty-seven porters in a harrowing river crossing— put their expedition a week behind schedule. That makes our trail adventure look like child's play.

Bachan, like some of the hill people in Afghanistan, represents the racial mix often found at the crossroads of culture. There are even legends of Macedonian blood in this region. At a spot only a few hundred miles from here, Alexander the Great made his farthest expansion into Asia, crossing east of the Indus River in 326 BC.

There, on the east banks of the Hydaspes River (now called the Jhelum River) a tributary of the Indus, he fought one of his greatest battles against the Indian king Purushotthamma in what is the modern-day Punjab of Pakistan. Alexander was victorious, but his army, perhaps tired after eight years of conquering the known world, refused to continue any farther into the subcontinent. The fact that they were met with terrifying Indian war elephants for a second time in six years, must have helped them make up their minds.

Alexander was dead three years later, and his empire was divided and dissolved. Despite that, his conquests had long-term cultural effects with the mixing of races, cultures, and the flourishing of Hellenistic culture clear to the fringes of Central Asia. It's not a stretch to imagine the spread of Macedonian blood to this region, since, according to Alexander historian W. W. Tarn, "Both flanks of the Hindu Kush [the mountain range several hundred miles west] were once full of hill chieftains who claimed descent from the man [Alexander] who left none to succeed him. On the Indian side they once ruled in Chitral, Gilgit, Nagir, Hunza [a province in the northernmost part of Pakistan] and elsewhere, and we ourselves have seen a Mir of Hunza who was descended from Alexander and bore a British title."

> *"There's something about human beings in the mountains, they seem to care less about the anchors other folks require. The result is they take on a curious lightness."*
>
> —Jeff Long, *Angels of Light*

CHAPTER 7

BREAKING POINT

At 9:45 AM we reach Paton, a small clearing with a teahouse located at a sharp bend in the river. We are getting out in the sticks, for amenities are getting scarcer and the "menu," a verbal list of what's available to eat, is translated by S. V. in a few sentences. I stick with tea, as Dipender sent us off in the morning with sack lunches. Today's brown bag consists of an apple, a foil-wrapped chapatti "burrito" with a spicy potato filling, a lump of cheese, a mini Kit-Kat bar and some biscuits (cookies in India's British English).

An hour later I pass the confluence of the Ralam River and the Gori Ganga. The clear blue waters of the Ralam tributary, surge into the milky torrents of the Gori Ganga. The wild and deafening cascades are a sight that even the locals give pause to appreciate. I bump into a cluster of porters admiring the sight while taking a bidi break. They are part of the 107 men hired by the Italian Nanda Devi East team. They are headed down, without loads and thus a happy bunch who take time to point out the details of the scene, with waving fingers and a few words of broken English. My Hindi is pathetic, less comprehensible than their English, so our exchange is limited to smiles and general nods of approval.

Another trail, one that started across the river at Munsyari paralleled our path since the trek's beginning. It's invisible to us in bamboo thickets and forests of towering Nepalese alder, called *uti*. That trail diverges and heads roughly due north and east for ten kilometers up the Ralam River valley to Ralam village. If known for anything, Ralam has a reputation for an off-the-beaten-track ruggedness. It's so pristine that, at nearly 12,000 feet, not even packhorses can make it up there. In recent years, Ralam's reputation has suffered as thousands of people swarm the region from April through June to collect one of nature's weirdest medicines—a medicinal fungus that grows on caterpillars, called Yar Tsa Gumba.

The fungus grows on hibernating pupae. Were the caterpillar to develop, unmolested it would metamorphose into an elegant white ghost moth. Instead, after ingesting a fungal spore, the caterpillar is consumed and mummified by fungus. Then, a worm-shaped stalk about the length of a cigarette grows from the body, poking through the ground. The stalk resembles a blade of grass, sometimes turning iridescent blue. It's that color—and the fact that yaks seem drawn to it—that key searchers in on its whereabouts. Folklore has it that fungus was discovered in the Tibetan mountain pastures 1,500 years ago when even old yaks got feisty after eating the fungus stalks.

The Latin name for this entomophagous, or insect eating, fungus is Cordyceps sinensis. Chinese call it, "winter insect, summer grass." Cordyseps is found in Nepal, Tibet, Sikkim, Bhutan, and several provinces of China. In this area, it fetches 60,000 to 80,000 rupees per kilogram (about $625 to $825 per pound) locally. When it reaches markets in China, it's worth a whopping $10,000 per pound. As a traditional medicine, Cordyceps has been used over the centuries to improve liver functions, bolster immunity, and treat aging. At one time, the fungus was considered so potent and precious; it was reserved for China's Imperial family. In 1993, when the Chinese women's Olympic team, broke three world records at the World Outdoor Track and Field Championships, the coach of the team claimed Cordyceps was the secret of the team's success. Says medicinal mushroom expert, Mark Kaylor, "when asked what their secret ingredient was, they said it was Cordyceps. We've found out it was Cordyceps, but it was also growth hormones, steroids and everything else, like we're seeing now with our baseball players in the U.S."

Whatever one's belief may be, Cordyceps value has reached the point that in the Kumaon, people swarm the 12,000- to 14,000-foot elevation alpine meadows, prematurely denuding the area. The usual harvests used to occur in July. In 2004, groups were in the area by April, effectively cleaning the fungus out by late June. About 20 to 30,000 mummified insects weigh a pound and, "If the trend continues for another two to three years, then this species will become extinct," says Dr. G. S. Rawat of the prestigious Wildlife Institute of India.

It's illegal to collect Yar Tsa Gombu, and despite regulations that forbid its trade, the ban is virtually unenforced. Administrative resources are limited, especially considering the poaching and cross-border black market trade. The instant windfall—like an American lottery—benefits few locally, and it's the out-of-town brokers who reap the profit. Still, Yar Tsa Gombu is a critical, if temporary, cash crop in a poverty-stricken area. Villagers have even demarcated areas in their local meadows as off limits to outsiders. It's this type of competition that has caused conflict, even two murders in the usually peaceful area. And for bad and perhaps good, harvests are diminishing. Annual yields have seen a reported decrease of 50 percent from 2002 to 2003.

Had I known of the miracle mushroom, I might have taken the detour and sought some myself in Ralam. I am catching a cold, and by the time I've arrived at a rainy Bodgwar, it's 1:00 PM, and I feel achy and dizzy. I take shelter under the awning of a stone rest house, one of a handful of buildings in this, an oasis of reasonably level ground at the 8,200-foot elevation. This stretch lies smack dab in the middle of the long passage of narrow gorge. The drizzle is steady, though it is so humid that it's hard to distinguish between mist, suspended moisture, and falling raindrops. As with last night, the mountaintops are hidden from view by clouds, but what still shows are the thousands of feet of impossibly steep vegetated walls hemming in our tiny haven on both sides. The effect is oppressive and mysterious.

I'm glad to have some shelter. The four-roomed building has white stucco walls, a tin roof, and an open courtyard of short green grass. The rest house was built by the Public Works Department of Uttaranchal province, which oversees construction, maintenance, and planning of roads, bridges, and government buildings, while employing more than 10,000 engineers, workers, and administrative staff. It is a prodigious task, considering that Uttaranchal, strategically located on the border of China and Tibet, needs roads that can accommodate the rapid deployment of military forces in the event of a repeat border war with China. This means plenty of rugged road-building in mountainous terrain up to 13,000 feet, plus a lot of sturdy bridges. There's enough seasonal flooding to keep repair crews busy all year round on the 14,000 miles of road. That's critical, as the PDW keeps the all-important tourist traffic going on Char Dam—the all-important Hindu religious pilgrimage to Badrinath, Kedarnath, Gangotri, and Yamnotri.

There's an Indo-Tibetan Border Police station a stone's throw from the PWD rest house. It's down the trail—a prefab Quonset-shaped hut—linked to a communications dish nestled in a pile of boulders a hundred feet uphill. The guy in charge of the post is short and stocky with a stern scowl. He's wearing a tan paramilitary uniform sweater and gives me the stink-eye as he walks by not once, but twice. I either look too Chinese—something he should be concerned about—or just suspicious enough to be a Yar Tsa Gombu smuggler. He finally yells in my direction as I sit under the awning. It could be something in Hindi or the local hill dialect, a fast mash of syllables with plenty of rolling r's. It might as well be Swahili for all I know. I shrug my shoulders with an incomprehension that's a bit too careless as his words get even louder and slightly threatening. Just then, the cavalry arrives in the form of S. V. Looking more like a tourist than an officer in the Gurkhas, the colonel sports a bright red civilian windbreaker emblazoned with a swept-winged Honda logo. Topping off his very unmilitary ensemble is a mesh-sided Marmot baseball hat I've given him. From the hat juts a rakish raven feather. He's sees what's happening and pulls the ITBP guy aside to assure him that I'm not a security threat or some kind of spy. The ITBP guy at first doesn't like the look of S. V. any more than he likes the look of me. It's a while before he can be convinced of our authenticity.

It's all too commonplace a scenario for me. After three trips to India, I am used to being mistaken for Nepalese, a Sherpa, or Garhwali. Sometimes, it's nice, like when a village lady gives me a kind smile, a greeting of "Namaste!" and tries to engage me in conversation. This often happens after the expedition is over, and I am invariably tanned as dark as the locals by the high altitude sun. Sometimes it's not so nice, as right now, when I am mistaken as an insolent youngster trespassing those unseen, yet powerful boundaries of caste or social status. It's not just in the hills that it happens either. On my last climbing expedition to India, I was taken out of line in the airport, had my bags confiscated and put through an extra security screening. My teammates, all Caucasian, wearing identical clothes and carrying identical luggage, waltzed past security without so much as a second glance. Another time, during a post expedition debriefing with a former Director of the IMF, I was mistaken for the Indian Liaison Officer!

Gabe and Jonny arrive shortly after the run-in, followed by Chuck and Sarah. Everyone is wet and tired from the hike that netted 2,500 feet of elevation gain in less than six hours. We still suffer from a little jet lag and the original zest of being on the trail is dissipating. The good news is we made the right choice by taking the more dangerous low road, as four of our bags didn't make it over the higher and longer detour. They'll have to catch up with us tomorrow. After dinner, Gabe and S. V. head to chat with the ITBP officer. Any prior misunderstandings are forgotten, and the pair spend the night in a spare floor space of the Quonset hut. S. V. provides Gabe with a display of martial prowess field-stripping and reassembling the officer's service automatic in less than a minute.

I wake up feeling out of synch. The illness from yesterday has subsided, but there's still that uneasy feeling at breakfast. Both Chuck and Jonny can put food away like no one else on the trip, and they more than make up for my lack of appetite. Sarah is more deliberate, carefully layering butter and jam on her toast while the others slather with gusto, then gulp it down. I dutifully shovel down some toast and porridge and excuse myself from the table. The morning hike takes us over some rough bridges crossing the gurgling streams that bisect the Bodgwar meadow. We walk past a teahouse and on into a narrow gorge, blasted by the continual roar of the Gori Ganga as it rages down an endless series of cataracts and steep steps. The vistas are incredible—polished alabaster boulders the size of three-story houses are jumbled in the tight V-funneled river course. The tan waters hammer down with violence made even more frightening by its unrelenting, mesmerizing continuity. Above, the bright green walls stretch to a distant slot of sky—this morning blue and clear. The only traces of yesterday's rain are the pockets of mist that hug the ravines and upper walls, which in turn are traced occasionally by white foaming rivulets issuing from unseen hanging valleys. These give way to ramparts of bare rock, bare only because they are steeper than vertical and bereft of the ledges or fractures that will allow any vegetation to gain purchase.

Our trail follows the left margin of this ferocious spectacle. It zigzags up steep grades, a slender thread weaving through an erratic hillside of indifferently tossed boulders. Our feet still tread block after block of granite pavement. The amount of labor required to lay these stones is unimaginable. After a few miles, the valley widens slightly, and the river, rather than forcing its way through a narrow defile, meanders about over a broad expanse of cobbled riverbed. It's a nice break from the tight confines of the gorge. I pass a rusted diesel compressor the size of a bull-dozer engine. I don't know how anyone was able to get this piece of machinery all the way up the valley, but I am thankful for the path it helped blast out of the cliff side. We've got it easy. In the past, due to rockslides or a wandering river, the residents of this valley were forced to use ropes draped on wooden stakes pounded in the rocks to forge a passage along the very margin of the torrent.

It's not the safest trail. That alone adds a little spice to the walking—an activity I've always thought as slow and boring. To add some zest, I periodically mince over to the trail's edge and peer over into the abyss. It's more than just a virtual game as countless people must have died in this gorge. In fact, it was near here that Kohli, leading the CIA expedition to Nanda Kot, witnessed just how fragile the thread-like path, could be. *Spies in the Himalayas* describes the scene,

Plodding along a narrow trail dug into a steep slope, Kohli fell midway back along their column and, looking ahead, saw one of the Tibetans coaxing half a dozen ponies, Suddenly, a cloud of white powder shot up in front of the Tibetan.

Where six ponies had been there was suddenly a void. Part of the trail had given way, sending the animals tumbling down the slope. They peered over the edge and saw a heart-wrenching sight. The ponies were in a bloody heap, their spindly legs twisted at unnatural angles. Several were barely alive, emitting human cries.

I hate to think what would have happened if the SNAP and its plutonium ended up on a terminal pony ride, straight into the meat grinding rapids below. Would the expedition members been able to retrieve the plutonium? Would the storage casing split on impact with the rock below, spewing a toxic mess into this pristine river? I pull back from the edge, reminded that the CIA, in their wisdom flew the SNAP, via helicopter, to Base Camp, just to avoid such a possibility. That was good thinking. What wasn't, was that they did not anticipate that the high tech SNAP, with all its seductive atomic age technology, still required low-tech tent pegs, rope, carabiners, and safety lines, to hold the transceiver aligned and in place. These simple, commonplace items were on board one of the six ponies that took the ride into the drink, and no one on Kohli's expedition was aware of the loss. They were later to pay dearly for this oversight.

Jonny and I are forced to stop at the beginning of a quarter-mile stretch of trail that's been carved, tunnel-like in the vertical rock walls. The holdup is a herd of goats, driven by two shepherds accompanied by a couple of dogs. The dogs resemble Tibetan mastiffs, standing about two feet high and weighing more than a hundred pounds. They are black with rounded skulls and blunt noses. Tan points of fur lie on their eyebrows, and the dogs wear a peculiar harness that wraps around their chest and ribcage. Later we'll see some actually carrying bags, the contents of which we can only guess. Some have chain collars and for the most part seem docile and obedient, though later I learn that they are notoriously aggressive. As reported in the 1908 edition of *The Kennel Encyclopedia*, "[The mastiffs) are exceedingly fierce. . . . A very large number were shot during the Expedition [a 1904 British invasion of Tibet] by both officers and British or native soldiers purely in self-protection. As one Officer remarked, they were far more troublesome than the Tibetans."

The dogs present us with no problems, but the goats, about a hundred in all, block the narrow path. The right side of the trail is a fifty-foot drop to the riverbed, and the left wall is solid vertical rock. It's a tight squeeze, and the goats apparently do not like human contact as some leap over the edge to avoid Jonny, the three porters, and myself. The agility of the animals, some carrying saddlebags, is incredible as their leap takes them off the precipice onto the tip of a jutting boulder fifteen feet below, and back onto some small footholds leading once again onto the trail. The movement is one fluid display of power—and fearlessness, as a miscalculation would dash them on the rocks below. They all have midlength summer coats that hang in loose dreadlocks of stained yellow or dirty black. The beards, expressionless yellow eyes and horns convey a classic satanic appearance. After ten minutes, the last of the herd passes in a clatter of hooves and cacophony of bleats and jangling bells. The dust settles as the herd rounds the bend below. We continue onward, but not before I make a mental note to ask Khem Singh to buy a goat for Base Camp before we pass beyond range of the grazing meadows. Besides the novelty of slaughtering an animal as a traditional sacrifice to Nanda Devi, it will be nice to have fresh meat in camp.

Jonny and I walk, chat and shoot pictures as the gorge bends, turns, and snakes its way ever upward. Gabe is somewhere out ahead. Every so often, he appears as a small dot perched on the edge of trail as it curves and disappears. Chuck and Sarah are behind us somewhere.

As a couple, the two have the unheard of privilege of sharing a Himalayan expedition together. They might never be lucky enough to have such a unique experience ever again, I feel that this will be one they will never forget. For the most part, they seem happy, an attractive couple, very much in love, but without the sappy doting common to new relationships. It's not without its challenges, as even at the best of times, a true intimate relationship is difficult. Throw in the stress of Third World travel, the inherent dangers of mountain climbing, and the intimidation of immersion in a foreign culture, and you have a scenario that exploits any hidden shortcomings.

Their relationship in many ways is still in its infancy. Almost immediately before dating Sarah, Chuck was immerseded in a dysfunctional relationship that went on for years.

Both their intense emotional issues dovetailed nicely with their desire to please and appease, sacrifice and suffer. She also had accompanying chemical issues and drew Chuck into the morass of that messy victim, rescuer, persecutor syndrome, and all its accompanying abuse and manipulation. It's a choice to be complicit in such a relationship, and it took Chuck's own sense of self-preservation to eventually extricate himself. Very shortly after he ended the relationship, he left Sarah a cryptic message saying he'd "be at Burning Man for the next two weeks." Burning Man, the annual festival in the Nevada desert, is billed as, "an experiment in community, radical self-expression, and radical self-reliance." In Chuck's case, it was a chance to excise an old reality, clear the emotional decks—and party his brains out. Sarah took this oblique communiqué as the green light to begin dating, and so they did upon Chuck's return. Sarah had patiently waited in the wings for many months. In fact, on her very last visit, Sarah had made her mind up that if Chuck hadn't become available, she would no longer pursue him.

Having been up and down the road with various relationships, I could see what was happening. I almost myself pulled the plug on my living with Chuck after his months of vacillating about terminating the old relationship, thus treading the edge of disaster. Now, though fully supporting Chuck in his new relationship, my concern was that it came, fast on the heels of a very searing and significant relationship. Only months prior, his ex-girlfriend had been pregnant—Chuck was going to have a child, get married, and in the eyes of some his friends, throw his life away. So it was with some relief that he courageously broke things off, but it was with alarming rapidity that he jumped head first into the next relationship.

Longevity is not necessarily the yardstick to measure the importance of anything. What I do know is that Sarah was the right person at the right time, especially compared to his ex. But her life as an engineer straight out of college has left her a bit inexperienced in the practicalities of the world outside of academia or profession. I worry because she is invited in many ways as a favor to Chuck, an opportunity for them to share time, especially when the trip shifts focus to Jonny's and my goals. I never anticipated that Chuck might not want to share such a trip with her and that he might not have the ability to tell her no. Both Jonny and I made it clear to our girl-friends that we did not want them to be on this particular trip—it would be too stressful and distracting to have them along. Both Stacey and DeAnn concurred, DeAnn so much as saying, "I don't want to be on a trip, but maybe something in the future." I assumed that Chuck, if he had any reservations, would make it clear. As it is, I've already got some indications that there were some reservations —one that he wants a separate tent from Sarah in Base Camp. Another that he insists he and I climb on Nanda Kot as a team.

It's proof that I should not make assumptions before jumping into the mix. But right now, hiking through paradise, all this is fine by me. After a few hours, Jonny and I reach an area where the trail is lost in a sea of hard sun-cupped snow several hundred yards long. Sun cups are depressions that develop in snow during intense sunshine and the expanses ahead are pocked with dirty white peaked rimmed pockets about a foot wide. The sensation is akin to treading snot-slick oversized eggshell foam. Our path becomes a groove worn into the surface by the passage of trekking boots, chappals, and thousands of goat hooves. Jonny ranges ahead and sets up his tripod on the opposite side of a gully, washed out by a raging side stream that races down to the Gori Ganga. He yells at me over the roar of water to go back and retrace a particular section once again. I dutifully do so. It's part of our working arrange-ment that takes into account the fact that we have to eventually rebound from our growing mountain of debt generated by the expedition. Jonny's got to sell pictures, and I'll help him get the shots that will sell.

It's a job full of unseen hazards. As I near the edge of the gully, I can see that the edge is undercut. It's like walking an ever-thinning plank, and at the very edge, I can see the light shining from below, through the snow. I gingerly traverse the edge, eventually gaining Jonny's position. I look back with a mixture of elation and horror when I realize that the area I crossed is actually a thin snow arch, no thicker than eight feet at its maximum, bridging a void that's sixty feet deep. This area is victim to an annual avalanche that buries the river, only to be eroded from below by the gushing spring runoff. By this time of year the Gori has undercut and finally swept away the snow dam, leaving large unmelted chunks on either side of the river. The mass we just crossed is intact, save for the vaulted tunnels carved out by the feeder streams gurgling down those very slopes. The slopes extend up for thousands of feet, denuded of trees and shrubs by the avalanches that created the glacier-like snowfields in the first place.

Besides the treacherous snowfields, natural wonders abound with a regularity that dulls the senses. Besides garlands of wildflowers and hanging fern gardens, the folded terrain hides wildlife like bear, endangered musk deer, wild sheep, and mountain goats. Tremendous waterfalls cascade down the gorge's sides with mind-numbing regularity. In the course of an hour, we see several that must plummet for hundreds of feet without touching the walls. These would be major tourist attractions in the States—one of these alone would be noteworthy enough to claim a spot as a National Monument or State Park. As it is, these falls don't warrant enough attention here to earn place names on the map.

The valley widens as the trail makes a sharp climb up the ever-present granite stair-steps. Hints of the great range—towering summits of the greatest mountains in the world—appear on the horizon. It's hard to tell if we are seeing dense clouds or the snow-capped peaks, but the vague outlines coalesce with every step. I'm feeling feverish as our team unites at a convenient set of boulders nestled on the banks of a crystal-clear brook. We sit streamside, filtering water and eating our brown-bag lunches. My appetite is dulled by what now feels like a vague delirium.

The others depart as I spend an uncharacteristic five extra minutes packing my backpack. For some reason, I've dumped the contents of the pack on the ground, and it takes a while to police it all up and repack it. Besides lunch and a water bottle, I am carrying an umbrella, extra clothes including rainwear, a headlamp, hat, gloves, guidebook, journal, camera, and an assortment of odds and ends that include my fanny pack with cash, wallet, credit cards, and passport.

A short while up the trail I catch up with Jonny who has stopped and is talking with three men. One is Indian and two are western. I can tell the white guys are European by their trekking boots, collapsible trekking poles—like ski poles with no snow baskets at the end—and bright clothes. Their tights are also a dead giveaway. Within a few seconds I can tell the Indian guy speaks more English than the Euros. He greets me with a warm smile. "Hello sir, I believe we've met before." It turns out that here on this remote trail, halfway around the world, I've run into a guy who helped me out in New Delhi six years prior. He is Mr. Shashank Gupta. Mr. Gupta of Rucksack Tours helped out when I got mired in the visa office. Were it not for him, my climbing partner and I would have spent the better part of the day standing in a sweltering administrative office—a fate worse than death as it was the midst of a particularly stifling summer.

Mr. Gupta explains that the trekkers are part of the Italian Nanda Devi East expedition. The European pair, nonclimbers were up for the trek, look antsy like they are in a hurry. I ask Mr. Gupta the question that's been eating up Jonny and me. "Is the expedition doing the regular south ridge route, or are they trying something new?" Gupta answers with a grin, "They are already climbing on the east face." He adds, "It has never been climbed!" Jonny and I share a brief glance of dismay. It's yet another piece of crappy news. Who would have thought that almost sixty years after the peak had been climbed that two teams, the Italians' and ours, have come from half a world apart to gun for the same objective. It would be like stepping off a spaceship expecting to be the first man to walk on Mars only to stumble over a pile of beer cans. Before marching down the trail, Mr. Gupta, who has no idea of our intentions, offers us some hope, "They are having a tough time with the lack of snow on the face." He adds, "They only have a month to climb it."

Jonny's quiet as we continue down the trail. I can tell he is bumming and retreating into himself. It's just another blow in a series of bad news, and we can only hope for the best. Hoping for the best entails wishing the worst for the Italians—that they fail and we cruise up with our extra weeks and finish what they've already started. Neither of us wants to generate any ill will for a bunch of people we've never even met. For one thing it's not cool, especially as climbers. For another thing, bad vibes tend to come full circle sooner or later. Our challenge is to let events unfold as they will, without bringing out the worst in us.

An hour later Jonny and I catch up to Gabe. At a bridge crossing of yet another crystal clear stream, he's engaged in a conversation with two women. They have broad cheekbones, full noses, and ruddy cheeks. The discussion consists of gestures and simultaneous monologues that neither nationality comprehends. They don't speak English, and he doesn't understand a lick of their tongue as they are Bhotia women—or people of Tibetan extraction who live in the mountainous crossroads of culture, neither natives of the sub-continent nor mainland Asian. The term "Bhotia" comes from "Bo" which is native Tibetan for "Tibet." These women are part of the old culture that spent summers tilling, grazing herds, and trading with the Tibetan Plateau. This seasonal migration ended following the war with China and it is only in recent years that limited trade encourages the ancient migrational patterns.

Gabe is sampling some sort of spicy chutney that the Bhotia women have mysteriously produced from their dusty robes. Their long black dresses are paired with similarly black vestments adorned with silver brooches and necklaces of rough polished stones. The stones are of all colors—some look like turquoise. The women are all smiles with cheery sun browned faces that crinkle with mirth. Their teeth flash with gold fillings as they give the traditional greeting of "Namaste!" as I walk past.

Namaste or Namaskar, as it is sometimes said, is a universal salutation used as both "hello" and "good-bye" would be used in English. The meaning is less off-the-cuff than our English equivalents, being the combination of two Sanskrit words: *nama*, and *te*. Simply, *nama* means "to bow" and *te* means "you." Pronounced "Nam-a-stay," the word is a reverential salute, emphasized by the accompanying gesture of bringing one's hands together near the heart—not unlike the posture of Christian prayer.

I'd love to stop and chat, if anything, to try the chutney, a yellow paste that soon leaves Gabe, sensitive to hot spice, red-faced with tears streaking his dusty cheeks. But I've got that ill feeling and am eager to get to our next camp. Khem earlier described the today's trek as "only ten kilometers," but it feels as though we've already gone that distance and more. Khem's a wily one and pulled this same sand-bagging on prior trips. Every time we round a bend in a hill, I eagerly look for our destination, the settlement of Railkot. But to my dismay, I am repeatedly greeted by nothing but the continuing trail as it traces a line contouring endless slopes of pale green knee high grass.

Finally at a quarter after one, we reach Railkot. The area is a plateau spread below a steep hillside that overlooking the river, several hundred feet below. To the south, in a downstream direction, there is a rough stone teahouse and a few other building in which the porters will stay. Thanks to S. V., who is pulling up the rear of our caravan with Khem Singh, we have permission to stay in the two ITBP huts that mark the northern boundary of Railkot's plateau. The huts are the same Quonset shape and were probably helicoptered in, as the sections, though lightweight, are half the size of a trailer home.

I lie down on a flat piece of bare concrete with my head on my backpack. Gabe is already there, and soon Jonny, Chuck, and Sarah straggle in, a trio of chatty happy hikers marveling at the sur-rounding splendor and crisp dry afternoon. Though the sun beats down through the ever-thinning alpine air—we are now above tree line at 10,000 feet—I lie shivering until I pull on my down parka and huddle in the fetal position. Even wrapped in goose down, I have a hard time fading off to sleep as my senses take on the distortion of a growing fever. I'm achy and voices seem to move in and out sometimes distant and sometime unbearably loud. I can hear the four others chatting and eating chocolate, but the words seem garbled and nonsensical.

Even under the hood of my parka, I'm starting to shiver. I've got my hat and gloves on now, though it must be above 70 in the bright sun. I hear the porters beginning to arrive, followed by Khem Singh and S. V.

S. V. commands me to lie down in the hut. I do so willingly as an afternoon breeze heralds the shift from sun to shade as the shadows creep from the base of the high hills to the west.

I try dozing off on a stack of foam pads. The floor of the hut is yellow prefab plastic, textured with the type of raised, no-slip bumps you see on industrial flooring. There are chalk arrows drawn on the walls where the joints meet. I look at the arrows with my head laid sideways, cradled in my arms, trying to decipher what the numbers next to the arrows mean. Suddenly, one of the porters lurches through the door. He barely notices me as he weaves an arcing path across the empty floor, as if avoiding unseen objects. He's obviously drunk—maybe on the local beer or rice wine. S. V. barrels in and steers the porter out later telling Khem Singh with the deliberation of a man who is accustomed to enforcing discipline, "I will beat that man if he tries to enter the hut again."

Our baggage finally arrives from yesterday's high detour. Not surprisingly, the luggage is wet from the continual rain. Khem Singh retrieves one of our tents from the duffels and sets it up while the others take stock of their gear. We'd neglected to pack everything in garbage bags before zipping them up. Some of our baggage was fairly watertight, other pieces—the ones with convenient twin zipper entries—leaked like sieves. Jonny and Gabe with their photographer's experience have packed well and suffer little.

But a wet shirt or two is the last of my worries as I crawl into my expedition weight down sleeping bag, so seized by fever chills, that I have all my clothes on. I close my eyes and start to drift off when it suddenly dawns on me that something terrible has happened. My fanny pack is missing. My "life," was in the bag. That means passport, all my money, credit cards, and visa. My first reaction is shock. My second is anger. After a few minutes I just want to lie there and forget about the whole thing. It would be so easy to fall asleep and pretend it never happened.

No amount of denial can keep me from crawling out of the tent and telling everyone what happened. Soon we are all searching the area, through the weeds, backpacks, and the huts. We find nothing, and I can feel the panic rise. In all my overseas travel including six trips to Asia, I have never misplaced or lost something this important.

S. V. pulls me aside and asks, "Where did you see it last?"

I answer, "I don't know," adding, "I think back where we stopped for lunch." S. V. shoots me a concerned look. He's noticing that my locution is garbled and semi-delirious. He asks, where did you stop?

It's at that point that the enormity of my mistake becomes apparent. As I later wrote in my journal,

> I realized to my horror that I'd left my fanny pack on the trail above a place called Mapang (the location of the snow bridge) at a nondescript turn in the trail as we were pumping

water. I'd been attempting to dry the wallet, money, documents, etc., out and in the emerging delirium of oncoming fever, left it sitting on the trail.

S. V. consults with Khem Singh who consults with Dipender. There's a universal shaking of heads. Khem Singh rounds up a couple guys to backtrack and search. It's a nice gesture. The men who are to search for my missing stuff have already carried a backbreaking load all the way from Bodgwar. To this day I am grateful to them, but from the outset, I don't have much hope. It is over four miles back to Mapang, and I can't give an accurate description of our stopping point as it is one out of dozens of such streamside curves. Even if someone were to have found it, the 16,000 rupees would be enough to tempt the saintliest of men and on the trail behind me there were scores of porters and a number of shepherds going up and down the trail.

Khem Sing asks a final time if we are sure that the fanny pack is nowhere to be found because as he puts it, "I am sending these men back and it is a far journey," hinting at what a bummer it would be if they left on the trek, only to have the missing pack turn up. I assure him that we've scoured everywhere. To underline his point, he asks to borrow a couple headlamps—a good idea since dusk will be on us in an hour.

The men depart. I sit in the tent absolutely disconsolate. This is just the latest in a series of hurdles that have plagued me for the last two years. Being denied the permit for Nanda Devi, losing permission to film, having the Nanda Kot permit revoked, then approved, finding out the Italians are trying the new line on Nanda Devi East, and the list goes on. Jonny, shares some words in this bleak moment. He walks up and squats next to the tent.

"Hey, Pete," he says.

"Yeah, Jonny?" I mumble.

He says, "Not to sound like it's not a big deal, but all that shit, it's all stuff that can be replaced," There's not a hint of New Age sentimentality in his words, and I remember that this statement comes from someone who has had to deal with the same dashed hopes and rollercoaster I've had to. Add to that, the fact that the 16,000 rupees coming from the expedition account is half his, gives the words some real weight. Before he stands up to leave, Jonny adds, "You should let go of it. It ultimately doesn't matter. It's just another thing to let go of."

Letting go is a great sentiment. Like many, I'm prone to give the notion lip service, but I am finding that when there's a lot at stake, it's a hard thing to do. In a way, the path into the mountains is always about letting go. One deliberately disengages with the familiar world, and with each step a small piece drops away, whether it's S. V.'s cell phone signal or a fistful of rupees. I've always felt that by the time you've said good-bye to friends and family, traveled to the mountains, and gotten four days into a dangerous climb, you've pretty much let go of everything. It's a progression—first the daily routine, then creature comforts, then basics like food and sleep, until by the end you've let go of the notion of physical safety. But none of that is of comfort to me right now. There have been only a few times in life I've wanted to give up and acquiesce to a situation that is unacceptable. This is one of those times, and the best I can do is say, "Fuck it." I curl up and pull the sleeping bag around my head.

Sarah Thompson on way to Camp 1 on Nanda Kot with the sun rising on Nanda
Devi East (24,389 feet), September 22, 2005. *Photo: Jonathan Copp.*

Religious pilgrim at the holy town of
Haridwar—the place where the Ganges
River emerges from the foothills below
the Himalayan mountain range. *Photo:
Jonathan Copp.*

Here I am digging a bivouac ledge at 23,200 feet on Nanda Devi East. Nanda Kot (22,510 feet) is the summit above my head. Below and left of the summit is the Dome, where the CIA climbers successfully placed the SNAP-19C and its transceiver. *Photo: Jonathan Copp.*

Me on Nanda Devi East in the early morning of October 7, 2005. *Photo: Jonathan Copp.*

Jonny Copp leads Chuck Bird and Sarah Thompson during Day 2 on Nanda Kot, September 23, 2005. *Photo: Pete Takeda.*

Religious pilgrims at the town of Rishikesh. Rishikesh is the gateway to the holy shrines at the tributary sources of the Ganges. Millions of people, including the Beatles in the 1960s, have spent time in this town. *Photo: Jonathan Copp.*

Porters from the Kumaon town of Lata. *Photo: Jonathan Copp.*

Kumaon man making gravel for road repairs. *Photo: Jonathan Copp.*

Himalayan peaks emerge from storm clouds. *Photo: Jonathan Copp.*

Climbing to Longstaff's Col on Nanda Devi East. *Photo: Jonathan Copp.*

Sunrise on Nanda Devi East (24,389 feet). The 1939 Polish route attempted by Copp and myself follows the left skyline, which also composes the western wall of the Sanctuary. *Photo: Jonathan Copp.*

I ponder the construction of the newly rebuilt trail on the trek out of Base Camp.
Photo: Jonathan Copp.

Me at second bivoac site (around
21,000 feet) on Nanda Devi East.
Photo: Jonathan Copp.

Jonny Copp in time lapse at night in Nanda Kot Base Camp. *Photo: Jonathan Copp.*

Takeda tranversing ridge on Nanda Devi East. Nanda Kot is visible in the left hand margin of the photo. *Photo: Jonathan Copp.*

Sarah Thompson straining hard on a beautiful boulder at Nanda Kot Base Camp.
Photo: Jonathan Copp.

Sarah Thompson bouldering in Base Camp, beneath a stunning mountain landscape. *Photo: Jonathan Copp.*

Looking across the moraine at sunset on Kuchela (20649 feet) with Nanda Kot (22,510 feet) in the background. Our Base Camp lies directly below Kuchela's summit, hidden from view by the moraine. *Photo: Jonathan Copp.*

The mythic Rishi Ganga Gorge, gateway to the Sanctuary, with Nanda Devi (25,643 feet) rising in the distance. The hike through the Rishi Ganga involves 30 miles of treacherous and sometimes deadly terrain. *Photo: Pete Takeda.*

Me descending ridge on Nanda Devi East. *Photo: Jonathan Copp.*

I try to invoke the power of Nanda Devi (25,643 feet) on the distant horizon.
Photo: Jonathan Copp.

Chuck Bird crossing washed-out trail on the second day of the trek to Base Camp.
Monsoon flooding swept away the granite staircase that usually crosses this section.
Photo: Jonathan Copp.

Nanda Devi East (24,389 feet). *Photo: Jonathan Copp.*

A member of the Indo-Tibetan Border Police stands watch on trail between Munsyari and Martoli. The ITBP presence is a constant reminder of the expedition's proximity to the border with Chinese-occupied Tibet. *Photo: Jonathan Copp.*

Takeda soloing on Nanda Kot. *Photo: Jonathan Copp.*

The team—Pete Takeda, Sarah Thompson, Chuck Bird, and Johnny Copp. *Photo: Jonathan Copp.*

Takeda climbs to Longstaff's Col on Nanda Devi East with Nanda Kot (22,510 feet) in the background. *Photo: Jonathan Copp.*

The Abode of the Bliss-Giving Goddess. Nanda Devi (25,643 feet) viewed from Lata Karak. The groove with shaded right margin dropping from gentle notch on the mountain's right skyline is where the SNAP-19C is believed to have fallen. Most of the mountain is not visible in this photo, as it is hidden from view. *Photo: Jonathan Copp.*

Storm clouds brew in the Lwanl Valley as Chuck Bird, followed by Sarah Thompson climbing steep snow and ice on Nanda Kot. *Photo: Jonathan Copp.*

I cross a snow arch formed by winter avalanche snow pack. A stream has undercut the snow mass creating the spectacular, and fragile, arch. *Photo: Jonathan Copp.*

Atmospheric moisture collects on the Sanctuary rim as Pete Takeda gazes out into Tibet from Nanda Devi East. *Photo: Jonathan Copp.*

Nanda Kot (22,510 feet). *Photo Jonathan Copp.*

Sarah Thompson buried in the avalanche. *Photo Jonathan Copp.*

Nanda Devi (25,643 feet) viewed from rim of the Sanctuary. The 1936 route (and CIA espionage route) follows the snow gully, right of left skyline to smooth-looking icefield directly above mid-height. The gentle notch above icefield is the last confirmed location of the SNAP-19C. The climbing route follows the skyline to the summit. *Photo: Jonathan Copp.*

Jonny Copp in a storm on Nanda Devi East. *Photo: Pete Takeda.*

Me digging out after the avalanche on Nanda Kot. *Photo by Chuck Bird from Pete Takeda Collection.*

Nanda Devi (25,643 feet) *Photo: Pete Takeda.*

Another view of Nanda Devi (25,643 feet, on left) and Nanda Devi East (24,389 feet, on right). *Photo: Pete Takeda.*

Jonny Copp stands before Nanda Devi East (24,389 feet). *Photo: Pete Takeda.*

Lt. Col. S.V. Singh rolls a cigarette while our Nepalese cook Dipender reads a two-month-old newspaper. *Photo: Jonathan Copp.*

The ice screw that saved Chuck Bird's and my life. *Photo: Jonathan Copp.*

Calm before the storm. The team on Nanda Kot peacefully cooking, hours before getting buried in the avalanche. *Photo: Jonathan Copp*.

"The power of such a mountain is so great and yet so subtle that, without compulsion, people are drawn to it from near and far, as if by the force of some invisible magnet; and they will undergo untold hardships and privations in their inexplicable urge to approach and to worship the center of this sacred power. Nobody has conferred the title of sacredness on such a mountain, and yet everybody recognizes it; nobody has to defend its claim, because nobody doubts it; nobody has to organize its worship, because people are overwhelmed by the mere presence of such a mountain and cannot express their feelings other than by worship."

—Lama Anagarika Govinda, a Western practitioner of Tibetan Buddhism

CHAPTER 8
MYTH BECOMES REALITY

I've hardly closed my eyes when there's a commotion down by the buildings where the porters stay. It's annoying because I'd just gotten to the point where I'd convinced myself that things did not matter—or at least enough to start to nod off anyway. It's obviously something important because there's about four of five different voices in the mix, all of them trying to get in edgewise. Pretty soon I hear Khem Singh, "Sir, please come." He's talking to me, so with a sigh I rouse myself from a cocoon of thermal underwear, nylon and down. The layers are already soaked in fever sweat.

About twenty feet from the tent are three porters. They are standing there with the two guys sent to search, plus Khem Singh and

S. V. One of the porters, a short guy with curly hair and broadnos-triled, almost African features, holds my fanny pack.

I have to do a double take to make sure that this isn't a hallucination. The curly-haired guy hands it over to me. As he does so, Khem Singh explains, "He found it on the trail." Curly, still smiling, makes the curiously Indian nodding gesture, tipping his head and rotating it in a figure eight pattern like a metronome. Like Stevie Wonder at the piano, his head sways in what, to our Western eyes looks vaguely like our head shake, as in "no." Over my last three trips, I've gathered that the head bob's many meanings usually have an affirming connotation like our own "Uh huh."

Curly looks to me, then looks to Khem Singh who says, "He didn't show it right away because he thought it belonged to the Italian team." The pack is dark nylon, supple and faded after years of use. It's been on several long trips, and as it's passed to me I can feel the weight of its contents. It would be rude to dive into the wallet to see if anything is missing. Instead I smile and thank the man. I turn to the would-be searchers who now hold out the unneeded headlamps. With great deliberation I unzip the pack, pull out my wallet and unfold the worn leather. There are threads poking out of the edges where the seams are because it's been years since I bought it in India. The leather is slightly slimy with wetness. At that moment, it strikes me as ironic that here, in a country that venerates the cow, one can get high-quality leather goods for a fraction of the price in the West.

The money is all there, crisp banknotes with the edges slightly tinged with damp. The circumstances of its return are a bit suspicious, as the pack wasn't offered up immediately. Maybe the guy was trying to make off with it and was held accountable by the two others.

But that doesn't make sense, since they could have just split the money and tossed the remainder in the river. As far as I can tell, it wasn't even opened. I peel off four 500-rupee notes and hand them over. I motion that it is to be split between the men. Curly raises the money to his forehead in what looks like half-Buddhist obeisance and half the sign of the cross. The head bobble speeds up, and the beaming Curly celebrates with a little dance step. I turn to Khem Singh and S. V., thanking them before stumbling back to my tent. S. V. comments laconically, "Well, Mister Pete, you got lucky today." Lucky indeed. Before collapsing in bed I zip the fanny pack securely into the top lid of my backpack. It's nothing short of a miracle.

I skip dinner. It's a real bummer because Dipender's made egg curry, boiled eggs swimming in a sauce of onions, garlic, tomatoes, spiced with a seasoning called garam masala. Garam masala's literal translation is "hot spices," and the blend includes cinnamon, cloves, nutmeg, pepper, cardamom, and so on. On past trips, the dish has been my favorite, but I'm far too sick to eat, much less sit up straight. Sarah is nice enough to come out with a bowl of soup. I can barely raise my head, and the bowl sits in the awning of the tent as I fade away into a soaking sweat. Every ten minutes or so I am paralyzed by uncontrollable shakes—like being possessed by a demonic paint mixer.

The next morning is September 4th. I feel like hell, but make my best stab at being civil at breakfast. Even then, I get up without a word after a few bites of toast and stalk off to pack. The others are still on their second round of chai. I can't tell, but as Sarah's journal notes, "Jonny getting really sick as well, rest of us trying to stay healthy." I have a really bad habit of withdrawing from the world when under duress—whether it is stress or illness or just a bad mood. That works to some degree as an individual, but as the expedition leader, it's not fair on everyone else. Part of it must be from being Japanese. My mom never complained, even when she was dying of cancer. My father always stressed being tough, tough meaning stoic, uncomplaining, never a burden on those to whom you are responsible. That all works great when the surrounding culture supports and understands the behavior, but here, it must be baffling and annoying.

Sometimes, I really sense some of what must be the immigrant dilemma, even though I am a generation separated from all that. Nevertheless, it's a worthwhile task to separate one's cultural circumstances from base-line human angst. Regardless of where the behavior originates—the effects are clear. Chuck later tells me, "You really tend to shut down to others when you are under stress. You really need to learn to reach out for help."

From 7:30 AM on, I stumble through one of the most picturesque regions of a land Peter O'Toole says is "where the extraordinary seems commonplace." It's a feverish limp through ravines and across steep hillsides that stretch down to the milky gray river. Sometimes, the vast scenery feels like a trek through Montana. The wind-stroked grass and craggy ridges set against intense skies of a blue that's unfiltered by the color-sapping dust and pollution so commonplace, as to lower our expectations of what a blue sky really looks like.

Above Railkot we pause at some ruined houses on a plateau with a view that extends several miles downriver. The vista gives us a perspective on the mighty Gori Ganga as it flows down the massive drainage. We can look back and see the broad valley we hiked up yesterday, gently snaking in wide curves before necking down into the deep, precipitous chasm of the Gori gorge. That's not all there is either. For the first time the snow-capped peaks of the Himalayas shine from both the east and north. I am reminded of Hotta's (the 1936 Japanese expedition leader) poetic understatement as they hiked this very path, "The grandeur of the Himalaya, the magnificent scenery of the great gorges, and the lovely snow-covered mountains . . . made a deep impression on us."

Hotta might as well have been standing right here, for indeed to the north appear some 20,000-foot peaks. They are majestic buttresses of dark gray rock, capped with diagonal sheets of white, rising to sharp curvy ridges terminating in points of snow. They are the guardians of the Tibetan plateau and mainland Asia. Impressive as they are, these mountains, higher than the mightiest ranges in North America, pale in comparison to what is about to come.

We straggle into Martoli village around midmorning. It's the Indo-Tibetan equivalent of an Old Western ghost town, with overgrown stone fences and dozens of houses in various states of disrepair. The walls of the abandoned homes are constructed layer by layer of dark gray rock. The stonework—unfinished rectangular and square blocks—range from fist to shoebox sized. There's an odd off-center vertical slit marking the rare side window. The front windows, larger and more profuse, sit adjacent to double-door entrances shuttered with weathered boards and framed with carved wooden coping. The walls rise to the height of two stories and are caked with yellow, red, and green lichen. The lichen and the unkempt thatches of wild grass soften the contrast of the man-made structures against the greenish backdrop of the rolling plateau. Upon this flat expanse that encompasses maybe several square miles, dozens of houses sprawl in an irregular and organic layout. The eerie spectacle gives the impression of man's labor being slowly swallowed by the earth itself. Indeed, from a distance the village, dwarfed by the massive mountainous landscape, appears to be melting into the ground, an effect enhanced by rooftops that sag, some to the point of complete collapse.

Prayer flags of pink, blue and yellow fly on wooden poles, marking two inhabited buildings. They are several hundred feet apart from each other, one near the southern outskirts of town, the other toward the center. I suppose if one had their choice of digs, they'd want to be close to their neighbor—but not too close. I follow a knot of porters, one carrying the skibag, towards the center set of prayer flags. He's easy to track as the long gray duffel bobs along like the conning tower of a submarine. I can't tell if it's the fever or the setting, but as I stroll through the surreal remains, I can almost hear the echoes of the life that once filled these ruined streets. The phantom cries of children, the clamor of cowbells, mingle with memory of wood smoke, incense, and dung.

Between May and October every year, Martoli boasted a seasonal population of several hundred people. It had its own stores and a school for the children. As a hub in the trade between India and Tibet, this village, 32 miles from the Tibetan border, was the biggest and most vibrant of all the settlements in the Upper Johar Valley. This was all to end after the 1962 border war. The abrupt closure of the border broke the rhythm of life, and Martoli was abandoned. The ruins I pick through today are only a few more visible bones of an age-old geopolitical conflict. The Bhotias, who lived as nomads traveled with pack goats and sheep, trading and grazing across the spine of the world from the lower foothills of India into Tibet. Mukti Datta wrote of the 1962 conflict in *The Mountain Forum* as a "great upheaval in the lives of the Bhotias. [For] Nomadic trade was in their blood." It was, so much so that they frequently risked life and limb, praying to Nanda Devi for safe passage over the hundreds of treacherous miles linking far-flung destinations like the Tibetan trade center of Gartok, to Varanasi, well to the southeast of Delhi on the plains of India. Homage to Nanda Devi for protection was understandable, since "bad weather on the frozen heights of the windswept passes caused many men and animals to perish."

Though some like the Bhotias paid tribute to Nanda Devi for protection of their lives, others ironically lost their lives attempting to pay tribute *to* her. In 1905, Dr. Tom Longstaff, on yet another groundbreaking exploration, happened upon an astounding, and gruesome sight. On an attempt to penetrate the Sanctuary from the south (he was eventually turned back), the red-bearded Longstaff crested a ridge about 15,000 feet above sea level, only to discover a small oval lake filled of hundreds of human corpses. The lake, more like a melt water pool the size of a football field, is called Rup Kund. Some corpses were mummified, others skeletal and later carbon dating showed the grisly find to be more than six hundred years old. Though speculation abounds, the most popular theory claims that the remains are what's left of a pilgrim party who were caught in an avalanche while off making a sacrifice to none other than Nanda Devi. That's a reasonable theory. To this day, a ceremony held once every twelve years, sees worshippers undertake a strenuous three-week pilgrimage called a Raj Jat in the same area, culminating in the release of a rare four-horned ram to the Goddess. What's more speculative is the notion that the corpses comprised a party of worshippers attempting to placate the angry Goddess after the prince of a local province had unsanctioned sexual relations with a neighboring princess. As *that* story goes, in her wrath, Devi swept them into the pit, with torrents of snow. It would all be so easy to disregard, were it not for the hundreds of corpses. They remain in the lake to this day, a mute testimony to whatever powers rule these mountains.

I want to stop in Martoli as I am fatigued by altitude (we've just climbed to 11,200 feet) and beset now by diarrhea that, as my journal notes, "is now the color and texture of wheat grass juice floating in a pod of gelatin." All this hiking is not making my health improve. I seem to have a combination of a cold and perhaps some food or water-borne illness. Getting sick on a mountaineering expedition is usually the kiss of death to any climbing ambitions. I have never gotten this sick on any previous expedition, and it's another crushing worry, since this might be the most important trip of my life. Of course, we say that about every expedition, but I also feel the burden of responsibility to my teammates.

Back in 1959, another young man, M. S. Kohli was in charge of another expedition to the very same mountain we are after. His burdens were arguably greater, because besides being the expedition leader he represented the Indian Navy. By implication Kohli also carried the dreams of his entire nation in an effort symbolic of India's emergence, not only as an independent entity, but also as a player on the world stage. At the time, mountaineering was a big deal, not just to its tiny eccentric clique of practitioners, but also to greater political prestige. The year 1959 followed a period of global decolonialization when Britain and other European powers dismantled their network of far-flung outposts, granting independence to the nations they once ruled. India, having gained self-government in 1947, sought to express her new identity. Climbing mountains that lay within her borders was in no small way a demonstration of her sovereignty and newfound pride. The Old World too, was looking for prestige and focus in a postwar identity crisis. The great evils of Nazi Germany and Imperial Japan had been vanquished, and countries like England looked for new struggles to define themselves in a new and uncertain world. Indeed, Edmund Hillary, who first climbed Everest with Indian Sherpa Tenzing Norgay in 1953, was hailed as a hero in Britain (this despite the fact that Hillary was a New Zealander rather than an Englishman) in the press—and in person. Besides being knighted by the Queen, Hillary recalled a particularly personal encounter that illustrated how something as absurd as mountaineering could capture imaginations and inspire the populace. He said, "The media created a Hillary and Tenzing that really didn't exist. They made us into heroic figures, and it didn't really matter what we thought or said or did. . . . The public really like heroic figures that they can look on with great admiration, and whether it's true or not doesn't seem terribly important. . . . We all went to Britain and there was a tremendous reaction. I can remember walking across the street and a London taxi stopped and the taxi driver—he was a tough looking cookie—came out and said, 'You're Hillary, aren't you?' And I said, 'Yeah.' And he said, 'Congratulations. You know, you've done a great job for us!' He got in his cab and drove off."

It's safe to assume that India was ripe to discover its own Hillary, and though nobody knew it yet, Kohli—the man of fate—was just the ticket. Though unaware, he knew on some level that he was indeed carrying the weight of the subcontinent's pride and aspirations.

One climbing friend compared expeditions to "a ship, whose inevitable leaks must be plugged with dollar bills." Despite all that responsibility, Kohli wasn't handed a corresponding wad of cash. For the entire Himalayan trip, he was on an allowance of 5,000 rupees, maybe 100 dollars in today's currency! That's not much, considering I'd lost more than three times that amount out of carelessness just yesterday. Back then, things were cheaper and Kohli, being in service of the government was spared the peak fees and other expenses that make Himalayan climbing such a financial burden today. Still, the team was so strapped for cash that they subsisted on "a few items of tinned foods and potatoes." The potatoes were a major windfall as Kohli remembers,

> I met a man in Martoli who learned we had so little. "How do you manage?" he asked, adding, "Do you want some potatoes?" He pointed to a field and said, "they are growing in the ground you can dig them out—take them free." We only had that few thousand rupees for forty-five days. So we agreed and we took I think two hundred pounds of potatoes out of the ground. We ate potatoes every dinner—potatoes this week, potatoes next week, potatoes in Base Camp, potatoes every day.

The fields where Kohli and company must have dug their 200

pounds of spuds are neatly fenced. Some are cultivated. The plots of land lie interspersed with the wrecked houses, and with the lack of people, there must be little competition over the land. The stone fences vary from three to five feet high and are made of what looks like rough slate slab of varying thickness. They too are covered with lichen, which indicates that this must be how things looked and how the land was divided for hundreds of years—certainly at least when Kohli passed through. If one were to mist things up a bit and throw in some guys with kilts, it would take on a Scottish Highland air.

Unlike Kohli, I'm under no dire threat of penury-induced hunger, and when I am offered food at "The Martoli Hotel," I'm not interested. The hotel is designated as such, not by a sign, but by the four-foot high letters hand painted on the front of the building. The letters, faded so that they are barely visible, sprout little tails where carelessly slopped paint must have run down the wall. The sloppy, unbalanced calligraphy is strangely fitting to the old building with its ornate yet crudely hewn woodwork and chock-a-block masonry. The wood framing the windows and doors is so old that the colors are long since blanched out by the high-altitude sun. The wood has been carved in decorative geometric and floral patterns. Occasionally the monkey god Hanuman cavorts, gesturing from atop the doorframe whose hinges and clasps are hand-wrought iron. Drying goat meat and bundles of medicinal plants dangle from ancient nails imbedded in the wood. I sit in the sun while Khem Singh explains that though we expected to stay here tonight, we will instead be moving up the valley that runs due west. "It's only several kilometers." He sits on the stone fence sipping a stainless-steel cup of chai, eyes hidden behind oblong wire-framed sunglasses. Khem Singh wears a waterproof safari hat that's a shiny burgundy color with a broad brim and shapeless crown. I gave it to him as a gift at the start of the trek, and he wears it with authority and that, combined with his bamboo swagger stick, lends a vaguely military air. There is a sense of forward momentum in the air—from Khem, Gabe, and S. V.

I'm bumming, but I have no choice but to continue. The others are keen and have that energetic spring in their steps, except Sarah, who suffers from oncoming aches and lethargy. Jonny, though getting a bug himself, outwardly betrays no symptoms. Another concern lurks in the back of my mind—the weather. Though we had some rain down low in the trek, the higher we get, the more stable the weather seems. The mountains hold little snow—compared at least to the shots I've seen of this area that were taken in years past. The brief trailside report from Mr. Gupta also confirms that there have been very few recent storms. What all that means is we are missing out on a big window of good weather—the one thing you can't have enough of. I've sat out more than one expedition to this region, with little more than brief spells of the mind-numbing clear weather we now enjoy. So, like a donkey chasing the carrot on a stick, I doggedly trudge onward.

The last leg of the day takes us uphill at a right angle to the generally northward travel of the last three days. Our new trail follows a gushing stream called the Lwanl Gad. "Gad" is to be the term for river in these parts, and it's Lwanl, a small settlement a couple miles distant, for which we are aiming. In about a half an hour, the trail narrows. It's now a foot-wide dirt single-track, sometimes vanishing beneath bower-like clumps of grass. The very tip of Nanda Devi and

Nanda Devi East should be poking out to the west, directly before me. But there's a layer of clouds up high, blocking the momentary line-of-sight afforded by the gap between the V-shaped rise of the walls of the Lwanl Valley. The trail curves through the regular folds in the hillside, and before the rearward view is obscured, I pause to look back. The town looks almost exactly as a thirty-three-year-old Robert Schaller saw it in 1967—a scattering of buildings on the raised plain, grasses yellowed in the late summer sun. Schaller's slideshow included a shot of Martoli, taken no doubt, when he trekked down from Base Camp—nearly ten miles up the trail— during his previous Nanda Kot trip. As he was helicoptered directly to Base Camp, I'm assuming that Schaller took this image when, as he later recalled, "I was excited and didn't want to miss a thing. If I wasn't at work on the mountain, I'd be climbing something else or hiking around. I remember sneaking out and went on numerous day trips in the area."

I remember from his slideshow, that Schaller's recollection was fuzzy from the forty ensuing years. Still though, if the details are lost, recorded accurately only in his journal, what remains is a blissful memory of a time when he could wander amidst the place he loved most—the mountains. Standing here, I can feel why, for him, it's not the journal and photos he really wants back. He wants back that part of his life, his identity, his memories.

There's a light breeze blowing, but other than that the panorama is crystal clear. Before me lies the same scene depicted in Schaller's faded Kodachrome image. It is virtually unchanged, perhaps more noticeably dilapidated. Martoli sits like a phantom town, laid out on a plateau carved from the earth by the Gori Ganga on the east and the Lwanl on the north. Were we to have continued up the Johar Valley instead of turning west towards Nanda Devi East and Nanda Kot, we would have crossed to the east side of the Gori Ganga and in seven miles reached the town of Milam. From what I've read, Milam is one of the most active villages in the Johar Valley, but like Martoli, it sports a mere handful of occupied houses plus the inevitable ITBP border post. Milam's etymological components, "Mi Lam" means "man road" in the local tongue—appropriate considering that the ancient superhighway we've just parted ways with, marches ever onward to the Tibetan frontier.

The most celebrated citizen of Milam was launched from obscurity as a schoolteacher on a transcultural mule path—to acquiring international acclaim as one of the world's great explorers. Nain Singh was awarded a gold Patron's Medal from the prestigious Royal Geographic Society "for his great journeys and surveys in Tibet and along the Upper Brahmaputra, during which he determined the position of Lhasa and added largely to our knowledge of the map of Asia." To give you an idea of what an honor this was, consider that such medals are awarded only to folks like Henry Morton Stanley (who found Dr. Livingston—who was in turn given a similar award by the Society), Dr. Louis Leakey, Richard Peary, and Jacques-Yves Cousteau. Singh was granted the award in 1877 after a series of clandestine exploration/mapping journeys across Tibet on behalf of the British Empire. These ran from 1865 to 1874. It seems that spying was as big back then as it was in the 1960s, only then it was Great Britain versus Imperial Russia—the superpowers of the era—with Tibet (in part ruled by China) stuck in the middle. Sound vaguely familiar?

The roots of Nain Singh's exploits began with the launch of The Great Trigonometrical Survey of India by British Colonel William Lambton. Though the survey traces part of its origins to 1767, it wasn't until the clearly articulated goal—map the subcontinent—became a reality in 1802 that the project was truly underway. This survey, born of scientific passion, political expediency, and military necessity, would employ ultimately thousands and demand a lifetime of dedication from some. It was fed with an almost missionary zeal and would lead to many things, not the least of which included the discovery of Mount Everest and the technical foundation of all subsequent topographical surveys.

By the 1860s, the British were urgently trying to develop a map of Tibet. But just as in the 1960s, the border was closed. Because Caucasians would draw unwanted attention in Tibet, Captain Thomas Montgomerie developed a plan to train indigenous hill people—in this case the Bhotias of the Johar Valley—to survey the forbidden kingdom. Nain Singh, his cousin Mani Singh, and other pundits, as they became to be known ("pandjit" is teacher or learned man in Hindi and "Pundit" was the codename used by the British when referring to Nain Singh), were taught to use the sextant and compass, and to determine altitude by observing the temperature at which water boiled. They learned to measure distance by using regular paces—33 inches in Nain Singh's case. To keep track of all those paces, the pundit modified a Buddhist rosary. Instead of the traditional 108 beads, his rosary had 100. Each bead counted for 100 steps and every tenth bead—larger than the others—marked 1,000 paces, about a half-mile. From the outside, his other recording device, a Buddhist prayer wheel, resembled the regular wooden-handled, copper-sheathed cylinder, spun by the devotee to release an inscribed blessing. Nain Singh's prayer wheel was the nineteenth-century version of Cold War microfilm—or plutonium tranciever—only this was a low-tech device fitted with strips of paper on which to record and conceal survey notes. The disguise was effective since the Tibetan-looking Nain Singh blended with the local culture. Thus he safely completed a total of three major penetrations of Tibet. His final espionage expedition took him 1,405 miles across the middle of Tibet, passing through Lhasa and ending in Northeastern India near Burma. Twelve hundred miles of his journey were a literal blank on the map averaging a bone-chilling 14,000 feet in elevation. Prior to his exploration, the areas of his survey had been completely uncharted, and Singh's travels were beset by the threat of starvation, the danger of being discovered, and spectre of death at the hands of the Tibetan authorities. It was no joke, as one fellow pundit was even sold into slavery before escaping and returning home.

India honored Nain Singh on June 27, 2004, with his own com-memorative stamp. His visage, with furrowed brow and focused measured, gaze stares out across the gulf of over 130 years.

Though our exploration won't take us over the once-again forbid-den border with Tibet, we still tread an area seldom visited. It's a per-sonal twenty-first-century exploration of an area that was virtually untapped by Westerners until 100 years ago. Though various parties in the mid-nineteenth century and a later group in the early 1900s explored this corner of the Kumaon, the accounts and maps left behind leave much to be desired. Even as late as 1936, Tilman and company got lost after their success on Nanda Devi, when they con-cluded their explorations by exiting the Sanctuary through this valley.

By early afternoon, I'm at the tail end of my energy. Even the wimpy pack I carry feels like a burden. Rounding a broad curve in the grassy hill, the area beyond hints at some sort of flat table of land, indeed I can see a few rough stone buildings in the distance. It must be Lwanl. In my feverish state, it looks like heaven. A hundred yards farther and I realize to my dismay that there's a deep valley to negotiate before reaching the settlement. Tilman wrote of this very stretch of trail,

"While yet some three miles from Martoli . . . I came suddenly upon a tributary river, and was dismayed to find the path turning off at right angles to follow this side valley for one and a half miles, where it crossed the river by a bridge and then came back down the other side for a like distance, before once more following the main valley back down to Martoli. This extra three miles was an unexpected blow. . . ."

It's an unexpected blow to me also. It seems that maps haven't improved all that much in the ensuing seventy years as my now well-thumbed *Lonely Planet* guide to trekking in the Indian Himalayas fails to note this pain-in-the-ass divergence from the straight and narrow. I'd foolishly convinced myself I'd be deposited in Lwanl without too much more effort. A teenager from Munsyari, acting as a porter for our expedition, has fallen in with me as I lag behind Gabe, Chuck, Sarah, and Jonny. With gestures and a few words of English, the kid, maybe eighteen years old, takes my pack, lashing it to the outside of his load, one that already tips the sixty-pound mark. At first I resist, but pride yields to physical reality, and as we make the steep descent to the bottom of the river valley, I hand it over.

We cross a stream called the Shalang Gad before a final steep climb up to the flat haven of Lwanl. The Shalang originates up a side valley hooking south then west to the southern ridges of Nanda Kot. That's not where we are heading, but I cast a wistful glance up the seldom-visited valley—another corner of the Himalayas that I don't have time to explore. For all I know, around the corner lurks a world-class alpine face. No doubt, there's a glacier that dwarfs anything in the Lower 48. It's the magnitude of terrain like this that puts perspective on things back home. It's easy to become parochial and possessive when we keep to the security of the local and familiar. There's nothing like these mountains to set that straight, inspire and broaden one's perspective.

Lwanl is a haven of a few stone huts—replicas of those in Martoli —along with some neatly tilled fields. To top off the pastoral feel, there are a few horses or wild asses, I can't tell which, grazing in an adjacent meadow. I lay out on a sleeping pad in the bright sun, tipping the boy—his named is Uttam—50 rupees, for his help. In doing so, I reinforce the notion that we from the West are made of money, but under the circumstances I have few regrets.

The diarrhea is coming on thick and fast, and for the second night in a row, I skip dinner while passing a clockwork-timed stream of hot mucous-laden fluid. The night closes in bringing a thick mist both outside the tents and inside my mind. The damp chills me to the bone, and a few times I nearly collapse in my own filth as ague-like chills render me weak and bereft of muscle control. I balance in a squatting posture as I gingerly wipe my inflamed butt, poised on a hillside dropping from a 60-degree slope of unconsolidated dirt and rocks. Pebbles tinkle and fall beyond the range of my headlamp into a black void for hundreds of feet before plunging to the Lwanl Gad. My sphincter feels as though it's extruding due to the violence and frequency of the diarrhea. It's not even a week into the expedition, and I'd give all my rupees for a Western-style, porcelain sit-down toilet.

September 5th dawns, and Gyan, Dipender's assistant comes around bearing a pot of chai for the morning bed-tea. It's about 7:00 AM, and I dismiss him with a grunt and fade back into a half sleep. Camp rustles with the sounds of a new day when Sarah arrives. "We've decided," she says matter-of-factly, "that we are going to take a rest day." I'm about to object, when she adds, "We know you won't make that decision for yourself, so we are doing it for you." Though outwardly I protest, I am relieved to be given some rest and also touched by the gesture. It's a good call, because I don't want to keep pushing and dig myself a physical hole I can't crawl out of. Besides giving me a chance to recover, it will help us all adjust to the altitude, now approaching 11,500 feet.

I am into my second day of taking Azythromicin, a broad-spectrum antibiotic that is the atomic bomb of expedition medication, treating everything from respiratory illness to gut ailments. I try to steer clear of such powerful antibiotics because the treatment kills the good microorganisms as well as the bad, sometimes causing stomach upset, and also leaving one sensitive to sunlight.

But the cure is not as bad as the disease, and though I still feel like shit, the drugs—and rest—are doing me good. The morning is clear as Gabe heads up with the porters to establish Base Camp. The rest of us stay in Lwanl, since we all are feeling the creeping crud to one degree or another. Jonny's cold has matured into a lovely respiratory bug, complete with high fever. Chuck claims to feel some possible funk, and Sarah still harbors the ill feeling she first felt the day before.

The sun shines as the team takes some time to leisurely reorganize and dry things out. Everyone seems to be getting along with each other. We are a varied group, "the most odd mix of people I've ever gone to the mountains with," Jonny notes. I can already see that there's good and bad to it. On one hand, Jonny and I are driven, passionate about the mountains, and know what we want. Between us, we have almost forty years of climbing experience, and countless trips spanning the globe. As far as climbing is concerned, Sarah is strictly recreational, and to a lesser degree, is Chuck, whose passion lies in ski mountaineering. Their experience is limited, and they prefer the higher recreational yield of skiing to the masochistic flogging of ice and alpine climbing. Neither burn for ascent and chances are, they would never have visited the Himalayas otherwise. On the other hand, the happy couple does not have the myopic megalomania that so rules the lives of many of us to whom climbing is a lifestyle rather than a hobby. Chuck has seen friendships, relationships, and jobs fall by the wayside because of his passion for skiing. And Jonny and I know what it is like to tread the fine edge of obsession that causes frustration and sometimes grief to so many, while affording a rare, though incalculably precious reward. For better or for worse, we are both committed—lifers. As Jon Krakauer wrote in his acclaimed expose of the 1996 Everest disaster, *Into Thin Air*,

> [climbers are] largely unnoticed and surprisingly uncorrupted by the world at large. The culture of ascent was

characterized by intense competition and undiluted machismo, but for the most part, its constituents were concerned with impressing only one another. Getting to the top of any given mountain was considered much less important than *how* one got there; prestige was earned by tackling the most unforgiving routes with minimal equipment, in the boldest style imaginable.

It's charming to note that climbers generally do not climb for the same type of rewards granted by traditional paths like a career or shopping for a soul mate. And as an athletic pursuit, the reward is the activity itself. Unlike football or basketball players, or even fringe practitioners of pseudosports like skateboarding or surfing, virtually no one—even the best of climbers—finds himself financially secure from climbing itself. Even I can lay claim to the title "sponsored climber," but even when supplemented by writing, I've always hovered at the poverty line. It sounds marvelously idealistic to the outsider, but at some point there comes the realization that the god to whom you've sacrificed everything, is neither commercially potent nor particularly benevolent.

Therefore, it's nice to have people along who don't have the heavily weighted intensity or accompanying neurosis of hardcore climbers. As I remarked to a friend after he returned in fall of 2004 from the Karakorum Himalayas of Pakistan, "A little levity on an expedition is a good thing." The remark came as my friend, part of a team of some of the world's best alpinists, returned a bit disappointed and disillusioned. It wasn't his performance in the mountains, but by the personal fallout with one equally intense teammate that left a sour taste in his mouth. Their trip, like ours, had multiple goals, culminating in two ascents of some remarkable rock fangs nearly 23,000 feet high; and two very daring attempts on an awe-inspiring 8,000 meter peak (8,000 meters is the gold standard of extreme altitude. There are fourteen in the world, all exceeding 26,300 feet in elevation). The six climbers all shared the similar vision of fast lightweight climbing, which, when it comes to the general public's perspective on mountain climbing, gets swept under the rug of Everest headlines and climbing challenges considerd dubious by the hardcore, like The Seven Summits phenomenon (in which climbers ascend the highest points of each continent, a feat first completed by the energetic and gregarious owner of the renowned Snowbird ski resort, Dick Bass at the remarkable age of fifty-five). I sense some hard feelings came out of that trip, some springing from partner jockeying and politics, as various members eyed the prize objective while seeking the most likely to succeed partner. It's a fine balance. The intensity needed to climb and enter the world of risk and chance is a necessary component to every expedition. As I sit in my tent, too sick to wander about, I hope that the balance between the remarkable individuals on our team can see us up Nanda Kot and fulfill the second objective of exploring the rim of the Sanctuary and perhaps climbing something like Nanda Devi East.

On September 6, after our day of rest, the crew breakfasts at 7 AM and hits the trail a half an hour later. Jonny conducts an interview of a man named Natu Singh. Singh, who must be in his sixties, is the oldest inhabitant of the area. Retired as a corporal from an Indian Army parachute regiment, Singh grows mustard, parsley, and other herbs, trading them in town when he, like all the other scattered high country inhabitants, winter in the lower elevations. It's a vestige of the old days of seasonal migration. Nain Singh who remembers the halcyon days of Indo-Tibetan trade, spends most of the translated interview requesting more government assisted infrastructure to support tourism. He vaguely remembers when, "In 1965 the U.S. men came to attempt Nanda Devi," as he lived alone, plowing the abandoned fields. But his recollections wander and keep returning to the need for more tourism and it's resultant income. He ends the dialogue with, "This is the land of the Gods. I pray to Nanda Devi for all the inhabitants of this place."

A short way up the trail, we catch our first glimpse of the Goddess to whom Nain Singh prays. Nanda Devi East rises before us, a gorgeous pyramid of rock and ice building from a broad base to a point, tapering like an inverted ice cream cone. The summit, standing over 10,000 feet above the valley floor, is capped with a jaunty beret of snow. From behind, the main summit of Nanda Devi pokes her head from just beyond and to the right. The effect is breathtaking, awe-inspiring and terribly frightening.

Not so awe inspiring is the goat wrestling taking place on the trail. I'd asked Khem Singh at the trailhead if he could score us a goat on the way in. As we pass a shepherd's camp, two miles or so above Lwanl, Khem Singh buys a goat for about sixty dollars. It seems like a good deal, as the animal must weigh as much as a very large dog. The goat was one of the very first animals to be tamed and bred by man over 10,000 years ago. It seems that despite the millennia of domestic pedigree, ours is completely uncooperative. Even the perpetually happy Dipender now frowns as he literally drags the stubborn animal through brush, over hills, and up sections of trail that teeter at the edge of big drop offs. The goat must weigh as much or more than Dipender, who stands barely five feet tall and probably tips the scales at a hundred pounds. He's got straight black hair cut in bangs and the classic Nepali features—high cheekbones, wide flared nostrils and shallow nose bridge.

Dipender is tough in that sinewy way you can only get by living in the hills all your life. Still, when at the base of a particularly nasty incline of mud and slick tree roots, Dipender, after a failed tug-of-war, is forced to pick the stubborn animal up and carry it bodily up the slope. Jonny strolls up. I think he's unaware that the goat was just purchased because he says, "He should just let it go because it looks like a pain in the ass to get that thing to Base Camp." I sympathize, but the novelty of slaughtering our own meat has too much appeal. We could slaughter it on the spot, but there might be some ceremony that needs to take place on the upcoming meadow of Naspanpatti, at the feet of the Goddess. Of course, I'm not the one doing the work, and Dipender, dirty and now covered with bits of wool and grease from the goat's shaggy coat, looks at us with a crestfallen expression. He understands more English than he lets on. He knows too, that, if at all cooperative, meat on the hoof is best moved under its own power. He tries a different strategy. Breaking off a tree branch, Dipender holds the green leaves in front of the goat's nose to coax it along. Having seen enough, Jonny and I take off up the trail, leaving man and goat locked in a battle of wills.

Chuck and Sarah wear tuxedo shirts. From a fashion standpoint it's a disaster, but under the blazing sun at 12,900 feet it's better than any sunblock on the market. Chuck picked up the shirts at Saver's, the Boulder equivalent of Goodwill. At a dollar apiece it's money well spent. The material breathes well, transmits perspiration, and the long sleeves protect the arms from the sunburn that bakes the short-sleeve crowd. Whether the mountains, work, or a night out, Chuck dresses in a bizarre hodge-podge of mismatched clothing that lean towards value, comfort, and longevity. Today, as we approach what should be Base Camp, his ensemble resembles something thrown together by a colorblind hiker. His baseball cap is lime green, the bandana, worn Lawrence of Arabia-style is an orange Denver Broncos commemorative logo hanky, his T-shirt is navy blue, and his shorts are tan. At least his socks match—a rarity from what I've seen, but as a pedorthist, Chuck usually pays close attention to everything from the ankles down.

The pair stride ahead about a hundred feet, white shirts billowing in the noticeably thinning alpine air. In twos and threes, the porters pass in the opposite direction. Having dropped their loads off, they race unburdened to the fleshpots of Martoli, no doubt eager to spending their hard-earned rupees on bidis and rakshi—the potent local rice wine. The valley, now a broad open expanse maybe a mile wide, is bare of the rhododendron and spindly Himalayan birch stands that stubbornly clung to the gullies and steep slopes of the lower Lwanl Valley. Instead, the surrounding hills have grown to rocky inclines extending to glaciated peaks rising in unbroken sweeps to summits exceeding 20,000 feet. Due west, the walls of the Sanctuary culminate in a toothed ridge anchored by the towering mass of Nanda Devi East on its northern extreme and linked with the imposing summits of Nanda Khat and Changuch, 21,653 and 20,741 feet respectively.

Nanda Kot, not to be mistaken with Nanda Khat (a peak we were almost erroneously assigned by the IMF), is set back to the south in its own glacial valley. The valley or cirque, in mountain parlance, is still hidden by its look-a-like neighbor called Kuchela. The two are so similar, that for a few minutes I am convinced that Kuchela, with a similar table-top summit plateau, is indeed Nanda Kot. Shortly thereafter, I realize my mistake, but not before losing a bet with Chuck, costing me a chocolate bar. At 20,649 feet in elevation, Kuchela is 2,000 feet shorter than Nanda Kot, but given the massive scale of our surroundings, it's easy to lose a few thousand feet in perspective.

We crest a low ridge composed of rocks and boulders heaped in a low longitudinal berm. In climber and geologist speak, these long heaps, deposited bulldozer-style by the toe of a glacier, are called moraines. The mother of all moraines lies about a half mile distant and is several hundred feet high. From that elongated salient of rubble, garnished with giant boulders the size of condos, issue forth several streams.

Splayed out before us is Base Camp, an angled strip of grass. Above are the lower stubbled slopes of what we've identified from the topo map as Kuchela. There are a few tent rings and fire pits indicating past human habitation. The trouble is, Nanda Kot is nowhere in sight, and from the looks of it this site would fast become a burial ground in a major storm due to the inevitable avalanche. This place could be a summer shepherd's camp, as it abuts the best-looking meadows. But the descriptions from other expeditions don't match. It's supposed to be, "at the foot of Nanda Kot," according to Kohli and in a, "valley . . . filled with huge stones fallen from the mountainsides . . . pitched in a hollow," according to Hotta. This place fits none of the descriptions, and worse yet doesn't provide adequate tent space for all of us to sleep on level ground. It looks nothing like the single photograph we have depicting Base Camp. Our photo, a black and white shot of the CIA field agent Sam Currie reclining on a flat rock in front of a makeshift kitchen tent composed of a tarp and aluminum poles. A goat lies in the background, and Currie grins behind a pair of wire-framed aviator glasses. What's telling is the presence of a huge boulder behind him. The rock is so big—maybe twenty feet high or more, it fills the entire frame and forms the wall of what looks like the kitchen tent—itself is over seven feet high. In the foreground stands the edge of another tent that indicates a large flat space. The biggest rock in our supposed Base Camp—now dubbed "Gabe-Camp" by Chuck, a name instantly adopted by everyone, much to Gabe's sheepish dismay—is chest high, nowhere near the size of the rock in the photo. The nearest rocks that size are about a mile distant, little mirages shimmering in the hot thin air.

It's soon decided to scout out the distant rocks, namely where they lie, a narrow valley bordered by the big moraine on one side and the toe of the hills on the other. I limp along, still feeling weak from the last few days, Finally, Nanda Kot comes into view, a spectacular, table-topped summit squatting atop a landscape of snow flutings and shingled ice cliffs.

I can see what's called the Dome, an obvious ice lump on the left-hand ridge below the summit. Little more the a thousand feet below the top, the rounded blob of ice, a few hundred feet in diameter, rises like a big white boil on the skyline, marking the spot where the CIA planted the second SNAP in 1967. The line of ascent, which traverses the Dome in the final stage of climbing, weaves up a faint ridge that drops thousands of feet from a saddle-like notch in the skyline below and left of the summit. That's the easiest-looking way to get up the mountain. It's the route taken by Hotta and later by Kohli, when CIA-sponsored Sherpas packed the few hundred pounds of spy gadgetry.

There is virtually no exposed rock on the entire route, and from that we can safely gauge that the actual climbing is technically moderate by modern standards. Snow won't stick readily to steep terrain and even in the old days, the dictum of our mountain climbing forebears was "where there is snow, there one can go." These days, climbers can go pretty much anywhere, given enough time and a sufficient buildup of equipment and supplies. In our smug modernity, it's also easy for the contemporary climber to forget that the tools and techniques we take for granted were not available to our predecessors. Things like nylon ropes, space-age clothing, and high tech climbing gear have changed what's possible. And, moderate or not, it is absolutely amazing that Kohli led four major expeditions to this one peak—climbing it in 1959 to start his climbing career, installing the SNAP in 1967, and returning twice in 1968 to unbury, and then finally retrieve the device.

We end up scouting the narrow valley. It is about fifty to one hundred yards wide and littered with boulders from the size of bowling balls to the mass of town-homes, carelessly strewn about like titanic dice. At one point, with the afternoon chill blowing in up the valley, I sit and wait for Khem Singh and Jonny to scout out a promising-looking spot. It's a no go, and finally we select a place nestled amidst a boulder field in the shadow of a 250-foot-high buttress of black, yellow, and gray rock topped with a standing cairn, or manmade stone marker. It has all the Base Camp amenities—protected from avalanche, flat, with direct access to the line of ascent. It also has great bouldering, a huge plus. As I've mentioned, bouldering is a subsport of climbing in which the climber pits him or herself against rocks that are small enough to negate a harmful fall. What it lacks in risk, bouldering makes up for in sheer difficulty and represents the highest level of technical difficulty in climbing. It's also fun. It has it's own place in expedition climbing—and while bouldering in Base Camp is kind of like going to a world class ski resort with plentiful off-piste terrain and spending all day in the terrain park, such fun is what we will need in the mandatory downtime over the next five weeks.

Upon return to "Gabe-Camp," we find that two porters have slaughtered the goat. I'm a bit miffed because it's something I'd like to have seen. It's not to get my morbid jollies, but to observe something we are insulated from in the West. How many of us have eaten a hamburger? And how many of us have seen the cow slaughtered?

Despite the fact that the goat's dead, there's plenty of carcass laid out and enough butchering going on to keep us thrilled. Sarah who witnessed the slaughter is visibly grossed out. Gabe keeps saying, "Wow, that was something else!" He looks a little shaken by the event, but that doesn't keep him from snapping pictures as one of the porters chops the ribs and haunches. The guy has captured the blood in a dirty tub and moves from chopping pieces to winding the intestines around his hand. The pieces of goat flesh are bright red with layers of white fat and fascia. They are laid out along with the head and a jiggling distended gut the size of the porter's torso, on a blue tarp. The acrid smell of burnt hair permeates the scene, as the hide was singed, post slaughter, to ease in the butchering.

The age-old drama is replayed for us, thanks to the miracle of digital technology. Gabe gives us the instant replay—shots of the ritual washing, what look like prayers of sacrifice, the shaving of the goat's neck and the blow of death done with a mean-looking three-foot-long knife. It's actually two blows of death. In the viewfinder, I can see the next shot of S. V. grabbing the tail and a porter the head, stretching the animal out as a third brings the heavy reverse-curved blade down on the back of its neck. The following pictures show gouts of blood as the animal pitches over—instantly dead.

We dine an hour later—alfresco—on whatever choice bits Dipender has picked out for us. It could be that I've only regained my appetite, but what appear to be kidneys, liver and pieces of flesh with charred hide still attached, seem marvelous. It's all swimming in a light-colored sauce with onions and garlic ladled over rice. There is a taint of burnt hair to the whole dish, but it doesn't stop me from enjoying more than my share. The others are not overjoyed with the meal and carefully push little bits to the edge of their plates in tiny piles of organ meat. S. V. passes on eating any flesh. Later, after the trip he reveals that he eschewed both meat and alcohol in the mountains. For S. V., man of the world though he is, the Himalayas is truly the abode of the gods.

> *"Security is mostly a superstition. It does not exist in nature, nor do the children of man as a whole experience it. Avoiding danger is no safer in the long run than outright exposure. Life is a daring adventure or nothing."*
>
> —Helen Keller

CHAPTER 9

NANDA KOT

The top is a body length away. The rock is crystalline, a flat pane of silver stone with little swirls covering the vertical surface—a veneer of tiny quartz flecks that sparkle in the bright sun. My feet are pasted on dime-sized edges, and the fingers of both hands bite into tiny door-jamb-sized indentations in the rock. The indents are at shoulder level. I bring my right foot up, apply pressure, and slowly stand with my left foot trailing behind, as I release my left hand and extend it to a dark blemish in the rock—what I hope is a big hold. My finger tips brush the blemish as my body comes out of balance. My fingers grasp the blemish—not even a hold really, just a sloping spot of texture. For a second they hold, as my ass starts slumping away. There's a moment of almost perfect weightlessness that seems to defy the laws of physics, then acceleration takes me, and I fall to earth.

I crash to the ground, nothing bruised except my ego. We are bouldering, clad not in bulky clothes or high altitude mountaineering boots, but skin-tight rock shoes and T-shirts.

I like bouldering. It's ironic that, having started out climbing as a boulderer over twenty-five years ago, I can fly to Asia on an expedition and come full circle. Back when I started climbing on those humble sandstone lumps in a quarry behind my family's house in Idaho, it was considered, at best—training for the "real thing," at worst a ridiculous aberration, pursued by those who wished to avoid the risk of true climbing. Years later, the activity is recognized and practiced as one climbing core disciplines, and one that is responsible for the acceleration of the sport's development. Still, the old attitudes remain. A few years ago, I interviewed Yvon Chouinard of Patagonia fame, asking about the impact of bouldering on our sport. He flat out stated, "Bouldering and sport climbing are not legitimate forms of climbing. Without risk—things like that are not really climbing." I then asked if he was climbing still (he's nearly seventy) and he replied, "I'm still climbing, but I had a big setback several years ago—I broke my elbow in three places." When I asked how it had happened he replied, "Hmmm, when I was bouldering . . . Ha, ha, I guess bouldering is dangerous."

The weather is bright and clear at 13,800 feet. This is Base Camp, and today, before bouldering, we shuttled loads from Gabe Camp to what is to be our home for the next five weeks. It's an idyllic location. Our narrow valley is covered with short grass sprouting the remnants of summer wildflowers—some small and purple—iris-like only tiny, others are yellow with a vague dandelion look, and others still, with pointed edelweiss-looking petals radiating from a core of florets, the width of a pencil. Bumblebees seem to run a regular circuit through the blooms often stopping on a colorful piece of clothing, as if mistaking the man-made objects for alluring blossoms.

A dry streambed runs the length of the valley, and it's by this foot-deep gully that I pitch my tent. Everyone spreads out, pitching tents at whatever choice location that they find. There's plenty of room. The centerpiece of camp is a giant rectangular boulder. The rock, maybe 20 feet tall has a shallow, fire-streaked cave on the south side. Ringed with a chest-high wall of rocks enclosing a rough courtyard of packed dirt, it is solid evidence of human habitation, at least for the summer months. The big boulder also looks suspiciously like the rock in the Sam Currie shot of the 1967 CIA Base Camp. On closer examination, we can't quite match up the subtle features in the picture to the rock, but one thing tells us for sure that it was used in the past. There's an inscription on the rock. "Indian Nanda Kot Expedition 1953." The shallow carving sports an inscribed trident above the chiseled lettering. There's a fleck of yellow lichen growing in one of the letters that authenticates the inscription's age.

Conboy's account comments that the CIA team "searched the nearby fields for a suitable landing zone and ultimately settled on a slightly elevated shelf that allowed for drainage off the edges." According to the field booklet S. V. draws from his pack, the minimum dimensions of a pad is several hundred square feet. The area was "cluttered with granite rocks and boulders that needed to be cleared," and for "four days, they lifted away all but the heaviest boulders." The ground surrounding our Base Camp is seldom flat. Neither on the hike in, nor during the explorations of the camp's immediate environs, is it apparent where they might have placed a pad. We also find no geometric-looking areas or telltale outlines of rocks that might have marked the spot. Due west, up the streambed the area is flat enough to accommodate a helipad. If that were the case, the boulders strewn along the flat plain could merely mark forty years of accumulation from rockfall, avalanche, and erosion.

On the evening of September 8, Gabe announces that he's leaving. He had scheduled a week in Base Camp to attempt Nanda Kot with us, but with everyone in various stages of illness, the chances of getting up the mountain in that time frame are dubious. Gabe himself has caught a cold. And his deadline comes from the fact that he has scheduled another expedition that is due to arrive in Lhasa in ten days. It seems patently absurd to all of us that he would schedule two major trips in a single season, but as it's his money and time, it's his choice. The other expedition—to a massive 8,000-meter peak called Shishipangma—sounds like a great opportunity. We are all bummed out that he's leaving. Gabe has that rare, hard to find, quality— happy, upbeat, and energetic in all situations. Even after such a short time together, he will be sorely missed.

Gabe made a timely choice. A few days after he hikes out of camp with Khem Singh and two porters, the weather changes from crystal clear to intermittent rain. Chuck and S. V. are sick, so on September 8th, Jonny, Sarah, and I climb to nearly 15,900 feet and located an old camp used by prior expeditions. Jonny came across the place. It's tucked away in a small hanging valley with a line of sight view of Nanda Kot's summit.

This spot was probably used as the Advanced Base Camp by most expeditions on Nanda Kot. Though accounts vary as to the altitude of past ABCs, ours might be the most accurate reading, as I get my measurements off an illegal GPS. Nowhere below is there a spot suitable to pitch multiple tents. With the snow long melted by the summer heat, we gleefully scour the barren turf and rocks for any tangible evidence of the CIA expedition. Like amateur archaeologists, our suspicions are confirmed when we unearth all manner of expedition detritus—old bottles, primus stove parts, tent stakes, ancient wooden box boards, and tin cans. We find bits of paper, one with an encouraging "1951" printed on the yellowed crackly parchment. The newspaper is brittle and fragile. Stuffed into a crack in a rock outcrop, it's been protected from the decades of harsh high altitude ultraviolet light. Another wadded fragment reveals a less exciting. I later write in my journal, "Aug. 27, 1997." "Every step of the journey holds its own barriers and own delights." We are on the right track as I match the old camp with a black and white image of the Japanese trip of 1936. It's strange to look back in time and to actually stand in such an obscure, yet historically important place.

Above there's more. In 1968, in the last chapter of the CIA espionage saga, the final Indian team climbed to the Dome to retrieve the second SNAP. The conditions encountered by the recovery team were taxing and fickle. They succeeding in retrieving the SNAP, the antennae, and one of the transceivers—they got lucky, crisscrossing hundreds of feet with probe-poles and shovels before finally happening on the device. But the climbers failed to locate one of the transceiver units. That unit, shaped like a microwave oven on stilts, is somewhere above us, still buried in the ice. Though we don't have much hope in succeeding where the Indian team failed, it's a mysterious prize worth searching for when we get up to those distant heights.

Before heading down, we stash a load of gear—a rope, cooking gear, fuel, three tents, and assorted food. We wrap everything in plastic trash compressor bags, shoving them into a niche in the rock outcrop. We also leave some climbing hardware, like ice screws—threaded steel tubes, twisted into solid ice as climbing anchors, and crampons—the toothy steel frameworks we'll lash onto our boots for purchase, when we assault the snow and ice that lies a thousand feet higher.

At some point on their way up Nanda Kot, Kohli's espionage expedition must have stashed the SNAP-19 at this very point. The "combined 125 pounds of sensor gear would require at least four climbers to haul at high altitude," according to Kohli. The human packhorse shuttle would no doubt have stopped here on the way up through the progression of four total camps that were established to climb to the Dome. Indeed, after the helicopter arrived, bearing the sensor, Conboy writes, "Kohli suited up and joined half a dozen Sherpas and the six Tibetans in making the supply shuttle up to Advance Base Camp." Before I leave, I picture this spot in mid-May 1967. There would have been six burly Tibetans of the Special Frontier Force, lounging around, plus over a half dozen Sherpas and climbers. There would have been backpacks strewn about, tents, and a telephone wire, laid by the expedition for radio contact to Base Camp. And there also would have been the packs carrying sensor loads. These packs were "reinforced cardboard boxes that fit on jerry-rigged backpacks." Long poles for mounting the apparatus would be poking out of duffels or luggage. There would be the box-like transceiver units named a tersely labeled B-1 and B-2. They'd be packed into bags carried by the Sherpas. And there would have been the SNAP itself, probably melting a hole in the snow, maybe surrounded by the Sherpas bickering—hands chopping the air, fingers waving, with verbal punches perhaps slightly deflated by the altitude. They would be arguing over the privilege of carrying the device they dubbed "Guru Rinpoche." Apparently, the Sherpas saw the SNAP with its unearthly heat, as something to be venerated, for Guru Rinpoche was, in Tibetan Buddhism, the second incarnation of the Buddha himself, who spread the religion across the Himalayas in the eighth century. Rather than venerating it, the Sherpas should have feared the nuclear heat. McCarthy's words echo in my head, "I guarantee you, none of them survived more than a few years."

Jim McCarthy feels that he came close to suffering the same fate—claiming he developed testicular cancer following his exposure to the SNAP's radiation.

McCarthy, selected for his climbing skill, had been instructed, as were the other Americans, in the use of explosives like C4 to excavate the set-up site. He'd also been trained by the Atomic Energy Commission to handle the plutonium. According to him, it was "Martin Marietta who trained me to place certain things in certain orifices." Connotations aside, McCarthy's reference is to his job of loading the SNAP generator with its deadly fuel rods. And it was he who ultimately loaded the glass-encased plutonium capsules into the battery pack. "In the Sanctuary, I was the only guy who handled the actual plutonium and I'm the one who loaded the device. I had to straddle the fucking thing. Let me tell you, the fuel rods were nice and wildly warm." McCarthy further says, "No question, there was no shielding at all and I got a large dose of radiation."

In 1971, while on a rock climbing trip to the Wyoming monument of Devil's Tower, McCarthy had finished climbing a route with his new wife, when he first discovered his condition. "I was in these painters pants and was changing them when I noticed that one of my testicles is greatly engorged. We drove straight back to New York, found the very best doctor in the Metro area. He says, 'This is not good.' Two minutes later, I'm in the OR."

McCarthy recovered, as his was the one type of testicular cancer treatable at the time. Kohli, as expedition leader says that there were safety precautions, including limiting the carrying time for the Sherpas to four hours, and pinning radiation badges to detect leaks. McCarthy has no recollection of exposure limits for Sherpas. "I never saw the Sherpas carrying it on the mountain. I did see them fighting over *who* got to carry it." He adds, "They had no idea of what it was. After it was loaded, they'd put the thing in the middle of their tent and huddle around it."

"There was absolutely no shielding," says McCarthy. "It was a field operation and when I look back on it, I can't believe I had no smarts enough to believe these shitheads." He adds, "If you challenge the Indians to prove any of those Sherpas are alive today, it can't be done. They are all dead. They were sleeping with the fucking thing."

To Kohli's assertion that there were radiation badges, McCarthy says, "There were absolutely no radiation tags—none whatsoever."

Schaller concurs, "I don't recall any radiation tags. There was some talk about them, but I don't remember ever seeing one." He definitively adds, "I know that I never had one."

As far as official oversight goes, Conboy's book states, and we can assume that these words are based on Kohli's recollections, "One additional American arrived with the rest [in the Sanctuary in early September 1965]. Introduced only as 'Jim,' he was from the U.S. Atomic Energy Commission. Soft spoken and polite, Jim would oversee the fueling of the generator. . . ." Regarding the presence of an official government technician to oversee the RTG, McCarthy scoffs. He states, "I was 'Jim.' I was the guy trained to load the device."

What is disturbing is that if his words are true, McCarthy, the trial lawyer and rock climber, is the guy tagged by Kohli as the man in charge of safe handling of the device in the field.

This means that when, "oblivious to any danger, the Sherpas snuggled up to the device, warming their hands and patting their face," it was a climber, not a qualified safety technician, who was claimed by Kohli, to have given assurances of the device's safety. Indeed, *Spies in the Himalayas* further states, "Despite Jim's assurances that the chance of dangerous radiation exposure was minimal, the friends and members were not inclined to join the Sherpas."

On the 9th, Chuck and Sarah hike to ABC—in part, to acclimatize and hike some food and fuel to stash. The afternoon alone also gives them a chance to be alone with each other, as it is their one-year anniversary. Sarah is hard to read. She says little of personal matters and whatever stress she might feel, is subdued by an impenetrable and rational, exterior. Later, she'll confide about having recurring dreams in which she is at work, attending a key meeting only to realize that she should be in India. "I'd walk out after filling out some paperwork and realize that I needed to be in Base Camp," she'd later tell me. "I would panic and start planning a helicopter trip to camp. Then I'd wake up in my tent—a big relief."

It's clear to me that Chuck finds it challenging to be with his girlfriend on an expedition. It would for anyone, given the risk, the deprivation and the testosterone-laden atmosphere. A compassionate soul, Chuck tries to find the balance between his and Sarah's needs. In doing so, he's set up a separate tent, one that is his, stuffed with his clothes, books, and personal items, though he invariably sleeps with Sarah. Later he'll say, "I felt some ambivalence. Plenty of times I liked it, plenty of times I didn't want her there. In some ways I never felt that I had the opportunity to tell her I didn't want her to go—so I felt railroaded by the inertia. In another way, I wasn't sure I didn't want her to go." He adds, "I guess in the end, I was empowered—so discussing it was an option."

Having solitude on such trips is the only way I've ever experienced. It provides great freedom with no distractions—other than the ones that dwell in my own head. Every high-altitude expedition I've undertaken suffers at some point from the sleepless, anxious grind of emotional head-tripping. Part of it, like Jonny's death dream seem to be evoked by place, as if the mountains are inhabited by things far older than we can imagine and things far deeper than the conscious mind can accept. Altitude stress, the hypoxia, and the body's physiological adjustment to thin air also seem to play a role. The panic often accompanies altitude gains, regardless of whether it's in Asia, Alaska or South America.

I spend the black hours of 1:00 AM to 2:00 AM on the early morning of the 10th wrestling with a shapeless nameless fear—it's an anxiety I've felt before, the feeling of absolute separation from God, man, and the universe itself. It's like being in hell, or the psyche ward—an irresistible claustrophobia from which there is no escape. Even the vague reassurance of dark expanses and open hillsides, faintly outlined beneath a cloud-draped quarter moon, do nothing to relieve my pounding heart, as I step out of the tent to urinate. It's not just me either. I've heard of men, under the physical and emotional duress of survival in the mountains, snapping under the strain. One attempted to cut his way through the wall of his tent in a high altitude blizzard. He had to be physically restrained, for destroying one's tent in a storm is akin to leaving one's foxhole in an artillery barrage. Another climber reportedly pulled a gun on one of his partners, reportedly in a fit of frustration over the choice of climbing route. That probably had less to do with the altitude than the fact that the climber, Aleister Crowley who—besides claiming the title Great Beast 666 and enjoying the tabloid appellation of "wickedest man in the world"—was, by all conventional standards, mentally unstable, a condition soon to spiral into heroin addiction. Still, his actions—he was disarmed and humiliated—are indicative of a mountain's power and its inherent stressors' ability to exacerbate psychosis and exploit emotional fractures.

As mine seems really altitude related. I adapt after a few days, but Chuck suffers from the same claustrophobia, though his is more acute—and chronic. On the one hand, Chuck loves the mountains. "They symbolize freedom to me—the furthest you can get from the enclosure of the day to day, physically and psychologically." But such freedom comes with its own psychic price tag for Chuck, as his nights are often hounded by "a confined panic that teeters on hysteria." It's a curse, one that often leaves him baggy-eyed and bleary in the morning. But ironically, his malady will ultimately save our lives.

Beneath his calm and frightfully caring demeanor, Chuck has a subdued tension, one that he has grown to manage over the years, through hard work, self-love, and the help of key people, especially his kind and loving mother. His childhood was marred by various experiences of sexual and emotional abuse. Details aside, I will say that most will never know what it's like to experience what he's experienced. Fewer still will know what it's like to survive and thrive as he has. And it didn't end there. Later his stepfather, "a cruel person," beat him, physically forcing him to submit to punishment—tantamount to breaking someone's spirit. The long-term aftermath left Chuck "an emotional wreck, paralyzed," and sometimes suicidal. There have been times he's almost succumbed to the power of a lie, those voices that tell you are worthless and powerless. Later still, Chuck, a very intelligent man, was struck in the head by a careless construction co-worker with a sledgehammer—disrupting his ability to think, drive a car, or remember simple things. Reflecting on the heap of misfortune, Chuck says, "There's been quite a few times I've become dangerous to myself." By that he means suicide.

"I had it all planned out. First off, you can't leave a bloody mess, that's bad form. The last thing you want is to leave something for someone to clean up." To address that grisly technical issue Chuck planned to wrap a pillow around his head, stand inside a shower stall with the plastic curtain drawn and blow his head off with a sawed-off shotgun. The reason for the shotgun was that "you might miss with a handgun." Still, the ensuing mess and the inaccessibility of his guns—Chuck prudently stores his firearms at his brother's house—negated the plan.

Hence Chuck's Plan B, "You go to Hawaii—it's the nearest access to the really deep water—and rent scuba gear. You swim out and deflate your buoyancy compensator (the inflatable vest that keeps the diver from either sinking down or floating upwards—called neutral buoyancy) and sink without a trace. Poof. No violence, no mess."

His deliberation is disturbing, but according to Chuck "it's not about giving up, or crying out for attention. It is about rage, about finally and totally controlling a situation."

But mercifully, there's a grace that pervades a select few lives, and Chuck's is one of them. It would have been so easy for Chuck to glide straight into crime, or the same abusive patterns. Still, no matter how far down the road he's come, there's an uncertainty and hesitance in the big picture things. For all his progress, his personal chaos is reflected in his inability to believe in a future enough to suffer through his impaired ability to concentrate, remember details, and focus. His room is a mess, so much so that it's no surprise to me when I hear from his brother, "In college, Chuck was such a slob that his roommates once left an open can full of milk under his bed. It was weeks until he noticed it—and a few more until he did anything about it."

It's an issue, but the answer is coming. It will unfold in a manner completely unexpected. And if we knew how it would transpire, we would run for our lives.

By the next afternoon, we are more than ready to start up Nanda

Kot. The weather has been unsettled and patchy for two days straight, following our jaunt to ABC. Rare windows of stark blue greet us in the morning but are quickly overtaken by clouds that drop rain. It follows a pattern that starts around midmorning and quickly closes in around our camp by the afternoon. Our time is spent fretting over gear and playing cards with S. V. and Dipender. On September 12, we are packed and ready for an attempt on Nanda Kot.

At 22,510 feet, Nanda Kot is by no means a giant in Himalayan terms. It is, however, a dominant presence, towering on the southern skyline of our Lwanl Valley Base Camp. Such prominence is no mean feat, considering that the Lwanl's elongated basin is bounded by a staggering array of peaks whose sharp heights are laid out like successive rows of teeth in a shark's jaw. The valley's eastern terminus is marked by the massive symmetrical triangle of Nanda Devi East, rising a breathtaking 10,000 feet above the Italian Base Camp. Perched to our north is the 19,000-foot-high mushroom-shaped profile of Nanda Lapak—which means "The Goddess's Leap." Precipitous as it is, this snow-capped beauty presents a mere high point on the first in a series of rising ridges, and is soon to be lost in a sea of peaks—some exceeding 21,000 feet—that march ever-northward to Tibet.

The Kumaon Himalayas are marked by a palpable spiritual and historic legacy. They also stand as the proving ground for the most significant and groundbreaking ascents of a bygone era in Himalayan climbing. Nanda Devi, Nanda Devi East, and Nanda Kot all lie within a dozen-mile radius. From the summit of each, you can see all the others—provided of course you're not in a blizzard.

The first ascents of these mountains represent a triumvirate of cutting-edge difficulty and standard-setting style—all completed within a three-year period. As we've said, in its day Nanda Devi was the highest peak climbed—to those in the know, a landmark arguably surpassing Everest in difficulty and style. Sister peak Nanda Devi East, climbed three years later by the Poles, is a mere 1,200 feet shorter than its neighbor. Its ascent, made by the south ridge, made up for its lesser stature with unprecedented technical difficulty. The singular route, the first and only despite attempts (and deaths) by prominent climbers, remains the only route to the summit. When asked what his hardest climb was, Tenzing Norgay, first to climb Everest with Hillary, surprised everyone by answering, "Nanda Devi East," not the highest mountain in the world. (Norgay climbed Nanda Devi East with French climber Louis Dubost in 1951. Two other French climbers on the expedition died attempting to traverse the twin summits.)

Known locally as Kulhari from its axe shape (Khuladi is Hindi for axe), Nanda Kot was first climbed by a Japanese team almost the exact same month as Tilman and Odell triumphed on Nanda Devi—the Japanese expedition caught word of the Nanda Devi ascent as they were working their way past the 18,000-foot mark. The expedition, led by the redoubtable climber mentioned earlier named Y. Hotta, was not the first to eye the attractive hatchet-profiled peak—it had been attempted by the prolific Dr. Tom Longstaff in 1906. Longstaff and crew climbed halfway up the mountain before being turned back by formidable logistics, harsh weather, and technical terrain. The only feasible route of ascent, the north face, was also avalanche-prone. As British Himalayan climber and Everest suitor T. H. Somervell wrote in 1926, after scoping the steep icy face, "It seemed to us that the whole mountain was in danger of slipping down in snowy crashes."

Hotta and team were Himalayan rookies. In fact, they comprised Japan's first venture to the great range—the vanguard of the hundreds of Japanese Himalayan expeditions in the ensuing decades. Hotta wrote, "We were all of us young and without experience of mountains other than those of Japan, none of which exceeds 15,000 feet; so that we could not feel confident of a successful assault on Nanda Kot, some 7,000 feet higher. . . . We hoped that, if Western mountaineers trained in the Alps could succeed in the Himalayas, we stood some chance of success."

And succeed they did. After suffering setback by storm, the team endured altitude sickness, the threat of avalanche, and the climbing challenges posed by a series of ice cliffs near the 19,000-foot mark. These took days to overcome. At one point, a mere 500 feet shy of the summit, the team was forced to beat a hasty retreat in the face of a storm. With admirable persistence, and only days left before their scheduled departure and impending winter, five Japanese climbers and Sherpa Ang Tsering, stood on top. The date was October 5, 1936.

Hotta's ascent was a remarkable climb for the times. It was steep and hard, with sections of near vertical ice that had to be climbed with only the rudimentary climbing equipment available in those days. Indeed, it was seen as significant enough to warrant the solicitation of an article in the prestigious *Himalayan Journal* where Hotta's painstakingly translated story was included among a handful of full-length expedition accounts.

Looking back, Himalayan climbing of the 1930s was an age of innocence, a prewar watershed where exploration for its own sake and lightweight style was with few exceptions, the norm. Indeed, the late 1950s through the mid-1960s was the postwar, "Golden Age" and saw with only a few notable exceptions, the full-on siege assault of Himalayan giants like Everest and K2. Gone was the shoestring planning and budgets, replaced by heavy-handed siege style, military logistics, and unbridled use of supplemental bottled oxygen. Perhaps it was the convergence of strategy and technology emerging from World War II that brought about the new approach, an approach many believed necessary to conquer such extreme peaks.

No less than M. S. Kohli had climbed Nanda Kot, eight years prior to leading the expedition that hauled the second SNAP-19 up the mountain during the CIA expedition. As it happened, Kohli was posted to Indian Navy Ship *Kistna*, in 1959. The *Kistna*, an antisubmarine frigate, was captained by Commander John Atkinson, himself a keen mountaineer. By luck, Atkinson was aware of Kohli's budding career in the mountains. He called the young lieutenant to his cabin and said, "Last month I was in Nainital [a town in the Himalayan foothills] with my children. We climbed up the ridge nearby and had a glimpse of Nanda Kot. I was attracted to the mountain, and I would like to lead a naval expedition to this peak. Would you like to join me?"

Kohli recalls that, without any hesitation, he replied, "Aye, aye, Sir."

Fate was to dole out a few more surprises, ultimately leaving the man of destiny in command of the expedition. Atkinson discovered a heart ailment, minor enough to not warrant dismay, but significant

enough to preclude a risky strenuous adventure at high altitude. As
Kohli recalls, "He called me to his cabin and said, 'Kohli, my wife
Barbara and I feel I should not go to this expedition. I believe you
are the most experienced mountaineer in the Indian Navy today
and I think you should take over the leadership.' "

It was a huge opportunity for a young naval officer still in his twen-
ties and one he "could not have said no to." With a vigor and determination that would later become his hallmarks, Kohli, accepted the
tiller of the expedition and began the process of selecting who was to
go and where they were to get the necessary equipment. Travel from
Delhi, the trek to Base Camp, and stocking the initial three camps on
the mountainside took over a month. Besides having little to eat,
Kohli and his six-man crew were beset by blizzard, avalanche, and
gales up to thirty-five miles per hour. Finally, after a several weeks of
effort, he, Sherpa Ang Tshering, and a fellow sailor, K. P. Sharma
headed for the summit. Recalls Kohli of that day,

I was like a man possessed. We seemed to be on the frontier
of life and death, but there was no question of turning back.
At 2:20 PM, after three hours of a breath-taking climb, I
found myself below a large cornice extending from the
summit. I made a hole in it and lifted myself through it. I
express my gratitude to Guru Gobind Singh and shouting
'Nanda Devi Ki Jai" (Hail to Goddess Nanda Devi), I
crawled on to the summit of Nanda Kot. Tears welled up in
my eyes, tears of joy. It was amazing to find Sharma, who I
had reckoned would take some time, crawling up the summit
within three minutes.

On the long hike back to civilization, Kohli picked up a newspaper in a trailside teahouse and was startled to find that he with his climbing partner, K. P. Sharma, had made the cover of the *Times of India*—comparable to getting one's mug pasted on the front page of the *New York Times*. Upon return to Delhi, he was congratulated in person by no less than Prime Minister Jawaharlal Nehru himself. Nehru, a political titan and India's first prime minister had always maintained a real interest in mountaineering. It was Nehru who founded the Himalayan Mountaineering Institute in Darjeeling, and it was such an acquaintanceship that would later draw Kohli to service of a different kind in those very same mountains.

Kohli later wrote, "I did not realize at the time that, with the Nanda Kot Expedition of 1959, one of the most glorious chapters in naval mountaineering had opened." Kohli's triumph propelled him into a limelight that would lead to more expeditions to mountains like Annapurna III and Everest. It would also take Kohli back to Nanda Kot by the mid-1960s, this time on behalf of the Indian Intelligence Bureau and the CIA.

Our first attempt on Nanda Kot kicks off around 11 AM on September 13. As mentioned, the 8th was the last fully sunny day with the 9th through the 12th a mix of overcast with intermittent clearing and general afternoon rain. That meant snow up high. Chuck went up to Camp I a day prior, radioing back that there were three inches of fresh snow draping the rolling slopes above. He then opted to spend the night in a tent at 15,700 feet on the pretext of acclimatizing better. It makes sense on one hand, but I question how effective that strategy is, considering that the mountain is

22,510 feet high, and 15,700 feet is a small fraction of the required elevation gain. We'll be spending the night at 16,800 feet on our way up, so I don't see the point—unless there is the opportunity to come back down and sleep at a lower altitude prior to the summit push. As is, it sounds similar to running a dozen miles the day before you race in a marathon.

In my eyes, you follow the age-old dictum of high altitude climbing, "climb high and sleep low." The general guidelines for climbing above 10,000 feet are: limit your altitude gain by 1,000 feet per day—and for every 3,000 feet of elevation gained, take a rest day. The exception is if you ascend more than 1,000 feet in a day. Then you should come back down to sleep at a lower altitude. This tactic allows the body sufficient recovery in thicker air after the stress of high-altitude exertion. But every mountaineer knows that there are no such things as hard and fast rules, and that if everyone followed these "rules" nothing would ever get climbed. Neither the CIA expeditions, nor the first ascent team found it possible to adhere to such a schedule, a schedule that would demand a minimum of twelve perfect weather days in a row. Here in the Kumaon, you'd have better odds winning the lottery. What's worked for me in the past is 3,000 feet of elevation gain per day, provided one is not carrying an inordinate amount of weight. Usually, you can knock off a twenty-something thousand-foot peak in a few days provided it's not too technical. When you start planning on building a huge safety margin in terms of food, fuel, rope, and hardware, your exertion level rises, demand for food and water increases, and recovery time lengthens. What would take a few days becomes weeks. The take away lesson is that gear, food, and fuel are never a substitute for the ability to move fast and efficiently over whatever terrain you encounter.

But I might be biased, for as we start up the slopes leading to the mountain, I still feel under the weather as the lingering effects of my fever and gastric bug slowly subside. I can't be bothered to hike up and spend an extra night at 15,700 feet before continuing immediately the next morning. I'm also a bit worried because I've never gotten this sick in the opening days of an expedition, and I know full well that we are just getting started.

The four of us, S. V., Jonny, Sarah, and I head up with relatively light packs, as most of the weight in gear has been stashed in the rock pile at 15,700-foot mark. Jonny ranges ahead, stops and shoots some photos of us beelining up a hillside of drab brown scree and low-lying sedgy-looking plants. He then packs his camera and moves on with an easy lope that belies the difficulty of the terrain. Jonny repeats the process as the majesty of our valley and the surrounding peaks slowly reveals itself. Each step grudgingly yields a new perspective, and soon Nanda Devi, a glistening crystal on the horizon, comes into view. I recall Hotta's words as his Japanese team reached a point near this very spot over seventy years ago: "That evening the perfect form of Nanda Devi became visible. How lovely she was! Her rare beauty enchanted us."

I've seldom moved in disciplined formation while in the mountains unless I'm roped with others for the sake of safety in crevassed terrain. To my like minded companions and myself, climbing is not a military exercise or a guided excursion. So, while tramping up the lower slopes of Nanda Kot, our group spreads out as time passes, each in his or her own world and marching at their own pace. The weather is clear, though the ground is damp and there's fresh snow as we climb to a level 1,000 feet above Base Camp. The weather looks as though it might hold, and we will need at least three more days to get up and off the mountain. About 2,000 feet above Base Camp, I trudge up the steep rocky rib that guides us up. The air is thin, and I pause for a sip of water and a bite to eat. Gazing across the ethereal panorama brings to mind a dream I had last night.

In my dream, I was trying to buy a latte at a cash register, and my credit card wasn't working for some reason. I ended up becoming furious and berating the poor guy behind the counter out of frustration. I knew it wasn't his fault and was starting to feel really bad when the scenery changed and I was looking at a work schedule for my old table-bussing job in Yosemite. I was absent from the schedule for some reason, and the people I worked with, all of them long term co-workers, gave me the cold shoulder when I tried to find out why. They were moving like automatons with little visible awareness of their surroundings and stripped of their human qualities. I woke up with a sense of rejection and alienation to the disorienting sound of Gyan tapping my tent. He was asking if I wanted the chai from the pot he brought around every morning as our wake-up "bed-tea." I almost told him to piss off, but like the guy in the dream, he was only doing his job.

Altitude, namely its accompanying hypoxia, does funny things to the mind. The physiological change, combined with the deprivation of distractions like television, Internet, alcohol, career, and whatever static fills our heads often dredges up of all types of buried experiences, memories, and unmanaged emotions. Having been on more than my share of trips like this, I'm used to it. I've also seen more than one apparently well-adjusted climber, flip out and leave the expedition or become so antsy, he can't maintain the emotional resiliency and energy required to carry on with the program. The clichéd quote from Thoreau, "the mass of men lead lives of quiet desperation," rings true when someone implodes after being deprived of the creature comforts, routines, and daily structures that provide accustomed equilibrium. Such apparently isolated experiences reflect upon the real world because for everyone, not just climbers, there exists a delicate balance between choosing our path in the real world—or "doing" that rote set of daily activities that do not lead to a spiritual or emotional progression, but become merely another way to maintain our sanity. Do we work to live, or do we live to work? Do we strive and busy ourselves for status or security alone?

Are we chasing the tacitly false promise of that fantasy future where we'll finally stop and live? If so, then we are suffering as a society from a mass neurosis. A neurosis like that is revealed on an expedition with the subtlety of a bad acid trip. Author Wayne Muller once wrote,

> Brother David Steindl-Rast (a noted Benedictine Monk and fellow author/lecturer) reminds us that the Chinese word for "busy" is composed of two characters: "heart" and "killing." When we make ourselves so busy that we are always rushing around trying to get this or that "done," or "over with," we kill something vital in ourselves, and we smother the quiet wisdom of our heart.

I'm not claiming that hard work is bad or being busy is wrong—

on the contrary. But, I do question what drives our choices, and, if we have the courage to make any true choices at all. Though life is about compromise, it is also about being deliberate without falling under the pressure of coercion by one's own fear or vanity. Don't get me wrong, I've succumbed as much as any other to the temptations of the world, but there's always been a rudder that steered me back on course—climbing, something I love. Whatever pains or annoyances I must endure, they are mine and mine alone and, like my life—I'll do what I want with them.

The disturbing feeling lingered well through the morning. But lucky for me, hiking up a hill with a pack on in ever-thinning air gives a sense of purpose that works as well as any distraction in the world. I'm wearing plastic double boots—standard fare in high-altitude climbs. I've taken them on three prior expeditions so they are broken in and comfortable. The boots consist of a lightweight inner bootie—ours of Chuck's custom molded insulating foam, encased in a form-fit plastic shell that's durable and waterproof. Think of an alpine ski boot configuration, only lighter, shod with a grippy waffle-bottomed rubber sole, and topped with a flexible cuff to allow hiking. The cuffs squeak with every step, a sound that's more comfortable than annoying. Each squeak sounds off another pace in the cadence of ascent.

Between squeaks, I glance back down our line of ascent. It's as steep as one of those black diamond runs at the ski resort. Unlike Vail or Aspen, a lungful of air has 45 percent less oxygen than at sea level. S. V. is struggling. He falls farther behind with each passing minute and pretty soon he is a red dot almost fading into a mist that now accumulates on the mountainside. He's got a gimpy knee from a ski accident, and his military postings don't often encourage the best health.

A military assignment to an urban area in India, with all its accompanying air pollution—Delhi for instance—is like smoking a pack of cigarettes a day. Smoking is something S. V. does anyway, and though I haven't counted, he must smoke more than a pack per day. All that tar doesn't help his performance, and he's a good hour behind us by the time we reach Camp I. The camp, the flat expanse of talus we'd located on the 11th is now covered with three inches of wet snow. The rings of rocks, assembled by expeditions over the past decades, are now completely obscured, so rather than seeking out the level sections of ground, we pile snow up to create a platforms for our tents.

Oddly, Jonny and Sarah choose the top of a flat boulder for theirs, scraping off the snow to find a more or less level surface. More or less level doesn't work for Chuck, for among his quirks is the absolute need for a dead flat sleeping surface. He's been known to use an avalanche inclinometer—a device to measure the angle of snow surface to determine whether or not a slope presents an avalanche hazard (usually between 30 and 45 degrees)—to get a sleeping area level. It works for me as I watch Chuck painstakingly craft the ideal bivouac. He sluices a shovelful here and another dab of snow there, periodically crawling in the tent to feel how level the surface is. It takes half an hour before, finally satisfied, he unloads his sleeping pad and bag.

In the final wash of orange evening light, Nanda Kot's now familiar hatchet-shaped summit towers nearly 7,000 feet above our camp. We figure we're at about 16,800 feet. Jonny, Sarah, and I made the 3,000-foot climb in a little less than three and a half hours, a relatively fast time, considering we'd not fully acclimatized. We want to shoot for the 18,500-foot level tomorrow—nothing excessive, just a good solid day of slogging. I feel pretty good—my appetite is fine, and I'm suffering from no headache, though my resting heart rate is more than 80 beats/minute. Any higher would be cause for concern as it would indicate a lack of physiological adaptation as the heart pumps faster to make up for the lack of oxygen in each lungful of air. Sarah, despite her inexperience managed as well as any of us. And she might end up better than all us because her pulse is little more than 60 beats/minute, which is lower than most people's resting heart rate at sea level. Scratching my head, I wonder if Sarah might be one of those who have a predisposition for managing altitude—something that some have and others don't. And you can never tell. I've heard of Olympic-level competitive cardio athletes tank at altitudes like this and until one goes high, it's a crapshoot trying to predict what will happen. Later, Sarah tells me of her childhood asthma, postulating "nonscientifically" that her performance is in part due to her body's adaptation to oxygen deprivation as a child.

We set up S. V.'s tent as he takes a breather on a boulder. He's not looking too great as he puffs another Khukuri cigarette with his black Gore-Tex jacket unzipped to vent perspiration that pours off like steam. S. V. pushes his knit hat back from his forehead before removing it altogether. His hair, like the rest of ours is greasy from weeks without a shower, and thin traces of vapor waft from his head. Khukuri's are his brand of choice—a rough raw-bodied cigarette he probably favors because of its connection with his army regiment—

the Gurkhas. The Gurkhas are legendary for their fierce martial prowess over centuries of war and have been called the "bravest of the brave." The Khukuri, or more recently "Kukri" is the reverse droop-bladed knife that's as feared as the men who wield it. Legend has it that at close quarters, the blade is so lethal that it's impossible to parry when wielded by an expert.

I've not seen S. V. wave a Kukri around yet, but he sure wields a mean death-stick. He lights his cigarettes in succession. When one is almost finished, he jump-starts the other with the dying butt. I call it "chain-gunning," a military euphemism that S. V. likes, or at least grins at when I say it. As we were counting out GUs and Powerbars in Base Camp, he must have been counting out the red and white cigarette packs that are emblazoned with a pair of bent-bladed, knives, crossed like a Third World coat-of-arms. I usually allocate two bars and six GUs per day for a climb. I wonder if S. V. breaks out the cig count into seven per day? A dozen? From his rate of consumption, it looks like at least a pack a day, maybe two. It's a concern to us whether he'll become a liability, but I feel that he, like everyone else on this trip needs to be given the chance—at least on this peak—to go as high as he can without any untoward pressure to turn back. S. V.'s easily the most proactive LO I've seen, and without his help, we wouldn't have the concessions from the IMF to attempt anything but Nanda Kot. He's still puffing away as he lies down in the tent we've loaned him, wistfully blowing tendrils of blue smoke through the roof's vent hole at distant stars, which twinkle in a clear and cold sky.

Beyond the smog and light pollution of the world at large, the night sky is a vast panorama of sparkling constellations and a glimmering belt of the Milky Way. High above, the faint twinkle of a satellite adds motion to an otherwise static display. I recall from my notes, now stacked in a tent three thousand feet below, that though SNAP systems had powered remote buoys and satellites in outer space, the Nanda Devi unit was apparently the device's first earthbound deployment. According to official NASA records, the SNAP-19 RTG was officially deployed six times. Two were launches of Nimbus weather satellites in 1968 and 1969, one of which was aborted. The RTG on that mission was recovered and recycled, while the other operated successfully for years. That and other accidents however raise the specter of plutonium poisoning.

Critics point to the potential for human tragedy if the large amounts of plutonium-238—as much as 72.3 pounds on the 1997 Cassini space probe—were to meet a fate like the space shuttle *Challenger* in 1986, or the *Columbia* in 2003 (*Challenger* exploded shortly after launch and *Columbia* disintergrated upon re-entry). "NASA, incidentally, changed the odds of catastrophic shuttle accident soon afterward—from 1-in-100,000, concocted out of the whole cloth, to 1-in-76 . . . in light of the subsequent Columbia shuttle accident," writes Karl Grossman, professor of journalism and author of *The Wrong Stuff: The Space Program's Nuclear Threat to the Planet.* He further notes that *Challenger*, before exploding after launch, was scheduled to carry 24.2 pounds of plutonium-238 on its next mission and, "Far more than seven people could have died if the explosion . . . occurred during the next launch." He also adds, "If *Columbia* had had plutonium on board, radioactive debris would have been splattered over Texas and Louisiana."

Potential estimates of the worst case scenario for such an accident of say, the Cassini, range from 950,000 to 40 million deaths. The government staunchly decries such criticism, pointing to the three-decade safety record of nearly fifty American and Soviet missions utilizing nuclear power sources. Despite "several launch failures, failures to achieve orbit, and accidental re-entries through the Earth's atmosphere," one pro-nuclear space group states, "none of these accidents have caused measurable health effects in the human population, though some environmental contamination has occurred."

Regardless of the perceived danger, RTGs have provided reliable and long-lasting power for the spacecraft, running instruments, computers, and on-board radio transmitters, along with attitude thrusters, and reaction wheels. Besides the Nimbus satellites, they've also been deployed twice in planetary probes and twice to the surface of Mars in the early to mid-seventies. Perhaps the most noteworthy—and definitely the last operational—SNAP-19 deployment occurred in 1972. Four individual SNAP-19 RTGs (initially providing 155 watts, an output that declined as the nuclear fuel decayed) to the *Pioneer* 10 space probe. At this moment, a dying *Pioneer* is somewhere beyond Pluto, racing along at 82,000 miles per hour.

One NASA report states:

After more than 30 years, it appears the venerable *Pioneer* 10 spacecraft has sent its last signal to Earth. *Pioneer's* last, very weak signal was received on 23 January 2003. NASA engineers report that *Pioneer* 10's radioisotope power source has decayed, and it may not have enough power to send additional transmissions to Earth. Famed as the most remote object ever made by man through most of its mission, *Pioneer* 10 is now over 8 billion miles away. . . . *Pioneer* 10 will continue to coast silently as a ghost ship through deep space into interstellar space, heading generally for the red star Aldebaran, which forms the eye of Taurus (The Bull). Aldebaran is about 68 light years away and it will take *Pioneer* over 2 million years to reach it.

In case *Pioneer*—which for all the world vaguely resembles a diaphanous deepsea jellyfish complete with a few stiff and frail-looking stalks protruding from a shallow bowl-shaped body—encounters any extraterrestrial life, a plaque was mounted on the spacecraft body to convey a little something of our world to whatever is out there. The plaque is etched with drawings depicting, among other things, a man, a woman, and the location of the sun and the earth in our galaxy. It's tempting to speculate how an alien life form would receive such an interstellar message in a bottle. What's certain is that the sister SNAP-19s are both beyond the reach of mankind—one in the icy depth of Nanda Devi's inner space, the other in on a one-way trip to the oblivion of outer space.

I doze, wondering if any plutonium is circling overheard.

Our dinner of Maggi noodles—the ubiquitous Indian version of Top Ramen—mixed with tuna doesn't sit well in my gut. At around midnight, I roll over, unzip my bag and slide on my boots for an urgent call of nature. Getting up at night is one of those unsung ass pains of high-altitude climbing. If it's just a leak you need to take, then you usually pee in a bottle to avoid the hassle of getting togged up to step outside. On precarious bivouacs, like when your tent is pitched on a knife-edged ridge, a groggy, nocturnal ramble can have fatal consequences and is best avoided. This time around, the only shocker, as I fumble with the zipper and push my head out, is the snow that's started to fall. I save my psychological batteries by ignoring the weather. I do my business, step back to the tent and brush the snow off my fleece underwear suit.

I sit at the tent entrance, remove my plastic boot shells and stash them in the pack adjacent to the tent door. That will keep them dry. I then remove the foam inner boots and place them between my sleeping bag and Chuck's snoring form. That will keep them warm for the morning. I crawl in my bag and pull the top over my head. Then I pass into a dreamless sleep hoping for the best.

I must have slept soundly for Sarah recalls, "Starting after midnight I started hearing the avalanches going off." It was a disturbing experience because she says, "I'd never been in this type of situation, so I wasn't sure that the avalanches were going to come down and wipe us out. Plus, our tent was pitched on an angle so I kept sliding down into Jonny, who for some reason slept like a rock." Such fears are understandable. After so much time in the mountains, I'm conditioned to ignore avalanches so long as I go to bed knowing they are a good distance away. Chuck is out cold after taking some Ambien, the tranquilizer of choice at altitude. Other sleeping pills act as respiratory depressants, leaving the user ruthlessly hung-over the next day and dangerously groggy during the night. As I said earlier, stumbling about outside the tent in a narcotized haze can be a fatal proposition. And there are other less deadly but arguably worse situations that can arise from taking the wrong sleeping pill at the wrong time. Sleep or no sleep, at least we aren't swimming in someone's urine. As one of America's great alpinists, Mark Twight once wrote,

> Proper sleep is essential on a multi-day climb. Sleep deprivation kills. On stressful routes, and all the meaningful ones are, it may be impossible to fall asleep or remain asleep. . . . To illustrate the dangers of sleeping pills in heavy doses, Michael Kennedy told me a story about his route on the northeast face of Ama Dablam, undertaken with Carlos Buhler in 1985. Several bivouacs up the climb, Carlos, who was using Halcyon, rolled over to pee in his bottle, but fell back to sleep before capping it. Hydrated as he was, it turned into quite a mess, for both him and Michael.

But all those charming bodily challenges are forgotten along with our climbing hopes, when, in the morning, there's eight inches of snow blanketing everything. We spend a few hours shaking off the snow accumulation before Jonny makes the decision to go down. He, Sarah, and S. V. pack their bags and wade through the new snow back down to Base Camp. Before leaving, they stuff their gear into plastic garbage compacter bags—more durable than those flimsy trash bags—to keep clothes and gear dry. S. V. packs his personal gear, for sometime in the night he makes the decision to descend and not go back up. He has the heart of a lion, but his military command and last second call to act as a liaison officer didn't allow for the months of training we'd enjoyed in the States.

Chuck and I lie in our sleeping bags at Camp I, listening to the snow patter on the tent fabric. Those readers who have gone camping know that tents generally comprise a nylon body erected around a system of aluminum poles. The poles are usually threaded with rubberized shock cord running down their hollow lengths. The bungy-like cord keeps the individual segments together as a single unit, for there is nothing like chasing down loose pieces of slick aluminum tubing while stumbling around on a glacier. The cord also holds the fully assembled tent pole under tension so you can thread the pole through the fabric sleeves that criss-cross the tent body. To top it all off, you'll add a waterproof nylon rain-fly over the whole structure. The expedition tents pitched in Base Camp are made by Marmot and can accommodate two people with an overall weight of about nine pounds. This is light considering that old-school tents from Hotta's time and through the 1970s, weighed up to three times as much. The tents we use on the mountain itself, are even lighter. This is an absolute necessity given our lightweight approach.

These shelters, including the one Chuck and I doze in are called single-wall tents. They are made of a light fabric operating on the waterproof/breathable principle made famous by the Gore-Tex company. These fabrics are created with an expanded polytetrafluoroethylene (PTFE) membrane. Huh? In layman's terms, PTFE is a chemically blown out version of Teflon, which was invented in 1938. It's the same stuff coating your nonstick frying pan, except that it looks and feels like a really tough rubber membrane that' so thin that it's almost transparent—like the skin of a balloon. Unlike a balloon, Gore-Tex has nine billion tiny pores in every single square inch to prevent liquid water from penetrating (water droplets are 700 times larger than those pores and can't pass through even under high pressure) while allowing moisture vapor (whose molecules are smaller than those in a liquid state) to escape. This property allows sweat and in this case the condensation of our breath to escape. Federal OSHA regulations disallow companies like Marmot from making tents out of Gore-Tex. But manufacturers circumvent the issue by using similar PTFE whose membrane is sandwiched between fabrics that possess higher fire retardancy. Still as every storm bound climber can attest to—because boredom ultimately drives them to read anything, including the eye-level warning label—you're still not supposed to cook with a stove, or smoke, inside the tent.

We forgot to tell S. V. about the fire hazard, but regardless, the beauty of single-wall tents is their ability to shed snow and rain with a single layer, thus presenting the mountaineer with incredible weight savings. These are specialized tents, not to be used for casual outings as they cost a bundle and like buying bikinis (which I've never personally done), getting a lightweight tent is all about paying way more for way less. I figure, we spend $50 for every pound saved on our single-wall.

Chuck and I eat chocolate and nap before packing up at 2:00 PM to head down. The idea is to acclimatize a bit more, but it's really just an excuse to idly chat in the narcotic haze. Often on expeditions, you get little time alone with others, and each conversation is altered by the input or interruptions of others. Before we leave, we secure everyone's gear. In doing so, we make the big mistake of leaving two tents pitched. We don't know it yet, but one of the biggest storms we've ever seen is bearing down. And when we return when the weather subsides a week later, the tents will have been buried without a trace and crushed under a pole-snapping eight feet of snow. Hotta's Japanese team, Kohli's navy expedition, and the multiple CIA ventures expeditions to Nanda Kot all experienced these same brutal storms. They all risked life and limb when forced to retreat from high on the mountain. As we shoulder our packs, I recall a passage from Conboy's *Spies in the Himalayas*, which now sits in camp, three thousand feet below. Three of Kohli's climbing team members during the CIA expedition faced a steamrolling avalanche as they were coming down the very slope that Chuck and I now face,

> Terrified, the three turned around and tried to run—a near impossibility, given their padded clothes and the slippery, calf-deep powder. Roped together, they half-stumbled, half-dragged one another downward. With tons of snow bearing down, they instinctively knew they had no chance of outpacing the avalanche. In an act of desperation, Sonam—prayer flags fluttering from his rucksack—yanked them sideways. It was a calculation that saved their lives. By a mere few feet, they were out of the avalanche's line of descent. The snow tore past them like a locomotive, hitting them with nothing more than a light dusting.

We keep this in mind as we make our way through thick mist and down a rolling slope that gets progressively steeper as we zigzag our way down. Our snow is more like sludge compared with what was described by Conboy. It seems really well consolidated, without the layering effect that makes an avalanche probable. Still, it's a gingerly half-hour descent to the flat shallow valley that others must have

used as an ABC. A further hour later, we are down to Base Camp
—all the scenic marvels of yesterday obliterated by thick clouds and
myriad snowflakes. The damp air hovers at about 38 degrees
Fahrenheit, a real icky temperature because, at barely above
freezing, the air retains moisture, adding a bone-chilling feel.
Nothing dries out easily in the damp, and the snowline is just above
Base Camp around 14,000 feet.

The ever cheery and reliable Dipender fires up his stove for a few
rounds of tea and soup. Chuck and I crawl off to our respective tents
—the others have already retreated—to hunker down with books
and their own inner thoughts. We lie in silence, having faced the first
real setback of the expedition until Gyan announces dinner a few
hours later.

> *"I knew that courage came with less struggle for some than for others but I believed that anyone who desired it could have it. That the desire was the thing itself. The thing itself. I could think of nothing else of which that was true."*
>
> —Cormac McCarthy, *All the Pretty Horses*

CHAPTER 10

BACK ONCE AGAIN

Base Camp can be either bliss or hell, depending on what the weather chooses to dole out. For now, it's anything but heavenly. When I poke my head out of the tent on the morning of September 15th, the cloud level hovers maybe a thousand feet above. There's a heavy rain coming down. Last night, it snowed a few inches, and the slight elevation of daytime temperature has turned the snow into rain. The incessant splatter transforms the pristine white carpet into a gloppy mess of thick crud. I write in my journal:

> You can gaze down the Lwanl Valley and see the cloud ceiling press down like a gray velvet curtain. The fog obscures anything higher than 14,000 feet rendering all that's visible

in a dull monochrome grayscale, lacking even the singular distinction of true black or white. It's like someone took an inkprint of the slopes leading up to the mountains—lopping of the tops and bleaching the whole thing out.

The damp permeates everything within my fragile nylon bubble. My sleeping bag's nylon exterior shell is clammy, and my journal pages are warped, swelling the weatherproof cover. As I raise myself to one elbow, I notice a springy quality to the tent floor. There's water percolating beneath the tent, and after breakfast, I set to digging a channel to divert the now free-flowing melt-off. Chuck saunters over and asks with his wry humor, "Looks like a Bureau of Reclamation project." I reply, "Yeah, I woke up dreaming I was sleeping on a waterbed—turns out it's more like a stream bed." That said, I borrow a hoe from Dipender and carve a diversion channel. It's enough to stem the tide, providing the main channel doesn't flood. It's getting close. Our once dry streambed is turning into a regular creek, requiring a few strategically placed rocks to cross the five-inch deep flow. Burbling water laps the edge of the bordering streamside turf. I can almost picture some primordial creature swimming up the current, eager to spawn.

When we gather for lunch—the usual fare of rice, dhal, curried vegetables, and chapattis—it's a wet crew. Everyone is wearing their mountaineering double boots, insulated pants, and puffy down jackets. We sit in folding camp chairs—sized for dwarves—and hunch over the knee-high table.

"These are amazing," says Sarah as she pulls on her down booties. She's brought them in the mess tent to warm her feet as she sits knitting in the downtime between lunch and dinner. Besides a gathering point for meals, the mess tent acts as the social center of camp. The blue canvas structure, a billowy fabric version of one of those little Monopoly hotel pieces, doubles as the drying room for everyone's clothes. They hang on a piece of nylon climbing rope. As Sarah knits, the rest of us tinker with gear or play cards. We've forgotten to buy a short-wave radio, and S. V.'s phone has no reception at all, so there's no news from the outside world. One of our biggest thrills is turning out to be the morning visit to the latrine tent where we read the headlines from last month's entertainment section of the *Hindustan Times*. It's a soggy fifty-yard stroll to the loo, a square-floored, standing-height structure with a flat roof threatening to cave in under the weight of rainwater pooling in ceiling fabric. Squatting over the latrine—basically a rock-lined hole in the dirt—we each in turn read day after day, how Bollywood star Govinda is in deep financial shit and that actor Sanjay Dutt is getting ready to sing for some band called Zinda. But what we can't gather from the *Times* is what's happening outside the confines of our little valley. For all we know, there could be terrorist attacks, nuclear war, or the second coming of Christ, even as the rain pours.

Sarah the engineer puts up her knitting and starts building a house of cards. It's a testament to how bored we are when soon, everyone gathers to give unwanted advice. Our gazes hang on the fate of each card as it is placed, in turn. The rain sizzles on the tent fabric as Sarah gingerly builds teepees of cards, placing horizontal layers as the foundation for the next storey. She concentrates. She has a lighter duct taped to string that she wears, necklace-like. It sways as she leans over, threatening to knock her structure over.

"Watch out!" someone says. She shoots us all a dirty look as if to say, "Go find your own entertainment."

While we run thin on luxuries and entertainment, Indian-flown, Soviet-made helicopters afforded unheard of luxuries to the 1960's CIA mountaineers. They were supplied continual loads of fresh vegetables and live chickens and goats (the chickens tended to die quickly in the thin air, but the meat was still fresh). We make do with whatever we carried to Base Camp and our goat, nearly two weeks old, still makes dismaying appearances at the dinner table. But overall, our food is good, three square meals a day served up piping hot by our smiling kitchen staff. Breakfast is usually porridge with toast and eggs. Though the toast will run out soon, the eggs, as nature's perfect food, remain unspoiled throughout the trip. Lunch and dinner always include the ubiquitous dhal bhat (rice and lentils), with whatever vegetables and odd tinned meat gets rationed out. Chappatis, Indian flatbread, a thicker version of our tortillas make an appearance every other meal. To cap it off, Dipender serves us a spicy chutney of garlic, peanuts, chili, mustard seed, onions, and hot masala, he's made on a grinding stone in the cook tent.

The CIA expeditions were supplied by air. Ironically, it was the mix of American-made fixed wing aircraft, *and* Soviet supplied transport and helicopters including Russian made Mi-4 helicopters. The Soviet helicopters, known for their high altitude capability not only dropped off the American climbers and CIA-developed transceiver, but also case officer Sam Currie.

It must have irked the Cold War intelligence agent—who, like his predecessor William McKniff was unavailable for an interview—to be shuttled in a communist-made helicopter. It was an irony of *realpolitik,* and though the Soviets and the U.S. may have differed ideologically, it was in both their interests to find out what the Chinese were up to. But that fact, a political bombshell, could never be openly voiced. Even the alliance of convenience between India and the U.S. had to be treated with delicacy and constructed with built-in deniability. Wrote Howard Kohn, "The CIA had the unofficial cooperation of its Indian counterpart, the Central Bureau of Investigation (CBI)." Kohn's limited access to facts, might have led him to confuse the CBI, responsible for India's domestic criminal investigations, for the afore-mentioned IB, whose tasks mirrored those of the CIA.

But I am splitting hairs. The important thing is that, as Kohn further states "American undercover agents . . . co-opted Indian intelligence, setting up the arrangement on an informal basis to preserve the CIA's absolute authority over the project." That claim wasn't too much of a shocker, but Kohn's assertion that the CIA insisted on keeping the affair a secret from Indira Gandhi and the Indian government, is. M.S. Kohli notes that, "the plan was approved by a disillusioned Nehru." As the Prime Minister died from a sudden heart attack on May 27, 1964, months before the chance meeting between Bishop and LeMay—Kohli might be mistaken on who was in charge of India at the project's inception. Or perhaps the Nanda Devi affair had its roots prior to Shastri's ascension to Prime Minister.

Regardless, Howard Kohn continues, "The CIA did give President Johnson a general outline of the project, but that agency also asked him not to notify the Gandhi government. Whether aware or not, Indira Gandhi's government certainly had inherited the espionage plot. She became Indian Prime Minister on January 19, 1966. By that time, plutonium had already blighted the Himalayas."

Also, the allegation that the incident was "concealed from both President Johnson and Prime Minister Gandhi," has not, to this day, been proven. One can speculate that the intelligence organizations on both sides of the Pacific were, in Kohn's words, "concerned that the Gandhi government might veto the project as needlessly provocative," and that "the CIA did give President Johnson a general outline of the project, but . . . also asked him not to notify the Gandhi government." But those exact details, like the SNAP itself, are out of reach, in an equally inaccessible classified file at Langley.

What's certain is that to this day, the CIA will not reveal any involvement in the affair. In 2005, Robert Schaller attempted to recover his confiscated journal and film from the first Nanda Devi espionage expedition. His experiences underline the Agency's attitude towards the entire affair. In a letter to Dr. Schaller dated July, 21, 2005, Scott Koch, Executive Secretary of the Agency Release Panel wrote:

We are responding to your 21 April 2005 letter appealing our 7 April 2005 response to your Freedom of Information Act request for the return, or a copy, of your personal diary and photographs you claim to have taken while participating in a project in 1965–1967 on the summits of Nanda Devi and Nanda Kot in the Himalayas. Specifically, you appealed our determination that we can neither confirm nor deny the existence of records responsive to your request on the basis of Freedom of Information Act exemptions (b)(1) and (b)(3).

The Agency Release Panel has considered your appeal and has sustained the determination that the Agency can neither confirm nor deny the existence or nonexistence of records responsive to your request on the basis of the Freedom of Information Act exemptions (b)(1) and (b)(3). Therefore in accordance with agency regulations the Agency Release Panel has denied your appeal.

Says Schaller, "I've tried as an ordinary citizen to get back what was mine—I took the pictures—I wrote the diaries—they're saying that the whole appeal was based on the existence or nonexistence of these items. I'm not disputing that because I know they exist. I just wanted them back and this is the response I get—they're sending me to court and it frustrates me and it angers me and it disappoints me and I feel betrayed in this process because I can't see how my personal diaries and photographs would be of any risk to national security. And they certainly don't reveal anything about the operations of the CIA. So that's where I stand . . . I'm not optimistic that I'll get them back." He adds, "I still have that same strong feeling for my county but I don't have the same trust in the government that I did when I was a resident in surgery. I might have been young and naïve at the time but I did trust my government then, much more than I do now."

In my own query to the CIA, I received a prompt reply, thanking me for my request for information, and like Schaller, referring me to the Freedom of Information Act. Told that I might, "anticipate an unavoidable delay," I, like Schaller am not optimistic about my chances of acquiring any official insight from the Agency.

The next day, rain, mixed with snow, continues without pause. A gray mood permeates camp. Everyone deals with it in their own fashion. Jonny is ever antsy, arriving at breakfast and slurping chai, followed by some very strong coffee to which he adds hot chocolate and protein mix. Chuck sleeps a lot, shuffling between the mess tent where he eats, his personal tent where he keeps his stuff, and Sarah's tent, where he sleeps. Today, he petitions for an adjusted schedule of 10 AM breakfast, late lunch and late dinner. The request comes after he announces, after skipping breakfast, "I could barely drag myself out of bed in time for lunch today," adding, "I think I've slept thirty of the last thirty-six hours." He grins like a sixth grader anticipating a sick day.

It's a good chance to get to know more about S. V. When everyone wanders off to their sodden tents after lunch, the colonel and I sit in the mess tent, a blue canvas and nylon affair about the size of a small living room. He's a handsome guy about six feet tall, trim, with the authoritative bearing of one used to having underlings snap-to on demand. It's no surprise in India, with its unofficial, but very real caste system, plus his own standing as a senior officer. He's a man used to barking out orders, a habit I can tell he restrains in our company, but one that also cannot be entirely suppressed. At one point Gyan, the twenty-something cook's assistant mocks S. V. behind his back, miming a salute with all the officiousness a short stubble-faced young man—in dirty jeans, scratched faux-Hollywood sunglasses, toting a dented aluminum teapot—can muster. Ours is not to judge another culture, older than our own, through the flighty superficial sentiment of people treated like modern-day British sahibs. If anything, I've noticed that in our

American eyes, we misinterpret that which we witness, basing our observations on a cultural naiveté. As citizens of the wealthiest nation on earth, we can indulge ourselves in a distorted view of what's fair and what's not. It's easy to pass a moral judgment from the lofty perch of what is, for now anyway, a position of global economic dominance. The thing we don't often understand is that we judge what we see on the fact that we wring for ourselves an unfair percentage of the world's resources. And we might not last. The plutonium caper itself provides the damning evidence of our do-good intentions and fly-by-night commitment. We'll do what's right, and then leave, letting those who were there before live with the results.

S. V. won't tell me too many specifics about his military career, and the ones he does I am not at liberty to divulge. But we do talk at length. He smokes, ashing the butts, their final acrid tracers of smoke, trail off crumpled white stubs, the brown ends stained with tar. They accumulate in the ashtray. The conversation carries on, punctuated as one cigarette becomes another, then another, then another until the tray is full. The smoke fills the tent hovering like a lingering ghost. We finish as the light dims and late afternoon gloom darkens the tent.

S. V.'s rank and his command of a Gurkha unit suggests, that he has fought in Sri Lanka, in J and K (Jammu and Kashmir, a hotly contested region in northernmost India where border wars and ongoing insurgency have claimed thousands of lives) and on the highest-altitude battlefield in the world—the Siachen Glacier. All that information I confirm later through research. I look up his decorations from a photo, bedecked in camo and medals, taken in our first meeting at the IMF. His chest ribbons later reveal that during

his long service he won, among other things, the Siachen Service
Medal, High Altitude Service Medal, Sainya Seva Medal in recognition of nonoperational services under conditions of special hard-
ship and severe climate, the Videsh Seva Medal for service outside
India—probably for a multinational service in Sri Lanka, a Combat
Wound Medal, an award for gallantry, and another for service in the
border war in Kargil.

I can only assume that so much war must have taken its personal
toll. People try to kill you, you try to kill them. If you are lucky you
kill them first and then someone pins a medal on your chest.
Nothing wrong with that—except that S. V. says, as if alluding to
an unspoken assumption, "When you have seen what I have, done
what I've done—something inside you turns to stone. Something
dies." That said, he takes a final puff, butts the cigarette, and
brushes a thick shock of straight black hair from the left to the
right. He then gazes out the tent door through the gray drizzle and
beyond—into the past.

That night, the snow—more like slush—drops unceasingly. It's
not cold enough to turn to blowing powder, instead, the mercury
hovers just below the freezing point, laying the snow in a thick
heavy blanket that sticks in clumpy masses. The cook tent collapses
in the middle of the night, burying Dipender and Gyan. They dig
out, illuminated by the pathetic beam of their cheap plastic flash-
light, which we quickly replace with our extra headlamps. The two
tube tents, provided by our agency—including Chuck's tent (he's
not in it now that he's sleeping with Sarah)—are squashed under the
pole-snapping weight. They look like squashed caterpillars,
stomped underfoot by Mother Nature herself. The mess tent also

crumpled, pitching over and folding as we slept. Our storage tent is half crushed under the heavy snow—a big orange Marmot dome tent, like a dead elephant. Breakfast finds us kicking snow from underfoot. Our cameras, gear, and bags of food and fuel are soaked and scattered about.

S. V. had a rough night, "I was lying in my tent, put a candle on, smoking a cigarette and I was getting all those nasty black bad thoughts in my mind, right from my family, down to this Base Camp and it's been raining and snowing for the last three days suddenly there's a nice gust of wind and the rock, holding my tent comes and hits me almost in the head."

There's a certain tension required to give an expedition lift off. That afternoon, Jonny sits, making another coffee/protein shake. He peels open the dark brown packet, spooning one, then two, then three, scoops of the rich brown powder into his coffee press. I can see the reactions of everyone sitting around the table—Mr. Hyper needs anything but more caffeine, especially when we can't go outside and burn off any energy.

Jonny grasps the coffee press—its green anodized steel emblazoned with a sticker announcing a product called "Chai Agra," a spoof on India's national drink and her national symbol (the Taj Mahal is at Agra). He grasps the press with both hands, curling the device inward as if embracing the apparatus. That's Jonny, physically encompassing whatever task or object is at hand. He does so with all his energy and attention.

Soon he's mixing the protein powder—a whey-based supplement handy to keeping from turning into high-altitude scarecrows. Five minutes later, Jonny is hunched over a steel cup, banging a spoon on the inside. He holds the cup on the table with his left hand and rapidly wiggles the spoon back and forth. The staccato ttrrrrllll . . . is like a speed-core version of an Old West dinner bell. S. V. says, "I've seen your type of guy in the service. The one's that just can't sit still and always has to be moving around." You can tell he's slightly annoyed as his manner always energetic and alert is subdued in an almost patrician resignation.

Sarah grins, asking in her direct to-the-point fashion, "Did you get yelled at a lot as a kid?" There's a knowing quality to the question.

Jonny pauses the beat for a moment, looks up with a big grin, "No, actually not really at all."

And the bad weather continues. Antsy, the next day Jonny prompts me to climb with him, unroped, up the gully adjacent to the sinister buttress of black rock towering for 400 feet above camp. We literally climb up a waterfall before grappling with vertical mud-soaked loose plates of balanced rock. At the top we plunge bare hands into snow, teetering for purchase above a surely fatal drop. It's just the thing we need.

We are spared more such shenanigans when the skies clear the following day after nearly a week of incessant pounding by the snow and rain. The weather breaks on September 19. Chuck, Sarah, Jonny, and I spend a few days letting the sun bake what must be a dangerously avalanche-prone snowpack on Nanda Kot. On September 22, we saddle up and start climbing, arriving at Camp I at 8:45 AM. That afternoon, under a hot sun, Jonny, Chuck, and I reconnoiter the next day's climbing route. By the time we reach a rotten band of rock to stash some gear, the sun has turned the snow into knee-deep mush. Jonny and Chuck continue up, exploring the most accessible route up to where the mountainside grows steeper. I return to Camp I, wallowing like a pig in the thick wet snow.

Sarah wavers. She has some intuition about what's to come, and she says, "I don't think I am going to go with you guys," adding, "I think I'll sit here and just enjoy the view." Part of her hesitation is common sense. This is her first big-mountain experience, and these peaks, in the land of gods and goddesses, don't exude that feel-good vibe of the hills back home. Of those other hills, she recalls, "I remember being in the Utah desert with my sister. It was one of those places where in ancient people went to give birth and it felt safe and protected. But not here." Staring at the snow-peaked panorama Sarah also had, "the feeling that I was not supposed to be up there. The three sisters Nanda Devi, Nanda Devi East, and Nanda Kot were saying we don't need you around and we really don't want you here—definitely not that welcoming feeling I've always enjoyed in the mountains." Part of it might be her female's intuition, as the Goddess on Nanda Kot, whose name literally means "Fortress of the Goddess," was saying, as Sarah later recalls, "You can come up here, but don't call me sister. You are not welcome here."

We three men unaware of the feminine dynamic taking place, sort gear in focused ignorance.

We opt for an early start—to avoid the midday melt that would slow progress down to an exhausting snail's pace. The alarm goes off at 1:30 AM. I try to ignore it, hoping no one else has heard it. Chuck rustles and sits up. There's no avoiding the fact that the day has begun. We set to the bleak ritual of melting snow, eating, and struggling into the dozen articles of clothing before stepping outside. It's still pitch black outside and very cold. Our breath condenses through our facemasks as the crisp snow crunches under foot. The vapor from our breath smokes in the bright white light of our head-lamps. In an hour we have the tents packed and after another half an hour, we start the frigid day, toes numb, even in our double layer boots.

As we pass the cache we stop to divide the gear we'd stashed yesterday. There's a rope, some fuel and food, plus other bits and bobs. Sometime during the night, Sarah has decided to go up with us. I turn to hand some items to her. Jonny stops me and says, "She's not feeling great so you should take these up." I'm a bit taken aback. This instance, like her snap decision to climb instead of remain at ABC, reinforces a guide-client mentality. I have to remind myself that we are acting as a team.

Dawn breaks. The mountains glow in the burnt orange of the rising sun. We make tracks up a slope that grows steeper with each step. It's one of those passages you encounter in the mountains that can be so innocuous when the conditions are good, as indeed they are right now. The snow squeaks underfoot with comforting regularity as your crampons bite the surface—a quiver of ten butter knives driving straight into Styrofoam.

I picture this terrain in bad conditions. If a storm were to blow in, this gentle rise would be rapidly transformed into a death-trap.

So what is it about avalanches that make them so unpredictable and so violent? Snow is snow, and to the untrained eye it presents a cryptic and benign uniformity. Unlocking its secrets is more art than science for what matters is what lies *under* the snow. What you can't see is what will kill you.

Picture this. You are climbing the same snow slope. It looks like a steep sledding hill the size of three football fields. It starts snowing. The angle is low enough to catch and hold the delicate flakes but steep enough to build an accumulation. The snow amasses. Details of landscape are blotted out as shallow hollows fill and humps and ridges are blanketed. Over several hours, the flurry compacts into a cohesive mass—the consistency of the plastic-wrapped brown sugar you see on shelves at your local supermarket. The mass grows. With each passing minute, the snow surface strains with hair-trigger tension—like a drumhead. Any number of things—a falling cornice, a sonic boom, a careless climber—can start the entire layer sliding.

Death-trap or not, you've decided to go up, and once the decision is made, there's no turning back. If there was ever a time to sense impending doom, this is it. Each labored step sinks your boots halfway up your shins. You are almost to the top when you hear a *whump*. You are conscious of a sudden change in air pressure, as if the earth has just exhaled. The ground begins to sinks, the solid white surface cracking and collapsing for hundreds of feet in every direction. You try to figure out where to run, but realize you can't. You are being carried downhill.

Things start off slow, almost gentle. There's the sensation of sliding but that feeling is contradicted by what you see. Your surroundings appear stationary, but it slowly dawns on you that the surrounding landscape is moving *with* you. The illusion ends when the acceleration hits. In a few short seconds, you are sliding faster than an Olympic bobsledder, blasting down the hill with a locomotive roar. If lucky, you'll have your neck mercifully snapped in the jumble of crushing blocks. If you have crappy karma, you'll survive, grinding to a halt as the fluid mass slows, molding itself about your body like molasses. Upon settling, the snow, liquefied by the intense friction of the avalanche, instantly hardens into something resembling concrete. Locked in a freezing vicelike grip now, you open your eyes, but it makes no difference, as it's pitch black. If you'd been fortunate enough to claw an air pocket in front of your face before the snow solidified, you might have bought another fifteen minutes of life. But without rescue, those slow minutes are worse than being dead. One avalanche survivor has spoken of her ordeal in shuddering, b-horror movie terms: "There's no one there to hear you scream."

The day wears on. We surmount a steep ice cliff as morning merges with afternoon. Gazing across the breathtaking panorama, I take in the alluring lines of Nanda Devi. She stands in the distance, beyond the terminus of the Lwanl Valley enclosed by knife ridges of snow and battlements of black rock. One by one, my three fellow climbers emerge now over the lip of the ice cliff. First into view is Jonny. He pauses at the edge to offer encouragement to the pair below. As he strolls across the horizontal snow leading to my impromptu belay stance, the others begin to emerge too. Chuck, followed by Sarah. They group up, well clear of the precipice.

With everyone now safe, I unthread the climbing rope from the belay device and unwrap an energy bar. My head throbs with the dull pounding of a body trying to compensate for the lack of oxygen by pumping more and more blood through my internal network of veins, arteries, and capillaries. I try to help things along by breathing deeply and forcefully exhaling through pursed lips. It's called pressure breathing. The idea is to increase air pressure in the lungs, thereby forcing more oxygen through the walls of the alveoli. I can't tell if it really helps, but it's nice to feel that I'm doing something. I gnaw another bite off the food bar, tearing the pieces off the tasteless mass bar before grinding it into an acceptable pulp. The muscles in my jaw are sore from the effort. Mid-chew I notice for the first time that clouds are rapidly filling the valley below.

The four of us hold a brief council to decide our next move. The time is coming up on 1:00 PM That's pretty late by mountain climbing standards, so we decide to continue just a bit higher before scouting out a place to spend the night. It will be an early morning wake-up followed by a very long day so we quickly opt for a sheltered spot fifty feet higher.

The terrain is rolling snow inclined to about an average of twenty degrees. A white blanket coats an underlying ice sheet that must be hundreds of feet thick. The angled glacier reveals periodic fractures where the ice, on its inching journey down the mountainside, has cracked, forming cliffs ranging in height from the 200-footer below, to 20 and 40-footers that pock the slope ahead. These cliffs are called seracs, and they are infamous for randomly collapsing, crushing anything unlucky enough to be below with wrath-of-God-like fury. Some have deep crevasses and caves at their base, leading into black and unknown depths.

Fortunately, not all seracs are prone to crumble, and we choose to pitch our two tents under a stable-looking escarpment maybe forty feet high. It's slightly concave and overhanging—steep enough to shed the snow that's starting to look imminent—but not steep enough to cave in on us. Through gathering clouds that are rapidly engulfing the very mountain we stand upon, I can see the slopes above, gentle and low angle. Somewhere about 500 feet higher is the saddle that marks the crest of the summit ridge. From that point, it's 2,000 feet to the top. The terrain looks safe to me. "What do you think about here?" I ask. Jonny says, "This looks like as safe a spot as any." Chuck agrees with a nod of his head. That done, we set to digging out platforms upon which to pitch our two tents. Our sheltering cliff is banded with layers of darker crystalline snow interspersed with solid white or blue ice. These display a frozen record of the seasons, layer upon layer, spanning the years like the rings in a tree trunk.

I struggle to recall a slide image Schaller showed me. As best I can recall, his picture resembles our current camp, perched as it is under an ice cliff—one in a series of such formations. The ever-changing river of ice, and ensuing forty-year interval make determining the exact location a comical pursuit—like surfing a wave at the same break. Same location, different water. Conboy's book describes Camp 2 as below "a particularly nasty feature at the 20,000 foot level known as the Saddle." Conboy also mentioned that Kohli was greeted with the same foul weather we now endure. "The sun was completely obliterated, and the onslaught of snow had continued almost without pause since the previous afternoon." The difference when compared to our situation was that Kohli was on his way down, after unsuccessfully attempting to place the sensor on the Dome.

In an hour, the four of us have the tents set up and the stoves going. Our mountaineering stove burns canned butane fuel. The other option, white gas, is nearly impossible to find in Asia. Our stove is called a Jetboil. It uses a rippled aluminum collar that retains heat for maximum efficiency. The beautiful thing is we get a full day's worth of melted water and cooking from each can of fuel. And before we are through, we'll need every ounce we carry.

After such a long day, it's crucial to melt snow and ice for rehydration. Today's 3,000-foot ascent is a respectable gain considering we've not acclimatized to this altitude. Going high in a fast push is nice but the downside is the effect of altitude. Everyone feels the effects and I am the worst of the lot and spend a bleak half-hour face down in our tent with my boots poking out the front door. I have that familiar debilitated feeling I've had more than once while climbing high. It's like a hangover that won't go away.

The snow grows in intensity. It's enough to require zipping the tent door shut. Despite the sheltering overhang above, the weather, growing worse with every passing minute pours frozen pellets of ice, called spindrift, into the tents.

Chuck recalls, "We got beaucoup snow . . . I was having claustrophobia issues in the tent compounded by the heavy weather (one inch of snow per hour). The need to stay dry prohibited forays into the outdoors." While taking a bathroom break in the late afternoon, Chuck begins exploring an adjacent crevasse, a garage-sized gash on the left hand edge of the ice cliff.

As I lie in our tent Chuck is joined by the others. After some discussion they opt to move into the gaping hole. It's not entirely uninviting. Upon entering the mouth the cave, the chamber opens up to the size of a living room, were your living room to have vaulted ceilings bedecked with feathery crystals and toothy icicles. The floor, a deep deposit of snow supported by god-knows-what, slants at thirty degrees. The chamber arcs back at the rear of the cave, necking down in the V profile typical of crevasses. The constricted passage continues for 20 feet before opening slightly and diving down for a depthless plunge of what might be 100, or 200 feet.

I rouse myself from my tent-bound lethargy and join the others in excavating two spaces for our tents. We twist in some ice screws—and string them with rope upon which we hang our garments to dry. Then we eat. Tonight's meal is soup with noodles, some tuna, and a scrap of salami.

Chuck wolfs his food, a portion made larger by my lack of appetite. It might have been overeating—Chuck almost displays a neurotic tendency to rely on food as a bulwark against fatigue and stress; to me, it seems like a compensation mechanism, for eating is no substitute for the experience or mental resiliency required by climbing—or the altitude. But during dinner, "I began to feel really bad," recalls Chuck. It might have a premonition of what is to come, for "I threw up everything from that afternoon in Sarah's boots." The vomit, a pinkish mix of fish-scented noodles will later need to be thawed with hot water, but in the interim, Chuck's crestfallen face reflects continuing nausea, or regret at having lost his evening's share of calories.

We are in bed by 8:30, and sleep comes quickly after the strenuous day. At 11:30, Chuck wakes from his fitful sleep with a start. The glow from the last quarter moon is diffused by the thick storm clouds shedding little light. As if suddenly aware of the pressing blackness. Chuck let's out a panicked, "Oh God!" He'd been dreaming, something dark and nasty. When he woke the exclamation was so loud that Sarah, ten feet away, heard the words. She'd also been sleepless for some time and was contemplating the long process of unzipping layers and struggling into a position to urinate. As it is, I'm awake and annoyed. I don't vocalize it, but inside I say to Chuck, *What the fuck. Shut up.*

"By some miracle I fell back asleep," says Chuck. "And I usually have to take my clothes off to get rid of the claustrophobia. This time I didn't." Though he doesn't undress, Chuck does completely unzip the tent door, a noisy, involved process of propping up one elbow, fumbling for the zipper, and straining for leverage against the reluctant tent fabric. That fact alone will probably save our lives. Chuck also debates taking another Ambien. He decides against that—a choice that might also have saved his life. Jonny snores lightly, in deep sleep as Sarah settles back into the prone position closing her eyes—like me trying to fall back asleep. I'm anticipating a long day tomorrow and rest seems very important. The open tent door bathes me in cold air wafting in unsettling wisps. It chills my head—I'd left my thicker hat in Base Camp—but I close my eyes, hoping for a deep unconsciousness that never quite arrives.

We don't know it yet, but the storm that now bears down on us with growing fury is the leading edge of a massive moisture-laden front blowing across the distant plains of India from the Bay of Bengal. As we lie in our hypoxic stupors, the front has already killed scores of people in flooding across the plains of India and will soon claim the lives of at least a dozen climbers throughout the Himalayas. We are about to be engulfed. In retracing the steps of the CIA's most ambitious and daring espionage venture of the Cold War, we four will soon be fighting for our very lives.

CHAPTER 11
THE AVALANCHE

It begins with a jarring *crack* that shakes the mountain and immediately builds to a deep bass rumble.

My mind starts its painfully lazy swim up from the dark blue depths of unconsciousness. I'm aware on some level that the rumble —now a roar—is coming to kill us. My eyes pop open. The cave is pitch black, but I can feel the air pressure change—I don't know it yet, but hundreds of tons of snow are rushing towards the entrance. The race is on. The inexorable slowly unfolds as I sluggishly shrug off my sleeping bag. Even as my body begins the race for survival, my brain, shaken from a hypoxic torpor, begins to sift the possibilities.

My movements seem slow—languid, like those of a passenger

stuck in a low-speed car crash—each moment stretched into a small version of eternity. The brain fumbles through questions in what seems like a criminally slow process. Did our cave collapse? Are we to be crushed, screaming under tons of ice? Is the whole mountain sliding down? Are we to end up in a broken tangle three thousand feet below?

In real time, everything is happening in fractional moments, and it's no more than a few seconds from the first blast, that a deafening hiss engulfs our shelter. Our team—split into two pairs ensconced in two separate tents—is perched on the icy floor of a narrow, downward arching crevasse with a ceiling of ice about twenty feet above. Picture two tiny nylon bubbles nested in a jagged stab wound piercing the sheet of ice that flanks our 22,000-foot mountain. Then picture a colossal dump truck emptying a mammoth load of quickset cement into the hole.

As the snow makes its crushing onslaught, I'm halfway out of my sleeping bag, torso through the tent door. I'm almost out as the first swell washes over me. Instantly, I'm pawing through a crushing tide that's the consistency of fine sand. It's like swimming through glue. The weight is incredible—a remorseless, crushing tide. Behind my shoulder, over the deadly roar I can hear Chuck yell. The only clear word is a drawn out "Fuuuck!" The rest is a nonverbal grind of consonants drowned as soon as they become audible. He's behind me by no more than one second—an interval that, in this race, might prove fatal.

As it is, Chuck isn't fast enough. It's impossible to see what's happening in the pitch-black rush of action, but as I make my dash to safety the rushing white waves bury him as he struggles to kick his legs free of his sleeping bag. The pressure of snow smashes the tent and wraps his body, pinning his struggling limbs in an irresistible embrace. Then, like cement, the snow closes around Chuck's head. His mouth and throat fills with suffocating white death—even as he releases that last desperate cry of someone who's losing a life-and-death struggle.

For a brief moment the deadly flow diminishes—like the trough between two big ocean waves. I make an instinctive grab for the ice screw. I vaguely remember fixing the screw into the blue ice ace above my side of the tent during the prior afternoon—an eternity ago. It's a good thing. As my hand latches the frigid metal, a second, stronger wave swells, and I pull myself up with one arm, right hand locked in a death grip on the carabiner clipped to the ice screw.

Having something to pull on makes the difference between treading the snow's surface and being sucked under. My stockinged feet gain the top of the moving mass as the tide slows almost to a halt. Then as fast as it all started, it stops. Billions of ice crystals pay obeisance to the laws of physics as they meet, interlock, and come to rest at the angle of repose.

As for the others, they're gone, washed down the chasm towards the black and bottomless pit.

> *"We just get by however we can,*
> *We all gotta duck when the shit hits the fan."*
>
> —The Circle Jerks, "When the Shit Hits the Fan"

CHAPTER 12

SWIMMING AND DIGGING

Chuck and I collect ourselves in the darkness. A few short seconds ago, the roaring tide had us swimming for our lives. It's only through some incredible luck that we stand in waist deep snow, clad only in our socks and thermal underwear. We can't see it, but by touch we can feel the heavy, almost grainy-feeling knee-deep avalanche debris. It's suddenly really, really quiet. Deathly quiet. The pitch black space presses in—very cold, very still, like the world's been smothered under a black quilt.

Upon waking, I had the certainty that if anything was ever going to kill me, this deadly rumble was it. I was lucky that Chuck's nightmare woke me barely an hour earlier. I'd not fully fallen back asleep, but was merely gliding through the translucent blue that precedes the dive into deep slumber. That's when the avalanche came and the race started. The feeling of doom was terrifying. At the same time, there was no loss of control, no breakdown, no reduction to a panic-stricken state. The fear was translated into movement, a frenzied struggle made almost pathetic in the face of the titanic, heartless forces at work. In those moments, the formula for life became beautifully simple—do what you can, and the rest will happen on its own accord. I had no choice in the matter. It was a glimpse into what we'll all ultimately face—death—the absolute loss of control, the equalizer of all humans, the inevitable moment when all you've become accustomed to no longer works. As I struggled, I had the vision of my fate—crushed under the debris of a collapsing cave, the solid roof of ice falling with abrupt finality. In that split second I imagined the irresistible force of thousands of tons of ice, crushing me, popping my skull, breaking me like a stick. Even now, I shudder. Worse yet, the thought crossed like lightning, I'd be trapped, broken and screaming, ice pinning me in the snow, the weight not enough to kill me outright, but enough to render my last few seconds, or minutes, or hours on earth, helpless, immobile, with no escape, except the relief of dying. I would have been so smothered that not even Chuck, who'd be right next to me would hear my screams. Nor I his.

I've had two acquaintances die that way and had at least a half-dozen others I know perish in avalanches or under falling ice. One disappeared under a falling serac that nearly took his partner's life. How his last moments on earth transpired, I can't say. I only hope the end was quick. Another lay, "screaming like a girl" for hours as his climbing partner did everything humanly possible, which was precious little. I feel like throwing up as I write these words—the acid bile rising in a helpless, uncontrolled spasm that, during the avalanche and the aftermath, I could not afford to feel.

While swimming out of the tent, those thoughts only served to add a frantic speed to my efforts. As I grabbed the ice screw with my right hand, I yelled back to Chuck, "You're gonna be okay!" It was strange. The instant I had the metal ice anchor in my hand, my entire concern shifted to him. In past close shares—and I've had at least three—I felt nothing but an overriding sense of self-preservation. It always bothered me how selfish it had felt, for whether it had been an avalanche, getting hit by rock fall, or nearly freezing to death, there had always been a, "better him than me" element, even if just a passing feeling. It bothered me so much so that this is the first time I've ever admitted it, even to myself.

I don't think Chuck heard my voice over the rumble and the white deafening hiss, but I could hear him yelling, almost a scream as the snow rushed over his head. I could hear the edge to his cries—that panicky note of someone facing the specter of mortality for the very first time. Chuck writes that it was "an angry yell. A yell of ultimate effort and rage, like mother earth itself is killing me. A groan of disappointment [and] the realization of an ultimate fear." Whether he heard me or not I couldn't tell. Chuck's later writes, "As my head cleared the entrance of the tent my mouth and throat immediately filled with snow. I started choking" Like the rest of us, Chuck felt the elongation of time, for "what seemed like an eternity was only moments, but those moments expanded so there was time for many thought—one oddly enough was how I was a C-section baby, stuck in the birth canal for thirty hours." But in a final desperate gesture, his right hand shot through the snow, grasping up into the cold air. It was the last part of his body to remain unburied as the avalanche dragged to a halt. At that very moment, my left hand reached back and grabbed the first thing it contacted—Chuck's outreached palm. We locked in an instinctive fireman's grip—each hand grasping the other's wrist in a death grip. Strangely, I remember his hand was dry and warm, the palm rough almost leathery.

Still clasping the ice screw with my right hand, I gave an adrenalized heave with my left. Chuck, his furry nylon fleece pants clumped around his ankles, ripped loose right as the snow locked in a final deadly embrace. He popped to the surface, heaving and hacking, fleece pants stripped down to his ankles by the snow's grip— like a guy getting the surprise of his life while lounging on the toilet. Snow dislodged and shot from his trachea. He gasped for air and managed some words, "You saved my life."

"No I didn't," I retorted. If anything, it's Chuck's fortunate claustrophobia that saved our lives. I had just acted out as anyone else would have done under the same circumstances. Still semiconscious after being roused by his anxious "Oh God" exclamation at 11:30 PM, I heard and then felt the first cracking report as the avalanche broke free. That was maybe an hour after being awakened. Had I been fully unconscious, my dash for safety would have taken a few additional and perhaps fatal seconds. That Chuck had also completely unzipped the tent door made the sprint for survival, one that lasted no more than a few seconds, successful. The arch-shaped tent door was constructed with the body fabric attached by a horizontal stitch across the leading edge of the floor. In order to get the air required to fight down his anxiety, Chuck needed to unzip the entire flap. The remaining fabric, normally secured, lay like a limp dog tongue in the snow. That left the door entirely open. Merely unzipping the door would have, under the best of circumstances (fully conscious and in broad daylight), taken twice the time.

After his 11:30 outburst, Chuck had miraculously fallen into a sound sleep. He woke, as if from a dream, to the first sprinkles of snow hitting his face. "How nice," he thought. "It tickles." Then reality dawned on him, as the snow poured in and he fought with his sleeping bag. "The pitter patter . . . transformed into a light pressure and then suddenly a force the likes of which I had never felt before." In a second, Chuck was pinned from the left side as he "clawed and scraped" on his hands and elbows. The avalanche, coming in from his side of the tent, pinned Chuck before reaching me, granting another split second to escape. Of those moments Chuck recalls "it was beyond terrifying, almost absurd. When the tent began to pin me I thought, it's all over—my worst nightmare—being crushed and suffocated. The force was indescribable—like having a hippopotamus steamrolling me."

"I felt like my life was being taken away from me again. It wasn't fair," he'll later tell me.

Now, knee deep in the six-foot berm of avalanche debris, there's no time to reflect. As it is, we are entombed. It's a visceral certainty rather than a visually confirmed fact. That makes it worse. I feel incredibly calm, the kind of calm born of the certainty that there are few things you can do—but what you must do is clear and simple. It's also the calm that comes from knowing that no human effort will alter the bigger picture. The roof could collapse under the weight of new snow. Another avalanche could come and tip the balance, or worse yet, inundate the entire cave like water filling a sinking ship's hull. Either event would leave us crushed or freezing to death. We have nothing on our feet except for socks and it's pitch-black. Our headlamps—as critical a piece of survival gear, as oxygen is to an astronaut—are buried under the snow. We are jumpy—senses at full alert—I yell into the darkness at Jonny and Sarah. My voice is shrill and edgy. "Are you guys all right?" The words fly into the darkness, flat and toneless. The new snow and sealed entrance suck the life out of the syllables. There's no echo and no response. I say nothing, but I think to myself, *If they aren't dead yet, then they are probably dying under the avalanche debris. And there is nothing we can do about it.*

It's a minor miracle that I was able to pull Chuck out at all because we are both blind as bats. We don't know it yet, but the double-garagedoor-sized entrance to our cave has been reduced to a former five-foot-diameter hole. The storm unrelentingly dumps outside. Light—neither from stars nor the waning moon—can thread into our hole, much less illuminate our predicament. Without gloves or footwear we will not be able to search for Jonny and Sarah. If they are seriously buried, we'll need a shovel. Without light, none of that will happen. Having some EMT training and being the first responder to two major climbing accidents, I understand the rudiments of triage. Our first need is to avoid becoming victims. For that we need light, then gloves. A shovel would help, as would footwear—even just our foam boot liners or an extra pair of socks. But that might be asking for too much.

We hear nothing from Jonny or Sarah. In my head, the clock is running as, from somewhere in my mental litter-box, I know that after fifteen minutes, the search for an avalanche victim usually becomes a body recovery. My secret fear is that they've been washed into the bottom of the bottomless crevasse. For us to mount a rescue in that situation would require more than just a light and some gloves. But that's beyond serious consideration at the moment. Chuck is tense, but controlled and deliberate. With plenty at hand to manage, he is detached from the predicament of our teammates, despite his intimate connection with Sarah. He later writes,

> I didn't think at all about Sarah and Jonny after the avalanche. . . . Selfish? Maybe. Maybe I knew I couldn't help them until we were better off? Maybe I didn't care? It is weird to just not think about my girlfriend who could be on the verge of death ten yards away. I don't know—I do know that I was focused completely on Pete and me and on our predicament. It felt very single-minded. Very focused, and at the moment, completely guilt free.

Oddly, a different question that always bothered him is answered in that moment. Having attended avalanche courses, Chuck had always wondered why slide victims, sometimes found a scant six inches under the snow, were unearthed with mouths and throats choked of snow. "I always wondered why they just didn't shut their mouths," Chuck recalls. At that moment in the cave, he realizes, "They couldn't close their mouths. They were screaming."

Right then, a scream pierces the darkness. It's Jonny. For an instant, I shudder, wondering if he's crushed and momentarily coming out of shock. The tone registers an angry "Fuuuuck!" It comes from below. It is enraged—or in agony. And for a horrid moment I think to myself, "I don't want to go down there," as I am picturing a mess of broken limbs and mangled bodies.

After a few moments Jonny yells, "We could use some help down here!" The words are edgy but lucid. I can't remember exactly what my reply was, but went something along the lines of, we are in no position to help right now. Kneeling on the avalanche debris—poised as it is on the angle of repose—there's nothing we can do. To venture down, blind and bootless invites us tumbling into the abyss and perhaps knocking them down with us.

We dig with our bare hands. It's an effort to kneel, pawing blindly at the snow, trying to get to the tent door that is now nearly six feet under the snow. The avalanche debris is set up like wet sand. The effort feels fairly hopeless as my hands go numb. I pause, placing my frozen palms under my armpits. Chuck takes over. He, like me, is starting to feel the wetness and cold penetrate his socks and underwear as the adrenalin loosens its grip. Another thought crosses his mind, "If I can't find my boots, I'll lose my feet to frostbite." What's startling is that he instantly accepts the possibility, and with no panic—not yet anyway. The rhythm of his digging doesn't cease.

"I didn't feel afraid. I was just waiting for it to stop," recalls Sarah. When the slide hit, she, like myself, had never quite fallen back to sleep. "I heard the crack, then the slide, then the snow as it came around the corner of the ice cliff and into the cave," she remembers. "Then we started tumbling. Besides trying to stay upright, there was nothing I could do but hope it stopped before going into the crevasse."

Jonny, sleeping naked except for a T-shirt, remembers tumbling with no sense of up or down. Both he and Sarah were encased in the tent, a translucent nylon shell that only moments before had provided protection. Now it could kill them. In the midst of the slide, the two tumble like rag dolls, the enclosed bubble trapping them, preventing escape, or even a desperate swim for survival. Jonny remembers, "I woke up to the tent collapsing around me, then rolling and sliding down in the darkness. It was like being caught in the spin cycle of a big washing machine."

Both were helpless to steer any course other than down the cave, towards the gaping maw of the bottomless crevasse. Even as Chuck and I swim for safety, Sarah is trying to stay oriented upright, almost like a sledder about to take a tumble. Jonny struggles with the snow-loaded tent fabric like a man wrestling a giant waterbed. As the snow slowed and hardened, "I felt like I was in a cement mixer," recalls Jonny. "I fought as if it were my last fight." Surprisingly enough, fear was not the overriding emotion. As with Chuck and me, terror was translated instantly into sharp awareness.

"When I woke up, at first I had no recollection that Sarah was even in the tent. It must have been only a few seconds, but they seemed stretched out for minutes as we tumbled. My first conscious act was to keep an air space around my head. I tried to keep my hands in front of my face—something I lost a few times in the struggle. Finally the tent fabric was pressed against my face like a mask, and I thought there was no hope. The seconds were passing like minutes, and I could feel the snow slowing and setting up like cement. It was then that I felt a tent pole with my hands. It was right in my face and snapped the pole like a twig and ripped the tent fabric open. Then we stopped moving. My head was just poking out of the snow."

With a "few big swimming motions," Jonny, whose chest was being crushed by the vicelike grip of the avalanche debris, ripped clear of the slide. "It was like breaking out of the womb with a tent pole," he says. Then, reaching down, he felt for Sarah's face. "I knew she at least had an air pocket," says Jonny. That's when he called for our help. Jonny, barefoot and naked in the snow was handed some clothes by Sarah, who was still buried, four feet under the snow. Then, with the light of a headlamp that Sarah had tucked near her body, he dug his tent mate out. It was then that he realized he had a pain in his chest. "I must have separated a few ribs in the fight to get out," he recalls. Besides that, Jonny has pulled muscles in his back, no doubt when he snapped the hardened aluminum tent pole in the desperate effort to cut his way out of the tent. Later, I'll try to break a pole, as in Jonny's case with my elbows by my chest, hands gripping and thumbs locked on the thin aluminum about an inch apart. Try as I might, I find it impossible.

Jonny and Sarah had tumbled to the bottom of our cave, under the irresistible force of the avalanche. They came to a halt very near the edge of the bottomless crevasse. Two feet farther, and it would have been over. They would have either died from the tumble down the slick rock solid walls of the crevasse or been hopelessly wedged, alive, but slowly suffocating as their bodies inexorably slide deeper into the crushing depths.

We dig, pawing with our hands—first with the light of one, then two, headlamps. I am desperate to get something on my feet as the numbness creeps through my toes and up my ankles. I have Chuck's headlamp. It was accessible—in the pocket sewn into the tent body, near where his head lay. Soon we've cleared the area around the tent opening, the tattered remains now a flattened yellow tube of fabric with snapped poles poking at odd angles like fractured bones. It takes all willingness I can muster to crawl under the six-foot drift to retrieve whatever I can find. I know my headlamp is somewhere in my sleeping bag. I also know that my boot liners were in the very rear of the tent pressed between the toe of my sleeping bag and the rear wall—to keep them dry. I stifle a gag as I crawl in the space, about six inches. I can barely get my head past the door. I try to push upward against the weight of the snow. It is futile. The useless thrashing prompts Chuck, fearing that the snow has collapsed, to grab my ankles and drag me from the tent. The words come fast "Jesus, Pete," he says, shaking his head.

Plan B involves hooking the boot liners with a ski pole. The best I manage is to rip the fabric of the liner with a thin screech. They are hopelessly wedged. It is frightening how the snow's weight is absolutely immense—impassive and unyielding. Finally, I clear more snow, this time hacking at the hard mass with the butt of a ski pole. I then tug both sleeping bags out, creating enough play between the snow and the stretched tent fabric to grab my liners. I slide them on my feet. Chuck still stands in stocking feet. His liners and boots, as well as my boot shells were set outside the tent prior to the avalanche. They are either buried, or swept down into the hole.

Though some of our crampons, harnesses, and technical gear are clipped to a rope, strung between ice screws, no one has recovered their boot shells. Without boot shells, we can't affix our crampons, nor can we keep our feet from eventually freezing. In other words, without boot shells retreat is impossible, and we can kiss our asses good-bye.

Sarah locates her down booties. She hands them to Chuck. She's a full size smaller and cram as he might, Chuck can't fit them over his now frozen socks. "By that time, I was ready to lose my feet—a small price for survival" he recalls. "But only a matter of time."

"Mind if I cut these?" he asks Sarah. The words don't register immediately as the request is a foregone conclusion. "Of course," she replies. Chuck cuts the cuffs. The nylon tears with a thin ripping sound and the down explodes, weightless fluff immediately absorbed by the carpet of fresh snow. He pulls the blue nylon booties over his feet. Now like the rest of us, he's bought himself time.

Using our hands and ski poles, we finally discover the shovel. Now the excavation begins in earnest. It's been hours since the avalanche struck, and the unspoken fear of another slide or a roof collapse is sublimated by the comforting task of digging. By 4:00 AM, we've miraculously located all but one shell, the one for Jonny's right foot. I join Jonny in the search as Sarah fires up the stove to melt snow. We are dehydrated, tired, the adrenalin worn off and replaced by a heavy-limbed fatigue. Our words—at first sharp and antsy—start to slur, then take on a sleepy torpor. An hour later, a thin glow appears at the entrance of the cave, a gap, now no bigger than the diameter of a coffee table. We can see that the snow, in its downhill rush was diverted at a right angle as it entered our cave. Had the entrance been parallel to the flow, we would have been blasted by the full force of the slide. If we had not moved inside the cave, it is clear that we would be dead.

As we dig, Chuck comments that it reminds him of the worst job he ever had, digging holes for concrete forms to anchor residential homes. He notes, flipping a shovel full of dense snow into the black hole at the end of our cave, "It seemed like we had a six-foot deposition depth because that's how far we're digging to find our stuff." He adds, panting in the thin air, "It must have been a soft slab avalanche because these chunks are kinda soft." That was a good thing. Without time to heat and refreeze, our slide didn't produce the big hard bone-snapping chunks and none of the refrigerator, microwave, or other appliance-sized pieces that might have battered us to death.

None of us are strangers to avalanche. We all ski and climb in Colorado, a state with the highest incidence of avalanche deaths of any in the United States. "In looking at the long-term statistics on avalanche fatalities, Colorado has about twice the number people killed than Alaska, the next highest-ranking state," So notes glaciologist Richard Armstrong of the Colorado-based National Snow and Ice Data Center. He adds, "While there is a lot of variability in avalanche fatalities from year to year, we have the dubious distinction of leading the nation." A good number of accidents claim outdoor enthusiasts—snowmobilers, skiers, and climbers. A closer look however reveals that fatalities are not always snowmachine yahoos or knuckle-dragging backcountry snowboarders straying from the resort terrain park. Sixteen deaths occurred on Colorado's *highways*.

Avalanches can blast downhill up to 200 miles per hour, about as fast as racecars in the Indianapolis 500. Despite generally averaging half that speed, it's still fast enough to usually kill by trauma, rather than suffocation. By the time an avalanche comes to a halt, the snow, heated by the friction of its own speed, melted into something like a liquid, and then refrozen. On average, avalanches claim more than 150 lives annually worldwide. The storm that's buried us, and another yet to follow, is probably skewing the annual average. Though we don't know it, as we dig for long hours entombed in the crevasse on Nanda Kot, scores of people are dying in snow slides across the Himalayas. On September 24, as we desperately dig for our lives, six members of the Sikkim Mountaineering Association are killed on a blunt symmetrical peak called Chomiomo on the Sikkim-Tibetan border. Chomiomo lies on the east end of the Himalayan chain in India at almost the same elevation as Nanda Kot. There, Indian climber Paras Mani Das—who summitted Everest in 1996, the same year of the Everest tragedy portrayed in *Into Thin Air*—is killed with five others including two experienced Sherpas. Two others are caught in the avalanche but escape with injuries.

They are a competent team. Besides Das, two are instructors from the highly regarded Sonam Gyatso Mountaineering Institute in Gangtok. Gyatso as you'll remember was one of legendary climbers on the CIA expeditions, and himself an Everest summitteer.

The same heavy snowfall burying Das and us, falls as rain in the lower elevations. Part of a late monsoon blowing off the Bay of Bengal, our storm is an indiscriminant killer, equally deadly to non-climbers. Landslides triggered by the downpour kill three members of a family in east Sikkim—a married couple and their eight-year-old son. Their nine-year-old daughter miraculously survives. News magazine *Outlook India* later reports ninety-seven deaths from flooding between September 21 and September 23, including three women washed away by flashfloods near a village we'd driven through during our winding bus ride to Munsyari.

Our own Khem Singh later describes the havoc caused by the storm as he leads a group through another area of the Indian Himalayas. As we are fighting for our very lives on Nanda Kot, the same storm pins both climbers and trekkers in their tents as Khem Singh escorts a group near Tapovan meadow—100 miles to the west of us. It's a place I've frequented during past expeditions—one of the most beautiful meadows in the world—a flat, stream-laced, expanse of boulders and wildflowers surrounded by dagger-like 21,000-foot peaks. When the storm rolls in on September 23, the heavenly meadow soon becomes, like our own camp, a hellish maelstrom of blowing snow and sub-zero cold. Even as we dig, Khem is giving food and shelter to a group of German trekkers at his camp while the storm rages outside their canvas tents. That evening a porter, who apparently considers himself indestructible announces, "I am a Garhwali. I am not afraid of this weather and I will go down now!" Despite the pleas of both his fellow porters and the trekkers, the man plunges off into the blizzard.

Being Garhwali is no guarantee of survival, not in the face of such fury. The porter is found frozen to death on the path down the mountain as Khem Singh and his group beat a retreat during a break in the storm. So deep and treacherous is the snow that the entire team has to link arms to create a human chain. Upon reaching safety, one of the Germans breaks down, tearfully thanking Khem Singh for saving his life.

The early morning slides by. Finally we locate Jonny's boot—the last missing item. An almost comforting light glows faint at the entrance as I pause in the snow, forcing down an energy bar. "Were gonna make it," I think. Part of me is ecstatic, happy in having again met what I've chosen to face since the first time I ever climbed.

But the snow builds outside our tomb. The flakes are fat and accumulate with the faint background patter—billions of frozen particles landing and melding with no regard for the human drama playing out beneath the mountain's glinting skin, now pale gray in the thin light of dawn. The surface that slid, a rounded ice dome perhaps a few hundred feet above us, is growing heavy once more, white flakes accumulating like powdered sugar. Pregnant with new snow, the Goddess is reloading her arsenal.

> *"One thing that comes out in myths is that at the bottom of the abyss comes the voice of salvation. The black moment is the moment when the real message of transformation is going to come. At the darkest moment comes the light."*
>
> — Joseph Campbell, *The Power of Myth*

CHAPTER 13
BURIED ALIVE

We sit and drink liter after liter of water. A hot drink would be nice, but we'd use up too much fuel transforming snow into anything but cold liquid. As it is, I'm thinking we have fuel for three or four days and if the storm carries on longer, we might be forced to risk a descent—something that could prove fatal. I know this because Kohli almost died in an avalanche somewhere below where we now lie. That was during the 1967 expedition. He'd been retreating in a hellish storm after reaching the Dome, SNAP sensor in tow. He and the rest of his crew—the Indian cadre, the Americans, including Schaller, Frost, and Prather, plus the Sherpas—were descending the same steep snow that we four climbed only yesterday. Kohli, at the front of the group was caught in a slide, generated by the fresh snow.

His parka hood and stocking cap blocked his hearing, and while the others yelled a warning, he was caught by tons of cascading death. Much like us last night, he was terror-stricken. And much like us, he was helpless. After being swept 200 feet to the very edge of a crevasse, he, like Jonny and Sarah, miraculously stopped before taking the final plunge.

If his (and our), situation wasn't so mortally serious, I could almost laugh out loud in fatigued hysteria. For next, I recall that the CIA team, having dragged the sensor to the Dome, discovered that they lacked the tent pegs and simple cable necessary to erect the device. Imagine that, after weeks of effort, some of the best climbers in the world arrive at a place so remote that a mere score of human feet have graced its icy surface. They've lugged up the 125 extra pounds of space-age nuclear-powered sensor that no doubt cost millions to design, produce, and transport halfway around the world. Only then, with the device parceled out in the snow, do they find themselves lacking a handful of household items to set the thing up.

I can only imagine the finger pointing and eruption of jabbering in Nepalese, Hindi, and English. You couldn't make up something so comic, so utterly wretched. Superpower hubris in the lap of the Goddess at 21,000 feet. Standing in all my clothes, boots on, draped with my sleeping bag, I stifle the chuckle. Jonny poking around in the snow nearby hears nothing. I'm far too tired to laugh. I also don't want the others to think I've gone over the edge. We lie, side by side, a few feet above the slope that leads to the mouth of the crevasse. Chuck and Sarah sit on an elevated snow shelf twenty feet up the cave, towards the entrance. They whisper in soft syllables, like lovers before sleep.

Suddenly, another rumble shakes the cave.

I stumble across the flattened snow to the opposite side of the crevasse, a place that at least seems marginally safer, a place that, if the snow should come rushing in, might afford the slim chance of swimming afloat.

Chuck and Sarah are up now, but there's a recognized futility in their actions. They have nowhere to go. They can't go down. Going up is also out of the question—that's where danger now comes. Chuck recalls, "I was looking for somewhere to run. But there wasn't anywhere to run to." Jonny rushes to their perch as Sarah reaches out, grabbing his arm. The snow is starts pouring in—as if someone had backed a colossal dumpster at the cave mouth, and then released hundreds of tons of cement.

Everyone freezes as another moment of doom arrives. There's nothing to do but wait. As the rumble shakes our crystal bubble, the entrance fills with a torrent of hissing white death. And just like that, the lights go out.

It's pitch black again. Transfixed and helpless, we hold our breath as the hissing subsides. The rumble fades, a freight train fading in the distance. Once again, our cave is dark, and the eerie silence engulfs us. There's a rustle of nylon as someone fumbles in the dark and switches on their headlamp. Jonny speaks first. He says simply, "Holy shit."

There's a hint of awe in his matter-of-fact pronouncement. The rest of us are dumbstruck or maybe just terror stricken. I can hear my heart pounding, once again anticipating with razor keenness, the roaring collapse of our cave, at last succumbing to the fresh burden, the thousands of tons of new snow. Chuck pants, the adrenaline pumping for the second time in six hours.

The seconds tick. We each in turn switch our headlamps on. As if by unspoken command, we instinctively shine our beams at the cave entrance. It's a shocking sight. What was originally a forty-foot square maw, lined on its upper lip with jagged icicles—is now a solid wall of fresh snow.

We've been buried alive.

Were this a Hollywood film, one of us, the shameless coward, the fainthearted girl, the villain maybe, would start screaming or crying, suffering a nervous breakdown. They'd need to be slapped or physically restrained or both. Then they'd collapse in a blubbering tearful heap. But this isn't a movie, and I have yet to see in all my experience something so melodramatic. The reality is, there's no bravado, nor any hysteria. This type of thing never fails to bolster my belief in the hidden strength in human beings. I'm a short-term pessimist, but a long-term optimist. And times like these—these all too real situations—does nothing but validate my faith.

But trapped in the cave, nothing more than a crack where the river of ice is temporarily peeling away from the mountainside, I almost wish we were in Hollywood. Someone could yell, "Cut!" and we'd take a break, maybe grab some coffee from the caterer and freshen our makeup. That would be important because we'd probably want to maintain our drawn and haggard look, like soldiers in a war film.

"You've got to be shitting me."

That's all I can muster. The sound is flat, the vibration sucked into the snow.

It's a predicament. At some point we will run out of air. That is not good, because we'll be dead. Eventually too, if we ever want to leave this hellish suck-hole, we'll need to dug our way out. No one jumps at the obvious, so with an almost perverse anticipation, I strip down to my Gore-Tex layers, grab the shovel, and crawl up the fresh apron of avalanche debris.

The snow is not quite cement, again more like brown sugar though a tad more solid. The shovel bites off chunks with slick tinny slicing sounds. The loose blocks I carve begin to fall as I dig a few speculative feet. I fight off the urge to heave. I bore deeper into the wall, biting my lip at the concern that the tunnel will collapse. Jonny comes behind as I disappear a foot at a time, pushing the snow behind me. He in turn scoops it back with his hands. The claustrophobia prone Chuck is relieved, later saying, "I sure didn't want to go in there and tunnel. I was glad that someone else decided to do it."

I don't blame him, for it's a grim, confined space. At first, I burrow straight into the mass. After a few feet, I begin gently tunneling upward. The air seems trapped and stale. Sound is dampened in the closed space, and in an instant I'm a kid again, stuck in a culvert or trapped in an abandoned refrigerator. I panic and suddenly paw backwards—doglike, bumping Jonny who is clearing the debris behind me. For a second he thinks, "The tunnel's caved in." He grabs my ankles and pulls me back into the cave.

"That's creepy," I say, panting from exertion and nerves. But in a few minutes I am back at it. The tunnel grows—five feet, ten feet, then fifteen. I back out once again, certain in my mind that the air at the far reaches of the long hole is stale.

As all this is happening, Chuck and Sarah organize, moving gear out of the way of the cascade of snow we're displacing.

I crawl back in with Jonny once again following. We've now completely vanished from the sight of the others. Only the muffled scraping sounds and the faint bob of our headlamps, growing fainter as we bore deeper still, mark our progress.

I'm on my side scraping at the snow. "How damn deep are we buried?" I ask myself. The words are spoken out loud, but they are so deadened, that for a moment I ask myself, *Did I say that out loud?* Jonny straightens out my mind. "Keep going, dude, you're doing great," he says, thinking I was asking him a question. "Yeah," I reply, with no particular conviction. I shove the blade deep at an upward 45-degree angle. Snow collapses on my head, and for a grim second I think, "That's it. I hope Jonny can pull me out." When the snow settles I shove again, arm at full extension. Debris showers down, then clears. A gray dawn breaks through the one foot-round hole. I've punched out like a baby chick who has escaping an eggshell. I'm nearly twenty feet from where I started.

Fresh snow blows into the tunnel. The air is cold and bracing—a relief, but a relief with a sting in its tail. Spindrift, tiny windblown pellets of ice hiss into the channel. They flow in waves, driven by the maelstrom outside. Visibility from the hole is about thirty feet. Beyond that, any details of the landscape vanishes in the uniformly white surroundings. The bass rumbles—mother nature's pounding subwoofers—of distant avalanches audibly mark the unseen cliffs on either side of our escape hatch. There's nothing to see and with the thick snow, the next slide is only a matter of time. I retreat, widening the tunnel. We savor the tang of fresh air.

A mile distant, invisible in the furious blizzard, the Italian climbers have prudently beat a hasty retreat to their Base Camp. Nanda Devi's east face, bombarded with avalanche, is a death-trap in the raging storm. Says Piera Vitali, an attractive twenty-eight-year-old female alpinist on the Italian expedition, "The avalanches made us worried for ourselves and for your team!"

Their concern was extended to us, "because we had seen you climbing up to Nanda Kot and placing the tents in a serac. That was when the weather start changing. We could not see you any longer and we hoped that you were able to get down safe."

But her worries were soon shifted. At 4:35 PM of the 23rd, as we move into the shelter of the cave, Marco Dalla Longa, the sturdy five foot eight inch tall expedition leader, steps out of his tent, gazes up at Nanda Devi East, and without warning collapses. The mountain, which that evening is obscured by storm clouds, is one that the brown-haired Himalayan veteran has fallen in love with. Dalla Longa has a lucid moment about ten minutes after collapsing, opening his blue eyes and recognizing the circle of concerned faces. But no more than ten seconds later, he falls into a coma.

"At this time, the Goddess was not happy," S. V. says later. It does seem that she's meting out all manner of harsh punishment across her domain. Dalla Longa is healthy at forty-one years old. He's fit and shows no illness prior to being stricken. Though the initial speculation points to a stroke, it seems that cerebral edema might be the culprit. The illness, caused by the swelling of the brain at high altitude, can be a fast mover. It's also the most fatal of altitude-related maladies and virtually untreatable in the field. When he collapses, Dalla Longa is wearing a T-shirt with a line drawing of Nanda Devi East emblazoned across the chest. He's quickly bundled up and Dr.

Rosa Salvi, makes him comfortable and administers oxygen. Despite all her efforts, Dalla Longa dies at 12:55 AM. He takes his final breath shortly after we get blasted on Nanda Kot.

S. V. is down in our Base Camp wallowing in the heavy snow, wondering what's become of us. He's still heard nothing of Dalla Longa's demise, and the last he heard of us, we were heading up to Camp 1. That was two days ago on the 22nd. For the Colonel, it will be a long and fretful wait. His journal for the 23rd reads, "No contact with Camp 1." On the 24th he notes, "Heavy snowfall starts pouring at around 2100 h [9:00 PM] on night of September 23/24. Poured through the night and day." He ends with, "No communication in spite of hourly call."

We can't get a signal on the radio inside the cave, and, frankly, we don't even try. It's dangerous just to go outside. I'm not kidding. Around 7:00 AM another rumble rouses us from our stupor. We've been lying around, resigned to whatever fate might be doled out. I'm exhausted from the stress and and a night spent shoveling snow. When a third avalanche roars to life, I can barely conjure up enough adrenaline to stand. Jonny, zipped up in his sleeping bag a foot away, at first hears nothing. His eyes are closed. He might be dozing.

Then, in a flash, Jonny, suddenly aware of the rumble, hops to his feet. He's still fully enclosed in his puffy orange sleeping bag—looking by all accounts like a giant inchworm. For a moment, the sight is comical. He's a big orange question mark, knees bent, arms pinned to his side, with only his head lending a human accent. He hops to the far side of the cave, like a man in a sack race.

I just stand there, leaden-limbed, resigned to whatever intractable fate might transpire. Then something beautiful and frightening happens. The diffuse gray light illuminating our cave fades as the snow passes over the door of our icy prison. It's like someone is slowly twisting a dimmer switch. Grey fades to black—nearly as black as when we were first buried. And the effect is breathtaking. As the snow steals the light, the ambient daylight from outside our cave, highlights the fractures in the ceiling. A tracery of bright blue appears—glowing where cracks in the roof are sealed by only the thinnest layer of translucent ice. The fractures shine in momentary contrast to the darkness within. I've barely enough time to exhale a transfixed "Aaaahhhhh . . ." Then the avalanche passes, the dimmer switch reverses, and the light returns as the snow overshoots our tunnel, flushing downhill leaving only a fine dusting of powder in its wake.

One could say that the Goddess, unleashing her fury, is as S. V. says, "angry." If she is indeed anger, then it's an anger tinged with mercy. Though she's pummeled us, she's also nudged us into the only place on the mountain where we'd be safe. Like the SNAP device on Nanda Devi, Jonny, Chuck, Sarah, and I have been swept by avalanche, into the perilous, yet paradoxically safe haven—inside a heart of ice. As I doze through the midmorning hours following the third slide, I feel a peculiar kinship with the inanimate Nanda Devi SNAP. It too is locked away at this very moment, buried in a similar flow of a few miles due west. Kinship aside, there's small comfort, because the Nanda Devi SNAP has been safely tucked away for four decades. We'll be lucky if we last four *days*.

Morning drags on, and outside our haven, avalanches sweep the slopes like relentless packs of killers. I recall that, despite their blizzard, the 1967 CIA crew finally humped their loads back up to the Dome where they successfully installed the nuclear sensor. They left it silently scanning the horizon for radio signals originating from deep inside China. I recall an image Schaller showed us of either Barry Prather or Tom Frost standing in front of the SNAP. Bundled in park hats and dark mountaineering glasses, it was impossible to recognize their features, even for Schaller. The metal box, perched like a TV on a pole and supported by guy lines, spent a full year less than 2,000 feet above where we now doze.

Another shot showed the collection of components, resembling a weather station or some weird postmodern sculpture collection. What I couldn't see in the photo was an inscription made by one of the American climbers. Either Schaller or Corbett in a cheeky parting shot (I can't imagine the devout Frost doing such a thing), "took a piton and scratched the letters AMF (for adios, motherfucker) into the side of the transmitter casing," before the climbers began their descent to Base Camp.

After operating successfully for three months, the device inexplicably ceased transmission. A team had to climb all the way back up to check out the problem. Turns out the SNAP had been covered in blowing drifts and the high-tech device needed to be shoveled clear. That wasn't the end of it. The same thing happened again at the end of 1967. The now proven unreliability of the plutonium-powered sensor was the final straw. By spring of 1968 the sensor collection had yielded no useful data. It was decided to end what must have been one of the most expensive and dangerous installment and maintenance jobs in the history of man.

And the device itself was worth a fortune. Today's RTGs add millions to current NASA project budgets ($50 million for each of the three RTG's on the Cassini Saturn probe). By way of an estimate, adjusted to 1960s dollars, that figure equates to more than $10 million. It must have caused a fiscal sigh of relief when, recovered after a thorough search and no small amount of luck, the Nanda Kot device was returned on a special flight to the United States. Its malfunction hinted at the possible fate of its lost counterpart on Nanda Devi. Unattended, the SNAP had been buried, fast merging with the mountain's ice cap. The nuclear heat melted a spacious cavern, which upon being opened by the recovery team, released a wave of warm air. And there it was, sitting in a spherical shrine of its own creation. A later account compared it to "a religious icon in a cathedral of ice."

The storm rages on. Chuck and Sarah huddle on a balcony. They are wrapped in their sleeping bags with the tattered remnants of the tent acting as a ground sheet—a millimeter of fabric between their foam pads and the snow. They talk, a low hum of syllables. It's as if our calamity has clearly delineated the unseen lines that steer our lives. Chuck has a new lease on life—his desire to live has been absolutely confirmed—for the very first time. Sarah needs no such affirmation, but even now, as they sit talking in low whispers, the bond is stronger. Chuck, the man who insisted on sharing the rope and tent with myself, now, in the most natural and unaffected manner, goes to his girlfriend.

They murmur, sharing whatever two people who love each other share, while living under the gun.

I'm not really interested in what they are saying. I have few, if any, voyeuristic tendencies and maybe under the circumstances I cannot fathom anything more interesting than my own internal dialogue. Or maybe I'm convinced that experiencing is the only way to really know anything. The trouble is, is that I've experienced all this before—at least three times.

One time, I was struck by rocks, free falling over a thousand feet from the summit of Half Dome. Some idiot tourists had pushed the granite blocks off the top and the missiles rocketed down, coming within a few feet. A direct hit by any of the half-dozen would have exploded a skull or torn an arm off. As it was, I was struck a glancing blow on the arm and face by one projectile that exploded a few feet above where my partner and I cowered. I bear the scars to this day.

That incident happened so fast there was barely any time to ponder the consequences. Not so for another near fatal experience. Over a dozen years ago, I got stuck in a rain and snowstorm, high on a ledge on El Capitan. My climbing partner and I sat on the narrow shelf for thirty-six hours, he in a hammock-like portaledge and I, lying in a puddle of ice water with little to keep me warm. My thin sleeping bag was filled with ammonia smell as I huddled in the fetal position. Later I realized that the smell—for I'd not pissed myself—was the by-product of cold-induced catabolism where, fat reserves depleted, my body began to consume its own muscle tissue to fuel the endless shivering. That kept me just warm enough to survive.

I literally prayed, over and over, "If there is a God, I want to live and I want to know what it is like to truly love someone." It was an odd prayer, honest and desperate to the bone. Surprising even to myself, who might have predicted something more cynical—along the lines of "Please save me, and I'll be a better person," or some such appeal for mere survival. The short story is that the weather cleared for a day, enough to climb to the summit and descend before the weather got even worse. I also got trench-foot in the process. But I walked away with my life and an explicit yearning that would haunt me from then on.

So while lying there, hat pulled over eyes, to shut everything out, I consider the low drone of conversation to be more significant in the fact that it exists, than for its actual content. In some ways, I don't even know what such a conversation could possibly be. What do two people who love each other say when a hundred thousand tons of ice might come crashing down at any second?

For some reason, I'm not too worried about dying. I just feel tired. It's as if death could give me what life couldn't. It could give me closure, real closure, the kind of irrefutable absolution.

Like everyone, Jonny is in his own world as the seconds tick. The moments become minutes, then hours. He, like me, spends much of the time lying in his bag in self-sustained suspended animation. Like the rest of us, the thought of death never fully departs for him. He remembers, "We had lots of time to think in the cave. At first I thought about the ice walls collapsing in on us, about the avalanches, the storm, about better places to be about my family, and what it would be like to never make it out."

Still, though, Jonny has a practical side unburdened by darker thoughts. He and Sarah take turns listening to *Harry Potter and the Half-Blood Prince* on her mini-MP3 player. It's the size of a cigarette lighter—a tiny island of escapist fantasy. Jonny recalls, "I remember the Potter book, and how it was a great escape to have the head-phones on." Later he shifts to the internal mode. "I started having fun in my own head, imagining things, designing stuff, thinking about what makes people tick. Someone offered me the headphones and I didn't want them. It felt like a breakthrough."

My headache pounds, feeling like some sadistic bastard is squeezing the brain tissue behind my eyeballs. The metaphor is close to medical reality. The headache is accompanied by nausea and fatigue, all symptoms of acute mountain sickness, or AMS. I've had AMS before, and it's not anything to immediately fret over. What I'm worried about is cerebral edema, in which the brain swells due to fluid leakage. I swallow Ibuprofen at regular intervals, but the symptoms linger and flare like an infernal tide in my body.

Going out to take a crap is a great distraction. We are all peeing in the very back of the cave, down where the black crevasse hole drops beyond sight. But dumping demands a trip outside. I get dressed, pull my boots on, and use a lighter to melt the frozen laces enough to string them through the outer shell's eye hooks. All told, it's a chore that takes a half an hour. I stagger towards the entrance. I notice some dizziness that might, without too much of a stretch, be interpreted as the beginning of ataxia. Ataxia is the debilitating loss of coordination—a sure sign of edema.

I blurt out to Jonny and Sarah as I pass, "I feel like shit. If this doesn't get better I'll need to go down."

Outside is a tempest. I kneel at the base of our sheltering ice cliff, now half as high as when we first camped at its base because of the fifteen-foot accumulation of falling snow and avalanche debris. I drop my pants in a process made efficient by years of practice. It pays to have toilet paper portioned out and ready, plus a clearly defined target area. The rest is, well—a natural chain of events.

Business done, I scrape a pile of snow over the mess and compact it so that the next latrine visitor has a clean toilet. I stomp the mess. The snow keeps compacting until, it punches through a layer, falling through a hidden crack in the wall. "Lucky thing I didn't fall in there," I mutter as I make my way back to the cave entrance.

Before ducking back into the hole, I ponder the chances of going down alone. If I made it two thousand feet—maybe two hours of down climbing—I'd be sucking 10 percent more oxygen with each lungful of air. I'd be safe, provided I didn't get flushed away by an avalanche. Given the swirling snow and distant rumbles, a nasty slide would be a high possibility. But I figure if things get bad I'll have to try. The others would stand a better chance, going down later after the storm clears. If my condition spirals downhill, I would become a huge liability for the others. People with cerebral edema rapidly become little more than clumsy, and dangerous, baggage.

For a moment, the high clouds part in the distance, revealing the proud pyramid of Nanda Devi, a disembodied tooth of blue and white floating like a fairytale castle. For a moment I feel like I'm gazing at scenery on another planet. As fast as they parted, the mists return, congealing rapidly into an opaque mass. I turn and return to the cave. I don't feel so bad. My illness feels more like a hangover, and the more I move, the better I feel.

DeAnn is writing me a letter. It's part of a journal she can share with me when I get back. She sits in Boulder, pen in hand writing on a piece of blank notepaper. We are thousands of miles and twelve time zones away, wasting away in our cave.

One week was hard. [the] first week I mean. I thought, how the hell am I going to do this? It sucked, still does. In the first week I talked to my imaginary Pete . . . People ask me a lot, "Have you heard from Pete?" It's sometimes hard. Nice they ask, but I find myself saying, "No news is good news." I also find myself sitting numbly in your home office chair. It's the place in your house I most identify with you.

On September 26th, I lie in my bag, trying to will myself to sleep. Sleep is a balm—a beautiful dim land where time passes free from the interminable, lingering wait. Eying the elongated chunk of ice roosting directly above like a rickety thousand-pound suspension bridge—it's hard to sleep. It's our own private purgatory—a haven and a prison. I keep thinking of how I'm tired of being tough. It's one thing to survive, it's another thing to thrive. What will it be like to take this experience and make it part of life outside the confines of these cold blue walls?

We'll know that soon enough. The next day at 9:30 AM, we push our packs through the entrance. The four of us emerge from the oval hole of our cave—four tiny dots reborn into the world. The skies are clear, and now, with only a few shreds of food and the partial remnant of a single fuel can, it is now or never. Jonny recalls, "It was time to leave and we were not sad about it. Heading down was a relief. My big concern was staying out of avalanche danger."

We got S. V. on the radio yesterday. He's been worried sick, calling on the radio every hour day and night. Our calls, made infrequently, never got through, perhaps as the result of the weather. S. V. noted in his log prior to our successful communication, "If they don't come down today or communicate by 1800hr [6:00 PM], then will have to go for a search till Camp I." I later find out that by the time we connect on the radio, he's afraid of the worst.

Chuck is happy. More relaxed than in the last few days, he says, "No more worry about the ceiling collapsing, no more worry about an avalanche closing us in. No more worry about where to go poop safely."

I look at Chuck, his eyes glowing blue and happy, ready to face the challenge of a new day. "Well, looks like you'd rather live than die after all."

The air is biting cold, enough to cause a coughing fit upon exiting the cave. Oddly, a storm's final passage is usually the coldest part of the weather cycle. When a blizzard dissipates, the clouds no longer remain to retain heat.

The sun is warm, however. Even behind our glacier glasses, we blink. We look like extras in *The Dawn of the Dead*, our faces coated with zinc oxide, the pale gluey paste smeared like bad makeup. Chuck wears a balaclava with the lower mask and neck gaiter pulled up, a dorky black stovepipe jutting hussar-like from his head. We tie into each end of one of the thin purple ropes. Jonny and Sarah do the same with our other rope. We start down, boots punching through a foot of light powder snow laid over a solid base that crunches with each step.

Sometimes we punch through to our thighs. I'm not sure what the easiest line down is, so Chuck leads diagonally across, dropping over a rolling crest, terminating in a 60-degree slope. The slope, perhaps 150 feet in length, ends abruptly, dropping from sight as it plunges off the band of vertical ice cliffs almost 200 feet high.

After being stuck in a tomb for four days, the vast panorama sucks our breath away. In a 250-degree arc, we can see past Nanda Devi, clear into Tibet and into Nepal. Chuck gingerly drops over the crest onto the steep snow, the vertiginous exposure adding to the tension. If the slope should decide to slide, we are gone. Chuck diagonals, cutting the slope down and to the right, seeking the safest line through the vague dips and imperceptible eddies in a hidden mine-field. I follow each and every footstep, maintaining enough distance to keep the rope snug to Chuck, but not tight. I have my ice tool in my right—uphill—hand, the idea being, that if he should fall or start a slide, I'll plunge the tool's shaft into the snow to stop us. I'm glad he is going first. Over a dozen years of backcountry skiing has taught him to diagnose the subtleties of perilous slopes like this—it's a level of experience I as a climber cannot begin to approach.

There's a slight horizontal shelf skirting the dizzying rim of the ice cliff. Chuck zigzags back left, halting at a slight gap. I follow his steps as he pulls the excess slack from the rope, traversing right, then back left. As I arrive by his side, I glance up—our tracks have formed two sides of a right triangle. Jonny appears, followed by Sarah, a hundred feet behind. They are two dots, following an ant trail of pocked steps, orange and red jackets highlighted against the broad field of glaring monochrome white.

Jonny arrives. I stand on the far edge with Chuck between us. There's none of the hoped-for ice to anchor ice screws, so we perch, unanchored at the edge of the precipice. It's a 100-foot free fall to where the lower slope begins—in itself a near-vertical sheet of ice blanketed by a thin layer of snow. Beyond, the mountain falls away for several thousand feet, an expanse of white, broken with intermittent ice cliffs. Our plan is to rappel, then traverse hard left to regain the ridge we climbed four days earlier. Until we gain the ridge, we are exposed to avalanche. It's an imminent threat made all the more likely as the sun bakes the slopes, melting the fresh snow into a dense layer whose growing weight might spontaneously erupt into a lethal slide. We are running a very real gauntlet as Chuck notes, "I don't like the fact that the longer we hang out, the more these slopes are exposed to the sun." He gestures with his ice axe in a broad arc encompassing the terrain above and to our sides.

There's something I love about the tension of these moments. There's something so real, so immediate, and so alive. Pounding an ice axe into a shelf of hard snow I've cleared, I feel that seductive power of someone who knows what he is doing and why he is doing it. Despite the fear and fatigue, it is in these moments that I am sure I made the right choice—to do what I love, and to do it the best I can. Implicit in that feeling is the absence of subjective morality, irrelevant emotion, or the matrix of artifice through which we filter the majority of our actions. To myself I wonder, *Is this is what they mean by "self-actualizing?"*

Right then, a rush of snow comes to life. Sarah, has triggered the slope, just above and to the left of where the three of as stand, exposed and unanchored. A field of snow bounded by our traversing tracks releases with a hiss, building into a rolling wave. There's that familiar acceleration of mind. I calculate the odds of surviving the drop below. The notion treads the borderline of the absurd, but in a very clinical and detached assessment, I decide that it might not be guaranteed fatal.

"The snow gave way and I slipped in the moving snow," Sarah

recalls. "It was terrifying. For a moment I was afraid I'd killed you guys."

Mercifully, the avalanche is small and passes to our left. It's a surface slide of lighter powder that dusts us on its way by. It flies over the lip of the cliff, strikes the slope below and dissipates—the residual debris vaporizing, melding with the vast white of Nanda Kot's flanks with a static hiss. Chuck, Jonny and I shoot each other a look, but the expressions are all blocked and distorted by hats, zinc-oxide, and mirrored glasses—high altitude masks. It's another close call.

If anything, the fact that Sarah's weight (and she certainly does not tip the scales any heavier than either Chuck, Jonny, or me), when placed in the same footsteps as the previous three, triggers a slide, points to the unpredictability of avalanche.

Predicting slides is like black magic, more an art than science. They generally occur when the weight of an upper snow layer breaks the bond with whatever holds the mass in place. That can be a lower, deeper layer of snow, ice, rock, or the ground itself. Predicting that type of hazard is like trying to predict the weather, an informed guess at best, a total shot in the dark at worst.

Sarah arrives. She's shaken. Later she recalls her premonition at Camp I when she questioned whether to even attempt Nanda Kot. "Going down I said over and over, just give us the chance to get down with our lives," promising, "If we make it down, we are not going to go back up."

How shaken she is, I'll only discover later, but for the time being, there's a lot on my plate. To rappel, one must thread a rope through an anchor, whether that's an ice screw, nylon sling, or a few pieces of rock climbing gear. In this case, there's none of the above, since what's available is only snow, and none of it is firm and dense enough to create the fool-proof anchor I'd like. Still, what I create is sufficient, two ice axes pounded straight into the snow, shaft first, looped with a nylon sling that's set up to equally distribute the load between the two. The "load" in this case is me. With no discussion, I automatically nominate myself to go first, a crash test guinea pig. If the anchor pulls, I tumble for a hundred feet, slam the ice face and take a big ride for a few thousand feet. I ease onto the rope, grimacing at the anchor distastefully, as if daring it to pull out. Though it's never easy to go first on a dubious anchor, I am past fretting over the pros and cons. We need to move fast.

Moving fast with four people on a technical descent is no mean feat. I'm not there to witness it, but it turns out that Sarah, overwhelmed by the stress and fatigue, especially after accidentally triggering the avalanche, faints at the stance. Jonny says, "She wasn't looking too good there and then she blacked out. I had to hold her after Pete rappelled." Her faint spell lasts about fifteen minutes. She describes it as "like really bad vertigo, like I was hungry and hadn't eaten." Whatever the cause, Sarah recovers in time to rappel to where the rope ends—a platform we've kicked in the snow and placed two ice screws as an anchor. It is a tremendous effort, especially when one considers how overwhelming the situation must be for a first-timer in the big mountains. I reward her courage with an accidental sock in her nose with my elbow, while I'm removing a glove. It's a wonder Sarah doesn't break down and cry right then and there.

It's taken both ropes, tied together to reach the bottom of the ice cliff. As the last to come down, Jonny, rather than sliding safely down the rope has to down climb the entire two hundred feet to our stance. The upper section—rotten vertical ice and steep snow—would provide a stout challenge to the weekend warrior, armed with the latest technical ice climbing tools. By way of explanation, a technical tool is a short, meathook-shaped implement a little longer than a framing hammer. These purpose-made tools tackle steep terrain the way a Ferrari tackles curves—ideal for what he now tiptoes down. But as it is, Jonny's been left with only one technical tool and a regular mountaineering axe—better for pedestrian snow walking than real climbing. Watching Jonny painstakingly climb down the face with his inadequate gear is like watching someone tee off with a baseball bat, except if he falls, he'll break his legs, or get killed.

But Jonny arrives safely, grinning like a kid who just stole some candy—and didn't get caught. He then leads off to our right, rapidly disappearing around a shallow snow ridge. We follow, and with that we've successfully skirted the most dangerous passage.

Hours later we slog down slopes loaded with waist-deep snow. Wisps of cloud streak overhead as a rhythmic thump, thump, thump vibrates through the air. A helicopter chugs below, headed down valley. For a moment I think we're being rescued, but later we'll discover that the Italian team is being evacuated. Still descending to safety, we are unaware that Marco has died, or that the helicopter made a pass of our last known whereabouts, in a vain search for our bodies. Swallowed in our icy tomb, we were as lost from the inquiring eyes of man as the SNAP device itself. Unlike the SNAP, we've been released once more to the world.

We arrive in Base Camp just as the last rays of the setting sun gild Nanda Devi East. The molten lines fringing the mountain cool, then fade, leaving only a stern silhouette as we stumble into the welcoming embrace of friends.

CHAPTER 14

NANDA DEVI

Moments of complete repose are rare. That much we all get to enjoy for the next few days as we bask in the hot sun, eat good food, and play hours of cards—in this case, something S. V. calls "capture the tens." It's a bit like hearts, with the idea being to acquire as many of the tens in the deck as possible.

From past experiences, Jonny and I have a psychological box into which we can put our harrowing adventure on Nanda Kot. We've chosen our lifestyles, and long ago we both accepted such risk as part of the cost of climbing. Chuck, and especially Sarah, haven't the experience or background to shake the ordeal.

Sarah retires to her tent after getting down. Chuck vacillates, never verbalizing a direct wish to either go back to Nanda Kot or follow the plan we'd discussed as a group. Earlier, Jonny and I talked about attempting the East Face of Nanda Devi East, while Chuck and Sarah would either attempt Nanda Devi East's South Ridge or at least climb to Longstaff's Col to gaze into the Sanctuary. As it is, we have scheduled 36 days in Base Camp, of which we have spent 21 days in two attempts on Nanda Kot or waiting out bad weather.

Jonny and I now have to face up to the very real exposure to the same risk we just stared down, but this time on a bigger, badder objective. Somehow, it is lost on Chuck that venturing to the Sanctuary rim is as critical as any piece of the expedition.

It is a dynamic of the ever-shifting sands of an expedition. The fact that Sarah is spent, deprives Chuck of a partner. The fact that Gabe bailed out in the weeks prior and S. V. is content to stay in camp doesn't help. It came as a complete surprise to me that Chuck later feels deprived of another shot at Nanda Kot. The final arbitration comes when Chuck falls ill after we depart. From my perspective, gauging the level of stress he's experienced and his overall level of discomfort and anxiety, it is no surprise that he falls ill. As an experienced alpinist, it takes every iota of determination plus some prodding from a redoubtable Jonny, to tackle the next adventure.

Adding in the post-Nanda Kot rest days, we have about ten days to do something. That realized, Jonny and I pack up to climb to Longstaff's Col and check out the South Ridge. Weighing the risks, and risking the Goddess's wrath we depart in the chill dawn of October 3rd, four days after stumbling down from Nanda Kot.

In our packs we carry a sleeping bag each, an ultralight nonwaterproof tent patched and battered from the Nanda Kot adventure, plus food for five days that we hope to stretch out to seven if we get stuck in a storm. This for a peak nearly 7,500 meters, or almost 25,000 feet high.

Our fuel situation is laughable—three cans, versus the seven we had at Nanda Kot Camp 1. Our technical hardware is cut pretty thin. Instead of the barely adequate 8.8-mm diameter rope we carried earlier, we are carrying an absurdly skinny 7.7-mm rope—a very flimsy cord that wouldn't catch, in one climbers words, "a falling interest rate." In other words, we are taking less gear for something much higher, much harder, and—with over a half dozen recorded fatalities—much deadlier.

Walking in the predawn across the moraine, we carry with us more than our 30-pound rucksacks. A day after returning to Base Camp, we spoke with the field manager for the Italian team's Indian travel agency. "Please, please, do not go to Nanda Devi East," he implored. The twenty-one-year-old Karum Verma, having already witnessed Dalla Longa's demise also saw their Indian Liaison Officer take a near-fatal plunge. He reveals that Dalla Longa had been warned to steer clear of Nanda Devi East by none other than the head priest at the Nanda Devi temple in Martoli. In an eerie foreshadowing, the priest had intoned, "The Goddess does not like people standing on her head," adding prophetically, "One person from each expedition to attempt the peak will surely die." Later, my research will discover that the priest wasn't too far off. The 33 expeditions to both summits have claimed a recorded total of 14 fatalities (including Dalla Longa). That's not counting fatalities taking place on the approach in and out of the area.

Whatever the numbers, Jonny and I cannot even offer the Goddess a religious ceremony, or *puja*, since the priest in Martoli is gone for the season. We are left torn between our trepidation and our desire to pay homage. The compromise is to go to Longstaff's Col and see if the vibe is right to carry onward, up the South Ridge of Nanda Devi East. Sarah is worried later saying, "I dreaded your departure right after what we experienced on Nanda Kot. I sensed another disaster on the way."

Midmorning finds us at the Italian Camp. Once a village of tents in a wide bucolic valley with short-cropped grass and a meandering stream fed by Nanda Devi's snowfields, it housed fourteen climbers and a half dozen others only a week prior. Now it's a ghost town, buried under a foot of new snow that so far has prevented the porters from recovering what's left—two forlorn tents, the cooking shelter, and a blue canvas mess tent. Mice infest half-eaten bags of rice and flour, contrasting with the neatly packed and stacked red duffels and blue plastic drums of the Italians awaiting the human shuttle back to civilization. The place is haunted, the trampled snow is littered with empty fuel cans, food wrappers and some tell-tale emergency oxygen bottles bearing mute testament to the desperate efforts to save Dalla Longa's life. In the flat circular space of exposed dirt where Dalla Longa's blue nylon tent stood, a crude cairn is capped by a sandy plaque of yellowed rock. It bears the inscription:

Marco Dalla Longa
30. 12. 1963
24. 09. 2005

A day later we stand on Longstaff's Col. It's a grueling climb through deep snow and steep technical climbing to a knife-edged ridge dropping with a tremendous sweep on either side. There's barely a flat spot big enough to pitch our tiny battered tent, and it takes hours just to excavate a tent platform. It's our first glimpse into the mythic Sanctuary.

Nanda Devi stands in all her glory, laid out in such resplendent beauty that no picture or words could do her justice. Were we to be climbing the mountain itself we would not have such a stunning, awe-inspiring perspective. I can clearly see the ripple of the glacier and moraine that curves in tortured oxbows at Nanda Devi's base. Somewhere down there is where the SNAP-19 came to a final rest. Like a sluggish river, the glacier has carried the device perhaps a half-mile down valley. It must be in the glacier, for the three follow-up recovery parties found no surface traces despite their systematic, painstaking grid search assisted by helicopter surveillance, thermal sensing, metal detectors, and hand-held neutron counters. The neutron counters were a nice touch, but just like the coolant in a nuclear power plant, water—in this case glacier ice—is nature's most common and effective neutron absorber, effectively shielding the plutonium from discovery. Recalls Schaller, "We did use a Geiger counter across the bottom of the glacier looking for radioactivity, finding a few positive readings when the Geiger counter went shooting off and we were anxious and thought we found it." The readings were an anomaly. Though the neutron count spiked to two hundred times the norm—attributed to defective counters—the results were inconclusive. "We dug, dug, dug," says Schaller, "and we didn't find anything."

The CIA search team even used some ingenious, albeit ineffective, low-tech means to search for the device. Schaller showed me a picture of their jury-rigged hydraulic system funneling glacial melt water through linked sections of a tan fire hose. The idea was to blast loose rubble from the SNAP's potential lodgment, "like the early miners in California looking for gold." The result was as funny as it was pathetic. His image displayed a man holding the brass nozzle trikling water. The thin flaccid stream was about as effective as pissing on a hillside. "It just seemed like a hopeless thing to do and we all kind of laughed and gave up on that idea," says Schaller.

Two days later Jonny and I have gained almost four thousand more feet, climbing some of the hardest technical terrain I've tackled in the mountains. Jonny is in his element, climbing shattered shingled rock, bereft of its usual easy-to-climb mantle of snow and ice. The ridge leading to the summit is a tortured rib of endless crumbling rock draped with many thousands of feet of tattered rope, some dating back to 1951.

After three days of climbing, the rarified air reduces our oxygen intake to less than 40 percent of what's available at sea level. My mind, warped by hypoxia is crowded with a cast of *Loony Toons* characters, and the act of moving upward is accompanied by a zany internal chorus.

It's clear in all directions. At 23,000 feet, the sky takes on a layered range of hues. The horizon, where the distant snowy peaks meet the sky, begins as pale blue, growing ever darker until, if one were to stare straight up, the heavens are nearly black—the firmament of space.

Very early the next morning, we melt ice with our last can of fuel before launching into the pitch-black night. The temperatures are around minus 40 degrees, and it's not until the pale dawn blooms into full sun that we can feel the blood warming our toes. The climbing is steep, plenty of 70-degree ice with short vertical steps of hard quartzite rock forcing traverses that skirt precopitous drops of many thousands of feet. By early afternoon, we confront the last barrier between us and the top of Nanda Devi East. It's about 700 feet above us. It's the highest I've ever climbed, and the aura of the great mountain and the harsh, inhuman environment promote equal parts elation and nervous tension.

Jonny and I have drawn level to Camp 4 on Nanda Devi. We gaze across at the spot, which, though little less than two miles distant, is clearly delineated in the crystal air. I can see where the SNAP was abandoned, a slight depression in an otherwise flawless expanse of snow and ice that proudly rides the crest of Nanda Devi's South Face, two thousand additional feet to the summit pyramid. Dog tired and sucking the thin air of 23,700 feet, I find it nothing short of incredible that Kohli's CIA team managed to get the sensor to this altitude. I can see the fall line of the device, tracing it with dry blood-shot eyes to the glacier. Somewhere, 7,000 feet below the SNAP still rests, its nuclear heat destined to burn hot, hundreds of years after my time on earth ends and all memory of that passage fades.

In early September 1966, the energetic and hard-driving Schaller climbed from Camp 4 on Nanda Devi to her summit. Due to the secrecy, his ascent, to the 25,645-foot summit was never reported until nearly four decades later. Accompanied by Tom Frost as far as Camp 4, Schaller set off alone up the tricky snow and icy rock to achieve the most unheralded ascent by an American climber to date. He nearly lost his life in the process, slipping off a short rock cliff below the summit and falling into a patch of snow with thousands of feet of open air below. Standing on the summit was a deeply moving experience—and one for which he would gain no accolades until now. "The feeling of being on top was—well—I can't describe it in words—it was a spiritual feeling," he remembers. "It was spectacular. I felt like I was part of the mountain."

One the way down Schaller was saved by his faithful friend Tom Frost. Frost who had passed on the summit bid out of respect for the guidelines set down by the CIA, had waited patiently above Camp 4, for Schaller's return. "I stumbled a little bit just before camp. We had our headlights on at that point as I remember. I would have fallen 3,000 feet to my death had he not been short roping me," Schaller remembers. "That stumble frightened the hell out of me. I will never forget when he tightened up on the rope and pulled me back from what probably would have been a fatal slip."

Recalling that, Jonny and I set out for our own summit. Jonny leads an extremely difficult 200-foot section of rock, laced with thin wisps of gray bubbly ice. Past accounts describe copious snow and climable ice not present in this era of global warming. Back at the local cliffs, this passage would rate a respectable grade of WI 4 and M5. Translated, that means that the pitch demands vertical ice climbing with tricky scratching up bare rock, teetering with metal crampon points on small door-jamb sized edges, with ice axe picks slotted into quarter-inch wide fissures in the rock. At sea level, the performance would be respectable in any experienced climber's book. At 24,000 feet with a heavy pack and a glorified piece of dental floss to stop a fall, it's nothing less than heroic. To follow, Jonny winches me up as I shamelessly grab what little intermediate protection anchors he's placed.

The weather is changing. Earlier, we could look out and gaze over the vast sweep of India, awestruck as huge thunderstorms pounded the lowlands, the brown and black clouds illuminated by flashes of lightning. We are so high this morning that we can see the curvature of the earth, extending into Tibet, Nepal, and the Gangetic plains, hundreds of miles distant. Now, the clouds have closed in, wrapping us in a brisk wind that carries with it the threat of snow. As if to deny the deteriorating conditions, I say, "We have this in the bag," as we stand below the last step that bars us from the final easy snow walk to the summit. I add, "This will be the best thing I've ever done in the mountains."

The steep slope above is deceptively desperate. The recent snows have transformed into a quicksand-like mix of granular powder. Wallowing up the crud is like battling a near-vertical treadmill. The clouds thicken. I am so focused on the climbing that I don't even notice the snow start to fall. The wind whips the particles, lashing the face above. Though I am mere feet from the final summit ridge, the slope is obscured by the driving blizzard. Jonny yells something unintelligible over the gale. It's getting late in the day and our fast and light style—to save weight we didn't even bring helmets—leaves no room for even the slightest setback.

Twenty-four thousand feet above sea level, we have a heated discussion, before we agree to retreat. As it is, we endure an epic descent to our last bivy spot, over a thousand feet below. A few hours into our descent, the skies miraculously clear. We gaze wistfully at the summit, now radiant with the light of the setting sun. "It might as well be Mars," I comment. There's no going back up as we've given everything for our rapid ultralight push.

We are virtually out of food and have only enough fuel to last one day at most.

Hours later, with the western sky still outlined by the blood-red glow of the setting sun, we became separated. Jonny opts to rappel, 80 feet at a time on our single climbing rope. I downclimb by headlamp. Jonny wrestles with multiple rappels, some off single sketchy rock anchors slotted in the occasional outcrop. His path of descent teeters on the very edge of the 7,000-foot high East Face, the same wall the Italians failed to climb. For my part, I gingerly crab my way down, balancing on a few millimeters of steel embedded in the hard bulletproof ice. My world is reduced to the ten-foot radius illuminated by my headlamp. At one point, my bulky insulated pants, carelessly donned during the storm, begin to slip, creeping down my legs and threatening to trip me. When I first pulled them on, my bulky mittens made fastening the waist button impossible. Every time I stripped my hands down to liner gloves my fingers grew numb, threatening frostbite. Now, hours later, perched on the edge of the Sanctuary, a fall would be fatal, thousands of feet of tumbling over ice, and skull-cracking rocks. I plant my tools, balancing on delicate crampon points as I reach down to pull my pants up. The headlines flash through my dopey brain, "Fatal Bathroom Visit—Asian Climber Found Dead with Pants Around Ankles."

Hours later Jonny and I reunite, set the tent up and crawl in our sleeping bags. I am exhausted. The next day, we descend 9,000 feet to Base Camp, through an afternoon storm that dumps snow for several hours. We both run on autopilot, honed by years of similar grueling experiences. We arrive in Base Camp at 11:45 PM, after six days on the move. The remaining few days of our expedition, are crystal clear—sunny, warm, and absolutely maddening. As author and Devi devotee Bill Aitken would later comment in Delhi, "Looks like the Goddess gave you the brush off."

We finish our expedition, leaving behind new friends like S. V. and Dipender, saying good-bye to old ones, like Khem Singh and Mandip Singh. I'll see them again before it's all over.

Tragedy stalks the Himalayas, even as we board a 747 for home. The season of white death rages on, and one month after our epic on Nanda Kot, 18 climbers including seven French mountaineers and 11 Nepali porters and camp staff perished in another avalanche. The event was later called "the worst ever single loss of life in the mountains and a devastating blow not just to the victims' families . . . but to the close-knit global climbing community." On October 20, 2005, a massive slide, perhaps triggered by a falling serac, "took out the whole Base Camp." The French expedition's objective was a peak called Kang Guru, which, like Chomiomo and Nanda Kot, was just shy in elevation of the 7,000-meter mark. The only survivors were four Nepalese who happened to be outside their tents when disaster struck. It is alarming to think that merely being outside your tent can spell the difference between life and death. But it did, both for the Nepalese on the French expedition and for Chuck and me on Nanda Kot.

What's really alarming about the Kang Guru tragedy is that the disaster occurred at Base Camp—usually the safest place on the entire expedition. What's more, as with the Sikkim expedition on Chomiomo, the French were no lightweights. Their leader Daniel Stolzenberg, was one of the most senior instructors at France's prestigious National School of Ski and Alpinism, ENSA (l'École Nationale

de Ski et d'Alpinisme) based in the French Alps at Chamonix. ENSA
and the French mountaineering community are known in climbing
circles to be among the best in the world—whether climbing, skiing,
or guiding. If ENSA has an American counterpart, it would be
the American Mountain Guides Association (AMGA), though
Gallic disdain—not completely unfounded—might prompt the
French to look at their American counterpart as a well-meaning but
awkward junior sibling. Says AMGA Executive Director Mike Alkitis,
"Guiding in France is held with national esteem. Thus ENSA is state
funded [the AMGA is not] so they really walk the walk." He adds,
"One of their senior instructors would definitely be one of the best in
the world at what he does, and that naturally includes avalanche
awareness. A guy like that would not make a stupid mistake."

Indeed, Stolzenberg a sixty-year-old climbing veteran understood
nature's volatility. He once prophetically remarked, "There's no such
thing as a high mountain or a low mountain, there is only the mountain. And when she's angry—things can go very badly wrong."

What all this tells us is that even the most experienced climbers can
be caught off guard. Note that the French were killed in Base Camp.
Choosing camp is a premeditated act, one that allows ample time to
assess threats and isolate the safest possible location—unlike the calcu-
lated risks climbers must take when they are forced to climb or traverse
potentially hazardous passages. And, despite whatever precautions they
must have taken, the entire party was taken completely by surprise.
According to the UK *Guardian*, Sarki Tamang, one of the Nepalese
porters who dug his way out of the snow said, "I have never seen anything like it. There was a sudden loud noise and within seconds we
were blown to the side. We were lucky. The others disappeared."

> *"What is above knows what is below, but what is below does not know what is above. One climbs, one sees. One descends, one sees no longer, but one has seen. There is an art of conducting oneself in the lower regions by the memory of what one saw higher up. When one can no longer see, one can at least still know."*
>
> —Rene Daumal, *Mount Analogue*

EPILOGUE

To survive is one thing, what to do with the void it creates is another. Months later, Chuck, Sarah, and I sit in a counseling session with a therapist, reliving the bleak moments where life itself hung in balance. Sarah suffers from anxiety, listlessness, depression, and an inability to focus at work. She carries a guilt that many survivors bear, whether from war, violent crime, or in our case, a simple accident. "I feel I am constantly on edge and continually overwhelmed even when dealing with small details," she says. There are tears in her eyes, something that even during the most stressful moment of the expedition, I never saw.

Months after our return, while skiing, Sarah was suddenly and unexpectedly gripped by panic on the snow-covered, yet benign slopes of a local Colorado ski resort. She described her feeling to Chuck, who with little reflection stated, "I feel that panic all the time. It's been that way since childhood."

In the process of writing this manuscript, I spent hours reliving the events as I typed it out on the computer screen. Recalling the events, I nearly threw up, reliving the stress and the fear of those days spent in our near-grave on Nanda Kot. I realized that I too had never let go of the experience, returning to America after more than a week of hectic travel, interviews and exploration of the mouth of the Rishi Ganga and jumping straight back into a busy life. I felt an inappropriate personal responsibility for everyone's safety, and carried guilt for leading them into a near-fatal circumstance. I realized that the dissolute feelings and unmanageable anxiety might be post-traumatic stress syndrome.

I think the counseling helped. I had the chance to speak the as-yet unspoken, to tell both Chuck and Sarah that they had done an incredible job of surviving, of staying cool and of doing everything possible to help all of us survive. "You just came back from the closest thing any of us will come to a war," I said, "And now it's over."

They in turn relieved me of the burden of guilt I'd carried, and was still carrying, around. "The expedition is over, Pete," Chuck said. "You weren't responsible for our choice to be up there and you are not responsible for our safety anymore."

At the end of the session Chuck has a realization. "I've been in a holding pattern, living with the safety of barely making it—having potential, keeping expectations low and surprising people by occasionally delivering," he says as we get ready to leave. He adds. "My step-father would lecture me and hit me—open-handed—until I would submit. I knew what he wanted and I'd do it and I hated myself for that—I'd be furious and that's how I've lived my life. When I was getting crushed by the avalanche, I felt the same sense of futility, rage and forced submission that I felt when I was being abused as a helpless child. This time I fought back. I did not submit."

A week later Chuck, Sarah and I sit, watching Jonny speaking from a spotlit podium before a sold-out house at the local Boulder Theater. As the founder and director of the annual Boulder Adventure Film Festival, Jonny tries to strike the balance between his passion for climbing and the outdoors, with his heartfelt desire to share and make the world a better place. The goal of BAFF is to promote awareness of environmental and social issues, through participation in human-powered outdoor activities. And from the tears and laughter throughout his three-day event, it's clear that Jonny's work is a resounding success. Stacey, his girlfriend, stands in the wings. In her spare time from work as an environmental consultant, she's helping Jonny share his vision.

Chuck and Sarah hold hands. They whisper whatever two people who love each other whisper, when they are out for a night on the town. In a month, they are taking a big step—buying a house and moving in together.

And as for me? I've got nothing to lose anymore. Perhaps Nanda Devi has given me that final piece I need to carry on in a life that dwells less on myself alone, but on a future that puts other things—a wife, marriage again, perhaps children—ahead of a compulsion to obsess over whatever comes along. Not that I'll quit climbing, but maybe I'll build in another direction. But first there's one last thing I need to do.

Before leaving India, Jonny and I collected two bottles of water and sediment from Rishi Ganga River—at the point where the glacial waters of Nanda Devi first meet human habitation. It's where the Ganges begins its journey, through the deep valleys of the Himalayas, on its way to nurture India's millions.

My bottle, a ten-ounce glass container, formerly held green chili paste. It now contains an inch and a half of sand and sediment resting in a matrix of cloudy river water. It's almost the exact size and shape of the plutonium lozenges loaded by McCarthy more than foryty years ago. I am a writer, not a scientist. And I cannot afford to have this water and sand tested in a lab.

So I take the bottle uncapping it as it releases a tiny hiss as the air pressure of my home in Boulder equalizes with that of a high mountain valley half a world away. A faint smell of India—dung, spices, diesel—escapes. I shake the bottle stirring up silt the and before the foggy sediment settles, I tip the bottle back and drink.

Taking the gray-green liquid into my mouth, I savor the lukewarm flow. I crunch the mica-flecked soup of glacial meltwater containing dirt, minerals, and organic material—perhaps including a few atoms of Tilman and Nanda Devi Unsoeld—and perhaps a trace of plutonium from the missing SNAP-19. Is it a health risk? Later, I'll have nightmares that my guts are burning from radiation, that I've committed an unspeakable crime against my very body. But for now, I relish the gritty crunch and the rich earthy taste of life itself.

ACKNOWLEDGMENTS

Countless people helped on a personal or professional basis to make this book a reality. My sincere apologies to anyone I might have overlooked in the following. A very special thanks goes to friend and expedition member Jonny Copp, for his enthusiasm, unquenchable spirit, and breathtaking photographs.

I'd like to thank the other members of the 2005 Nanda Kot Expedition—Chuck Bird, Gyan, Dipender Rapti, Gabe Rogel, Khem Singh, Lt. Col. S.V. Singh, and Sarah Thompson.

Special thanks goes out to Tom Fritz and Tory Jackson at Marmot Mountain Ltd. Without their help, this project could have never succeeded. Gratitude also to Mr. Mandip Singh Soin FRGS of Ibex Expeditions.

More special thanks goes to author Jeff Long who gave me invaluable encouragement over the years. Special thanks also to my publisher John Oakes of Thunder's Mouth Press, and my agent Rob McQuilkin of the Lippincott Massie McQuilkin Agency.

Thanks to:
Barb Aeschliman, Bill Aitken, John Bercaw (Black Diamond

Equipment) Mike Alkitis, Brent Bishop, Hannah Brenkert, Bridget Burke, Majka Burhardt, Kristi Denton Cohen, Kenneth Conboy, John Cooley, Greg Crouch, Dr. David Dalke, Mr. Venkatesan Dhattareyan, Mark Day (La Sportiva), Jonathan Degenhardt, Michelle Ellsworth, Cameron Elmendorf, John Evans (Petzl/Carlet), Kevin Fosburg, Tom Frost, Eric Greene, Lindsay Griffin, Karl Grossman, Eric Johnson (Teko Socks), Mr. Harish Kapadia, Capt. M.S. Kohli, Gary Landeck, Kyle Lefkoff, Nancy Lehet, Paula Lehr, Melissa Lester, Dr. Iggy Litaor, Jim McCarthy, Roanne Miller, Renato Moro, Kim Morris, Paul Niland (Sterling Ropes), Stephanie Pearson, Duane and Lisa Raleigh (*Rock and Ice* magazine), Steve Rathbun, Caroline Rydberg, Dr. Robert Schaller II, Robert Schaller III, Stacey Schulte, Cynthia Sliker, Anita Singh Soin, Scott Sutton (Jetboil Stoves), Keith Takeda, Karun Verma, Piera Vitali, John Winsor (Radar Communications), Eric Wynn, and Nick Yardley (Julbo Eyewear).

SELECTED BIBLIOGRAPHY

PREFACE

Kohli, M.S. and Kenneth Conboy. *Spies in the Himalayas: Secret Missions and Perilous Climbs*. Lawrence, Kansas: University of Kansas Press, 2002.

1. THE GODDESS

Krakauer, Jon. *Into Thin Air*. New York, NY: Villard Books, 1997.

Fanshawe, Andy and Stephen Venables. *Himalayan Alpine Style*. London: Hodder and Stoughton, 1995.

Wolpert, Stanley. *India*. Los Angeles, CA: University of California Press, 1991.

Shipton, Eric and H.W. Tilman. *Nanda Devi: Exploration and Ascent*. Seattle, WA: The Mountaineers Books, 2000.

Hathaway, Bruce. "The Great Goddess Devi." *Smithsonian*, June 1999.

Mukerjee, Amitabha. "The Ganga Basin." July 16, 1998. March 5, 2006, http://www.cs.albany.edu/~amit/ganges.html.

"Peak In Himalayas Climbed By 2 Men." *The New York Times*, September 9, 1936.

Negi, S.S. *Garhwal: The Land and People*. New Delhi: Indus Publishing Company, 1994.

Roskelley, John. *Nanda Devi: The Tragic Expedition*. Seattle, WA: Mountaineers Books, 1st edition. 2000.

Roper, Robert. *Fatal Mountaineer: The High-Altitude life and Death of Willi Unsoeld, American Himalayan Legend*. New York, NY: St. Martin's Griffin, 1st St. Martin's Griffin Edition, March, 2003.

2. A COLD WAR

LeMay, Curtis E. *Mission with LeMay: My Story*. New York, NY: Doubleday, 1965.

Interview with Manmohan Singh Kohli, October 28, 2005.

Kohli, M.S. *One More Step: An Autobiography*. New Delhi: Viking, 2005.

Bishop, Barry C. "How We Climbed Everest." *National Geographic*, May, 1963.

Twitchett, Denis and John K. Fairbank. *The Cambridge History of China Volume 14, The People's Republic Part I: The Emergence of Revolutionary China 1949–1965*. Cambridge: Cambridge University Press, 1987.

Twitchett, Denis and John K. Fairbank. *The Cambridge History of China Volume 15, The People's Republic Part 2, Revolutions within the Chinese Revolution, 1966–1982*. Cambridge: Cambridge University Press, 1992.

Maxwell, Neville. *India's China War*. New York: Pantheon Books, 1st American Edition, 1970.

"Statement By Peking On Nuclear Test." *The New York Times*, October 17, 1964.

"China's Bomb." *The New York Times*, October 17,1964.

"Cable Number 347, Secret, excised copy, U.S. Embassy, Taipei, to Department of State, 24 October 1964." *National Security Archive*, January 12, 2001, http://www.gwu.edu/~nsarchiv/ NSAEBB/NSAEBB38/document20.pdf.

"Glenn T. Seaborg, Chairman, Atomic Energy Commission, Diary Entry for 17 October 1964." *National Security Archive*, January 12, 2001, http://www.gwu.edu/~nsarchiv/NSAEBB/ NSAEBB38/ document18.pdf.

"The Wandering Lake." *Earth Observatory NASA* http://earthobservatory.nasa.gov/Newsroom/NewImages/images.php3?img_id=6762.

Binder, David. "Shastri Asks Plea To China On Bomb." *The New York Times*, October 8, 1964.

Kohli, M.S. and Kenneth Conboy. *Spies in the Himalayas: Secret Missions and Perilous Climbs*. Lawrence, Kansas: University of Kansas Press, 2002.

"John Foster Dulles Obituary." *The New York Times*, May 25, 1959.

"Summary notes of 10/17/64 NSC meeting on the Chinese Communist nuclear weapons test." October 17, 1964. Declassified Documents Reference System. #CK3100278427.

"Curtis LeMay." *Wikipedia,* http://en.wikipedia.org/ wiki/ Curtis_E._LeMay.

Ullman, James Ramsey. *Americans on Everest; The Official Account Of The Ascent Led By Norman G. Dyhrenfurth*. Philadelphia, PA: Lippincott, 1964.

Hornbein, Thomas F. *Everest: The West Ridge*. Seattle: Mountaineers Books, Reprint Edition, 1998.

Taubman, Phillip. *Secret Empire: Eisenhower, the CIA, and the*

Hidden Story of America's Space Espionage. New York, NY: Simon & Schuster, 2003.

"Central Intelligence Agency, DCI (McCone) Files: Job 80-B01285A, DCI Mtgs with the Pres, May–Oct 1964. Secret; Eyes Only. Drafted by McCone on October 7." *Federation of American Scientists Intelligence Resource Program,* http://www.fas.org/irp/cia/product/ frus_30_055.htm.

Interview with Jim McCarthy, May 17, 2005.

Kohn, Howard. "The Nanda Devi Caper." *Outside* May, 1978.

Kohli, M.S. *Miracles of Ardaas: Incredible Adventures and Survivals.* New Delhi: Indus, 2003.

3. THE MISSION

DeBrosse, Jim. "Dayton Shunned, Stunned By Exclusion From Bomb History." *Dayton Daily News*, December 8, 2004.

"Military-Industrial Complex Speech, Dwight D. Eisenhower, 1961." *The Avalon Project at Yale Law School*, October, 1996, http://www.yale.edu/lawweb/avalon/presiden/speeches/eisehower001.htm.

"Nuclear Power In Space." *U.S. Department of Energy Office of Nuclear Energy, Science, and Technology*, http://www.ne.doe.gov/pubs/npspace.pdf.

Rowe, D.M. *CRC Handbook of Thermoelectrics.* Boca Raton, FL: CRC Press, 1995.

"The History of Electricity." *Tom Henry's Code Electrical Classes Inc*, 2006, http://www.code-electrical.com/historyofelectricity.html.

Letter No. 255/33-1. May 11, 2004, from Jyotsana Sitling, Director/Forest Conservator, Nanda Devi Biosphere Reserve, Uttaranchal, India.

Interview with Dr. Robert Schaller II, August 14, 2005.

Interview with Dr. Robert Schaller II, January 15, 2005.

Interview with Dr. Robert Schaller II, August 13, 2005.

Interview with Tom Frost, January 16, 2006.

Interview with Paula Lehr, February 28, 2006.

4: A DEADLY SUBSTANCE

Hecker, Seigfried S. "Plutonium—A Historical Overview." *Los Alamos Science, Number 26—Challenges in Plutonium Science,* 2000.

Michaudon, Andre F. and Ileana G. Buican. "A Factor of Millions— Why We Made Plutonium." *Los Alamos Science, Number 26— Challenges in Plutonium Science,* 2000.

Clark, David L. and David E. Hobart. "Reflections on the Legacy of a Legend, Glen T. Seaborg (1912–1999)." *Los Alamos Science, Number 26—Challenges in Plutonium Science,* 2000.

Michaudon, Andre F. "From Alchemy to Atoms—The Making of Plutonium." *Los Alamos Science, Number 26—Challenges in Plutonium Science,* 2000.

Bortz, Alfred B. *The Neutron.* New York, NY: Rosen Publishing Group, 2003.

Grossman, Karl. *The Wrong Stuff: The Space Program's Nuclear Threat to Our Planet.* Monroe, ME: Common Courage Press, 1997.

Britt, Robert Roy. "Nuclear Power Poised for Re-Entry into Space." *www.space.com,* June 25, 2001, http://www.space.com/businesstechnology/nuclear_space_010625-6.html.

Martin Zeilig, "Louis Slotin And The Invisible Killer." *The Beaver,* August/September 1995.

Rhodes, Richard. *The Making of the Atomic Bomb*. New York, NY: Simon & Schuster, Reprint edition, 1995.

Interview with Jim McCarthy, March 8, 2006.

Welsome, Eileen. *The Plutonium Files: America's Secret Medical Experiments in the Cold War*. New York, NY: Dial Press, 1999.

Seddon, Tom. *Atom Bomb*. New York, NY: Scientific American Books for Young Readers, 1995.

"Leó Szilárd." The Columbia Electronic Encyclopedia, Sixth Edition. Columbia University Press, 2003, *Answers.com,* March 7, 2006.

"Leó Szilárd." *Wikipedia*. Wikipedia, 2005, March 7, 2006, http://www.answers.com/topic/le-szil-rd.

Laurence, William L. *Eyewitness Account of Atomic Bomb Over Nagasaki*. War Department Press Release, September 9, 1945.

Kohli, M.S. and Kenneth Conboy. *Spies in the Himalayas: Secret Missions and Perilous Climbs*. Lawrence, Kansas: University of Kansas Press, 2002.

Interview with Jim McCarthy, June 20, 2004.

Gofman, John W. *Radiation and Human Health*. Berkeley, CA: Sierra Club Books, University of California Press, 1981.

Interview with Dr. Robert Schaller II, January 15, 2005.

"Appendix"—Report of the Committee to Indian Prime Minister Desai under Notification No. 1/1/3/78-CF, May 4, 1978. *Spies in the Himalayas: Secret Missions and Perilous Climbs*. Lawrence, Kansas: University of Kansas Press, 2002.

Augusta Dwyer, "Playing with Radiation," *MacLean's*, November 2, 1987.

Gorman, Christine. "A Battle Against Deadly Dust: Doctors Join Forces to Treat Radiation Victims in Brazil." *Time*, November 16, 1987.

Patel, Gordhan N. "Counterterrorism Technology: Picking Winners and Losers" Testimony Before the House Committee on Government Reform, Subcommittee on National Security, Emerging Threats and International Relations. September 29, 2003, http://reform.house.gov/UploadedFiles/Patel%20 Testimony.pdf.

Karon, Tony. "The 'Dirty Bomb' Scenario." *www.time.com*, June 10, 2002. http://www.time.com/time/nation/article/0,8599, 182637,00.html.

Interview with Dr. Iggy Litaor, July 9, 2004.

Kelly, Henry. "Dirty Bombs: Response to a Threat, Testimony before the Senate Foreign Relations Committee on March 6, 2002." *The Journal of the Federation of American Scientists* March/April, 2002, Volume 55, Number 2, http://www.fas.org/ faspir/2002/v55n2/dirtybomb.htm.

Bhatia, Shyan. "The Missing Radioactive Sensor." *Deccan Herald*, April 25, 2004, http://www.deccanherald.com/deccanherald/ apr252004/fp2.asp.

5: TO INDIA

Wolpert, Stanley. *India*. Los Angeles, CA: University of California Press, 1991.

Keay, John. *India: A History*. New York, NY: Grove Press, 1st Grove edition, 2001.

Weare, Garry. *Trekking in the Indian Himalaya*. Oakland, CA: Lonely Planet Publications, 2002.

Abram, David, et al. *The Rough Guide to India*. Fifth Edition. New York, NY: Rough Guides, 2003.

Tharoor, Shashi. "Brown-Out in Calcutta." *Newsweek International*, August 29, 2005.

"Statement Made by the Indian Prime Minister to Parliament, 17 April 1978." *Spies in the Himalayas: Secret Missions and Perilous Climbs*. Lawrence, Kansas: University of Kansas Press, 2002.

Borders, William. "Desai Says U.S.-Indian Team Lost Atomic Spy Gear." *The New York Times*, April 18, 1978.

"Senator Cranston receives letter requesting information on truth of article that appeared in the Journal 'Outside' stating that the CIA placed a nuclear powered spying device on the Himalayan peak Nanda Devi in 1965." Declassified Documents Reference System. #CK3100219512.

"CIA responds to 4/14/78 letter regarding the CIA placing a nuclear powered intelligence device by telling writer that it is CIA policy not to publicly comment on speculations about its intelligence activities in the Himalayas." Declassified Documents Reference System. #CK3100219513.

Darian, Steven G. *The Ganges in Myth and History*. Honolulu, HI: The University Press of Hawaii, 1978.

Aitken, Bill. *Seven Sacred Rivers*. New Delhi: Penguin Books India, 1992.

6: FROM THE TRAILHEAD

Interview with Dr. Robert Schaller II, August 14, 2005.

Collins, Larry and Dominique Lapierre. *Freedom at Midnight*. New York, NY: Harper Collins, 1997.

Bonington, Chris. *Mountaineer*. London: Baton Wicks, 1996.

Fanshawe, Andy and Stephen Venables. *Himalayan Alpine Style*. London: Hodder and Stoughton, 1995.

Datta, Mukti. "The Bhotiyas of Kumaon." *The Mountain Forum Online*, 1997, http://www.mtnforum.org/resources/library/dattm97a.htm.

Knaus, John Kenneth. *Orphans of the Cold War: America and the Tibetan Struggle for Survival*. New York, NY: PublicAffairs, 1999.

Tilman, H.W. *The Ascent of Nanda Devi*. Cambridge: Cambridge University Press, 1937.

"India." *CIA—The World Factbook*, May 2006, http:// 198.81.129. 100/cia/publications/factbook/geos/in.html.

Kohli, M.S. *Miracles of Ardaas: Incredible Adventures and Survivals*. New Delhi: Indus, 2003.

Kohli, M.S. and Kenneth Conboy. *Spies in the Himalayas: Secret Missions and Perilous Climbs*. Lawrence, Kansas: University of Kansas Press, 2002.

Kapadia, Harish. *Across Peaks & Passes in Kumaun Himalaya*. New Delhi: Indus, 1999.

Keay, John. *The Great Arc: The Dramatic Tale of How India Was Mapped and Everest Was Named*. New York, NY: HarperCollins, 1st American edition, 2000.

Tarn, W.W. *Alexander the Great*. Boston, MA: Beacon, 1st Beacon paperback edition, 1956.

7: BREAKING POINT

Interview with Piera Vitali, February 26, 2006.

McKie, Robin. "Tibetan Poachers Target Bhutan's 'Miracle' Fungus." *The Guardian Unlimited*, September 11, 2005.

Asher, Mansi et al. "Livelihoods in Transition: Agriculture in the Alpine Villages of Malla Johar, Western Himalaya." *Foundation for Ecological Security*, November 2002, http://www.fes.org.in/documents/paper5.pdf.

Adams, Mike. "Interview: Medicinal Mushroom Expert Mark Kaylor." *Newstarget.com*, October 27, 2005, http://www.newstarget.com/012788.html.

Hobsbawm, E. J. *The Age of Extremes: A History of the World, 1914–1991*. New York, NY: Vintage, 1996.

Kohli, M.S. and Kenneth Conboy. *Spies in the Himalayas: Secret Missions and Perilous Climbs*. Lawrence, Kansas: University of Kansas Press, 2002.

Briggs, Andy. *Newsletter of The Tibetan Mastiff Club of Great Britain*, December 2004, http://www.tibetanmastiffdogs.com/Newsletter%20and%20cover-smallerDec%202004.pdf.

Aitken, Bill. *The Nanda Devi Affair*. New Delhi: Penguin Books India, 1994.

8: MYTH BECOMES REALITY

Hotta, Y. "The Ascent of Nanda Kot, 1936." *The Himalayan Journal Vol. IX*, 1937.

Emmons, Arthur B. "The Highest Mountain Ever Climbed." *Natural History*, April, 1938.

Datta, Mukti. "The Bhotiyas of Kumaon." *The Mountain Forum Online* 1997, http://www.mtnforum.org/resources/library/dattm97a.htm.

Aitken, Bill. *The Nanda Devi Affair*. New Delhi: Penguin Books India, 1994.

Bernbaum, Edwin. *Sacred Mountains of the World*. Berkeley, CA: University of California Press, Reprint edition, 1998.

The Greatest Adventures of All Time. Time Life Books, 2001.

Interview with Dr. Robert Schaller II, January 15, 2005.

Weare, Garry. *Trekking in the Indian Himalaya*. Oakland, CA: Lonely Planet Publications, 2002.

Krakauer, Jon. *Into Thin Air*. New York, NY: Villard Books, 1997.

Interview with Natu Singh, September 6, 2005.

Babicz, Jan. *Peaks and Passes of the Garhwal Himalaya*. Krakow: Alpinistyczny Klub Eksploracyjny, 1990.

9: NANDA KOT

Kohli, M.S. and Kenneth Conboy. *Spies in the Himalayas: Secret Missions and Perilous Climbs*. Lawrence, Kansas: University of Kansas Press, 2002.

Interview with Jim McCarthy, March 13, 2006.

Interview with Jim McCarthy, March 8, 2006.

Interview with Dr. Robert Schaller II, April 22, 2006.

Languepin, J. J. *To Kiss High Heaven*. London: William Kimber, 1956.

Blake, S.B. and Jakub Bujak. "The Polish Ascent of Nanda Devi." *The Himalayan Journal. Vol. XII*, 1940.

Kohli, M.S. "A Vision on Nanda Kot." *Sikhspectrum.com*. Issue No. 14, November 2003, http://www.sikhspectrum.com/112003/nanda_kot.htm.

Grossman, Karl. "Fire in the Sky." *Boulder Weekly* July 7–13, 2005.

Pioneer Home Page. *Spaceprojects.arc.nasa.gov.* http://spaceprojects. arc.nasa.gov/Space_Projects/pioneer/PNhome.html.

Twight, Mark F. *Extreme Alpinism: Climbing Light, Fast, and High.* Seattle, WA: The Mountaineers, 1999.

10: BACK ONCE AGAIN

Kohn, Howard. "The Nanda Devi Caper." *Outside*, May, 1978.

Kohli, M.S. and Kenneth Conboy. *Spies in the Himalayas: Secret Missions and Perilous Climbs.* Lawrence, Kansas: University of Kansas Press, 2002.

Letter from CIA, reference: F-2005-00976, July 21, 2005.

Interview with Dr. Robert Schaller II, August 14, 2005.

Letter from CIA, January 12, 2006.

Schimelpfenig, Tod and Linda Lindsey. *NOLS Wilderness First Aid.* Lander, WY: NOLS, 1991.

Fredston, Jill and Doug Fesler. *Snow Sense: A Guide to Evaluating Snow Avalanche Hazard.* Anchorage, AK: Alaska Mountain Safety Center, 4th edition, 1999.

McClung, David and Peter Schaerer. *The Avalanche Handbook.* Seattle, WA: Mountaineers Books, 1993.

11: THE AVALANCHE

None

12: SWIMMING AND DIGGING

Armstrong, Richard. "Colorado Most Dangerous State in Nation for Avalanche Fatalities." *Cooperative Institute for Research in*

Environmental Sciences Newsroom December 28, 1999, http://cires.colorado.edu/news/press/1999/99-12-28.html.

Daffern, Tony. *Avalanche Safety for Skiers and Climbers.* Seattle: Cloudcap Press, 1983.

"Sad News." *Himalayan Club E-Letter, Vol. 2*, September 2005, http://www.himalayanclub.com/pdf/e%202%20finale.pdf.

13: BURIED ALIVE

Kohli, M.S. and Kenneth Conboy. *Spies in the Himalayas: Secret Missions and Perilous Climbs.* Lawrence, Kansas: University of Kansas Press, 2002.

Interview with Dr. Robert Schaller II, August 14, 2005.

Interview with M.S. Kohli, October 28, 2005.

Interview with Piera Vitali, February 26, 2006.

Interview with Karun Verma, September 28, 2005.

Astrada, Rodolfo. "Cassini Meets The Ringed Lord." *Suite101.com* June 28, 2004. http://www.suite101.com/print_article.cfm/astronomy_astrophysics/109551.

Berhorst, Bruce. "Safety Considerations in Space Nuclear Operations." *Nuclearspace.com.* http://www.nuclearspace.com/A_RTG_DOEVIEW2_FIN.htm.

Hultgren, Herb. *High Altitude Medicine.* Stanford, CA: Hultgren Publications, 1997.

14: NANDA DEVI

Interview with Karun Verma, September 28, 2005.

Shipton, Eric and H.W. Tilman. *Nanda Devi: Exploration and Ascent.* Seattle, WA: The Mountaineers Books, 2000.

Interview with Dr. Robert Schaller II, January 2005.

Kohli, M.S. and Kenneth Conboy. *Spies in the Himalayas: Secret Missions and Perilous Climbs.* Lawrence, Kansas: University of Kansas Press, 2002.

Interview with Dr. Robert Schaller II, August 14, 2005.

Interview with Bill Aitken, October 28, 2005.

"Kang Guru Accident Update: Scarce Hope for 7 French, 11 Nepali Team Members." *Mounteverest.net*, October 24, 2005, http://www.mounteverest.net/news.php?id=969.

Bierling, Bill et al. "I've Never Seen Anything Like It. We Were Lucky. The Others Disappeared." *The Guardian*, October 29, 2005.

EPILOGUE

None

INDEX